NEW CROSSINGS

NEW CROSSINGS

CARIBBEAN MIGRATION NARRATIVES

ANTHEA MORRISON

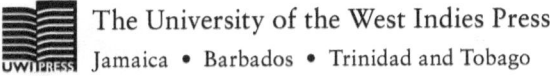
The University of the West Indies Press
Jamaica • Barbados • Trinidad and Tobago

The University of the West Indies Press
7A Gibraltar Hall Road, Mona
Kingston 7, Jamaica
www.uwipress.com

A catalogue record of this book is available from the
National Library of Jamaica.

ISBN: 978-976-640-735-3 (paper)
   978-976-640-736-0 (Kindle)
   978-976-640-737-7 (ePub)

Cover photograph © Kishan Munroe
Cover and book design by Robert Harris
Set in Scala 10.5/15 x 24

Printed in the United States of America

For my mother
and
for my son, Tarik

CONTENTS

ACKNOWLEDGEMENTS

HEARTFELT THANKS TO ALL THE FRIENDS AND COLLEAGUES who supported and cheered me on in various ways, even when this project looked like a dream, slow in realization. The words of gratitude are so many that I hesitate to name names, but I must make mention of Evelyn O'Callaghan, Rachel Moseley-Wood, Nadi Edwards, Velma Pollard, Swithin Wilmot, Lorna Goodison and Tracy Robinson.

I remember here Michael Dash, in gratitude for his tremendous example, and for his generous support when I was just beginning my career.

I must record my appreciation too for the remarkable scholars whom I was fortunate to have as lecturers, and who contributed to my love of language and literature, especially Gertrud Aub-Buscher, Merle Hodge, Joe Pereira and Jacques Chevrier.

I am grateful for the dialogue with my students at the University of the West Indies, Mona, which teaching afforded me: with them I discussed some of the ideas about diasporic literature developed in this book, and their comments and insights were always thought-provoking.

A special word of gratitude goes to the staff of the University of the West Indies Main Library, and especially of the West Indies Collection – particularly Cherry-Ann Smart and Jewel-Ann Garvey-Miller.

I am indebted to the University of the West Indies for the Principal's Research Fellowship in 2009–10, during which I began work on this project; to the Department of Literatures in English at Mona, which has always provided me with a stimulating and nurturing institutional home; and to my colleagues at the Cave Hill campus, for all the years of collegiality and friendship.

I take this opportunity to express my appreciation of the accessibility of the five writers whose work made the study both a challenge and an ongoing passion. Special thanks go to Maryse Condé, who was so generous with her time, many years ago, in enlightening conversations in New York and in Guadeloupe, and during her visits to the University of the West Indies at Cave Hill, Barbados.

Thanks to the team at the University of the West Indies Press, especially to Shivaun Hearne, for her patience and her invaluable editorial support.

Last, and in fact first and always, my gratitude goes to my family: to my mother, for so many gifts of love, showered on her children throughout the years – and for constantly believing in me; to my son, Tarik, companion on many journeys, whose humour and love have distracted and sustained me; to my sister Petey, who has supported me in so many ways – including reading the manuscript and rallying me in anxious moments; to my brother Dennis, on whose calm and positive words I have always been able to depend; and remembering our father, himself an early migrant of sorts – born in Panama because his own father travelled in search of a better life.

INTRODUCTION

Home? If only I knew where home was.
Chance had it I was born in Guadeloupe.
—Maryse Condé[1]

It is time to plant
feet in our earth. The heart's metronome
insists on this arc of islands
as home.
—Dennis Scott[2]

THE YOUNG PROTAGONIST OF CUBAN AMERICAN Cristina García's *Dreaming in Cuban,*
at the end of a fruitful first visit to her parents' birthplace, and after a warm
reunion with her grandmother Celia, gives voice to the angst of competing
affiliations which many Caribbean migrants have experienced: "I'm afraid
to lose all this, to lose Abuela Celia again. But sooner or later I'd have to
return to New York. I know now it's where I belong – not *instead* of here, but
more than here."[3] Different versions of this duality of allegiance constitute a
major thematic concern in recent Caribbean migrant literature. Of course,
the potent charge of "home", remembered/imagined from abroad, is hardly
a new preoccupation in Caribbean literature: a history of displacement, of
migrations more or less freely chosen after the vast historical uprooting that
was the slave trade, has ensured that all who inhabit a once-alien region now
claimed as home are aware of the proximity and even attraction of "other"
lands. During the colonial period, the myth of affiliation with a European
"motherland", coupled with the reality of scarce economic opportunities

1

in small territories only nominally emancipated from plantation life, impelled the movement of many West Indians in a northerly direction.

In the case of the anglophone territories, the first, "Windrush", generation (beginning with the 492 travellers who set out on what would become the iconic SS *Empire Windrush* in 1948) headed for England in the postwar years, unsure of their welcome but convinced of the need to search for a better life beyond seductive but limiting island shores. From the beginning, West Indian writers traced that movement and honoured those expectations in fictions such as Selvon's memorable *The Lonely Londoners*, and the work of George Lamming, and – despite their troubling assumptions – V.S. Naipaul's early narratives, such as *Miguel Street*, in which many of the characters dream of escape from colonial Trinidad. Perhaps the aspirations of that first generation are best summed up by Caryl Phillips, the St Kitts–born "black Briton", in his powerful memoir/travel narrative *The Atlantic Sound*: "West Indian emigrants, such as my parents, travelled with the hope that both worlds might belong to them, the old and the new."[4]

For the inhabitants of the French West Indies, the controversial and in some ways revolutionary *loi de départementalisation*[5] of 1946 bestowed on the former colonies – Martinique, Guadeloupe and Guyane – the status of "overseas departments" (*départements d'outre-mer*) of France, which, theoretically at least, removed the inequality inherent in the situation of the colonial subject and gave French West Indians (transformed into *"des Français à part entière"* [full Frenchmen][6]) the capacity to travel freely and to work in *la métropole*. In addition, the establishment in 1963 of the BUMIDOM,[7] a French government agency created to facilitate migration, provided institutional promotion of and support for the relocation to France of thousands of West Indians. Other Caribbean travellers moved to what would become new, North American, diasporas. The Cuban revolution of 1959 and the establishment of Castro's socialist regime led to the exodus of thousands of Cubans, many of whom settled in Florida; Haitians fleeing the country's poverty and the brutality of the Duvalier regime hoped for new opportunities in the United States and Canada. Thousands of nationals of the Dominican Republic sought refuge up north before and during the Trujillato, the long and wounding Trujillo dictatorship (1930–61); they would represent a fast-growing migrant group by the late twentieth century, with the numbers of Dominicans obtaining permanent resident status in the United States totalling 221,552 in 1980–89 and 359,818 in 1990–99, according to the US 2013 *Yearbook of Immigration Statistics*.[8]

For natives of Puerto Rico, movement to the American "mainland" was facilitated by the close political ties inherent in that country's status as a commonwealth of the United States. And by the end of the twentieth century, as the former British West Indies became less closely linked to England, North America emerged as the destination of choice for many migrants from the anglophone territories. Indeed, considering the Caribbean migration story from the other side of the border, and contexualizing it in relation to a wider world, it is noteworthy that the postwar period saw the dramatic opening up of the United States to searchers of fortune from different parts of the globe, who would transform America's identity – and American literature – even as they themselves assimilated elements of the host culture. In this regard, Gilbert Müller makes an interesting point about the influence of those on "the margin" in *New Strangers in Paradise: The Immigrant Experience and Contemporary American Fiction*: "Immigration in postwar American fiction reflects a national myth or narrative undergoing transformation as the margin modifies the mainstream and cultural Others alter the ways in which both their identities and American identity are defined, for their odysseys of dislocation are also odysseys of evolving national consciousness."[9] The breadth and implications of a global migratory movement are also underscored by Elleke Boehmer, who identifies the literary repercussions of this late twentieth-century postcolonial phenomenon, which she describes as "energized migrancy": "Cultural expatriation is now widely regarded as intrinsic to the postcolonial literary experience, impinging on writing and the making of literature world-wide. . . . For different reasons, ranging from professional choice to political exile, writers from a medley of once-colonized nations have participated in the late twentieth-century condition of energized migrancy."[10] Boehmer goes on to cite, inter alia, the Caribbean writers Derek Walcott, Jamaica Kincaid, Caryl Phillips, (Marlene) NourbeSe Philip and Olive Senior as examples of this second wave of travellers.

In the final decades of the twentieth century, Caribbean literature continued to privilege both the "native" and the "other" lands in its exploration of the migrant condition – a dual preoccupation still manifest in the early twenty-first century. For the present-day traveller, leaving home might not seem as formidable an undertaking as it had been for those intrepid voyagers of the 1940s, who set out on banana boats, often inadequately prepared for the cold awaiting them. In the first text of Curdella Forbes's 2008 volume of linked narratives, *A Permanent Freedom*, the male protagonist, reluctantly contemplating his imminent departure to New York, tells the woman he must leave behind that "plane cross water".[11] Indeed, it might be justifiably assumed that the sense of rupture, of painful separation, of nostalgia for the bounty of Antillean landscapes experienced by the travellers of the first generation would lose its potency in the contemporary period, as possibilities for relatively cheap travel and the general accessibility of electronic communication (the latter facilitating the creation of virtual "imagined communities"[12]) might lessen the distance, both affective and spatial, between migrant and land of origin. Conversely, Robert T. Tally Jr has argued convincingly, in his preface to the text *Literature's Sensuous Geographies: Postcolonial Matters of Place*, that "the suppression of distance by modern technology, transportation, and telecommunications has only enhanced the sense of place, and of displacement, in the age of globalization".[13] What is clear is that the concept of "diaspora" continues to compel the attention of creative writers and their audience, the condition of the migrant powerfully conjuring up notions such as those of belonging, hybridity and self-identification, which preoccupy even those who remain at home.

Furthermore, the theme of journey and migration can hardly lose its hold on the collective imaginary as long as the phenomenon of seeking one's fortune away from home remains current in Caribbean societies, in which most families can rely on relatives in North America or Europe to keep the dream – and the possibility – of flight alive. Kezia Page's illuminating study *Transnational Negotiations in Caribbean Diasporic Literature: Remitting the Text* uses as central metaphor the ritual and the fact of the remittance – the dispatch from abroad of money, which is a token of the continuing concern of the migrant for those left behind. Page makes the compelling point that there is "mutual inter-dependency" between homeland and diaspora: "A study of the literature shows that writers and citizens alike exhibit and practice not the ascendancy of diaspora but the mutual inter-dependency of the two locations; further, as Curdella Forbes has pointed out, they trouble the idea of diaspora and exile as conditions that are historically separate and diaspora as a seamless, ameliorative condition."[14] The texts studied in the following chapters remind us that Caribbean migration should be seen as part of a continuum of life-changing experiences, ranging from forced departure, as in the situation of political refugees, at one extreme (particularly in the cases of Haiti, Cuba and the Dominican Republic), to travel for reasons of study and work at the other. While some Caribbean nationals leave home to escape repressive regimes (a motivation less common in the anglophone territories), for most emigrants from the region, self-transplantation to a northern location, usually an urban centre, is an imperative born of economic difficulty or deprivation. One may argue that the prospect of departure occupies a real if not openly acknowledged place in the consciousness even of West Indians determined to stay in the region. Thus, popular expressions of fidelity to homeland, such as the 1982 patriotic song by the reggae musician Pluto Shervington, may betray this awareness of the allure of "other" lands:

I man aan ya
I man born ya
I nah leave ya
Fi go a Canada
No way sah
Pot a bwile ya
Belly full ya
Sweet Jamaica.[15]

Despite such potent articulations of the "sweetness" of home, for some anglophone Caribbeans, the post-independence period saw the emergence, in the last decades of the twentieth century, of a certain disenchantment with the dream of sovereignty and prosperity; in fact, Shervington's words were deemed ironic, though not necessarily insincere, by many Jamaican listeners when the musician himself moved to Miami in the early 1980s. Thus, "foreign" (the Jamaican Creole term for extra-regional countries), while hardly seen as land of milk and honey, became for many a necessary site of compromise in the face of economic challenges and uncertainty.

In the poem "Making Life", Lorna Goodison's whimsical pondering on an apparently inveterate restlessness among Caribbean peoples hints at the diversity of motives informing individual decisions to leave a familiar island; the poet-persona speaks in both the individual and the collective voices:

> is it because we came from a continent
> why we can't settle on our islands?
>
> Did our recrossing begin with deportation
> of maroons to Liberia via Nova Scotia? . . .
>
> I first came north to paint pictures, but
> maybe I wanted firsthand acquaintance
>
> with the fanciful places named in songs.
> Isle of Joy, the song said Manhattan was.
>
> I'm from island in the sun, I had to come
> and my sweetheart poetry joined me.
>
> Not really exiled you see; just making life.[16]

The five authors chosen for analysis in the present study are also "not really exiled"; rather, they reflect a range of migratory choices and experiences, for several reasons, including the fact that the book embraces three language areas of the Caribbean: anglophone, francophone and hispanophone. It focuses on the significance of travelling – as trope but above all as reality – in postcolonial literature born of Afro-Caribbean experience.[17] The writers in question represent migration as a choice or as a necessity which does not necessarily compromise belonging to one familiar rock. One notes that the term "migrant" itself demands guarded use, remembering that the migration experience is as varied as the islands of the Caribbean archipelago, which, even though they share a common history of colonialism, are distinguished by specificities of language, culture, government and ethnicity. While postcolonial theory and the cultural theory of hybridity provide a useful framework for reading these texts, it is evident that the range of thematic concerns explored necessitates an inclusive approach which recognizes the fertile intersection, in Caribbean literature as a whole, of issues of class, race, gender and postcoloniality.

The concept of "diaspora", with its biblical origin, its place in Jewish history and its various and complex contemporary applications, is of course relevant to this study, with the essential reservation that its resonance is informed by specific historical and cultural contexts. James Clifford insists, in *Routes: Travel and Translation in the Late Twentieth Century*, on the need for precision in diaspora discourse, cautioning inter alia against the conflation of "diaspora" and "travel": "Diaspora is different from travel (though it works through travel practices) in that it is not temporary. It involves dwelling, maintaining communities, having collective homes away from home (and in this it is different from exile, with its frequently individualist focus)."[18] In the case of the five writers discussed in this study, however, the terms "migrant", "traveller" and "diasporic subject" might apply in one instance, or in one text, but not in another. Three of the five authors left the region not as a personal choice but as a result of their parents' migration, while the other two travelled away from home alone; and the fictions they create represent both diasporic communities, in the precise sense of the term, and individual odysseys – though implicit in the latter are often the adventures of the group. Avtah Brah reminds us, pertinently, that "the identity of the diasporic imagined community is far from fixed or pre-given. It is constituted within the crucible of the materiality of everyday life; in the everyday stories we tell ourselves individually and collectively."[19] She goes on to further explicate the meaning of diasporic journeys: "all diasporas are differentiated, heterogeneous, contested spaces, even as they are implicated in the construction of a common 'we'".[20]

In accordance with the study's interdisciplinary orientation, it draws on a pan-Caribbean corpus of texts, representing the anglophone islands of Jamaica and St Kitts, the former French colonies of Guadeloupe and Haiti, and the hispanophone Dominican Republic – territories which exemplify, in their diasporas, the quality of heterogeneity alluded to above. This analysis of recent migrant literature will discuss both the traveller's memory/imagining of the native land and also the experience of that *other* land in which the second journey, the journey of assimilation and adaptation, takes place; but its main focus is on the former – on the possibility of continuing to inhabit, in psychic and emotional terms, the land left behind. Thus, I am primarily concerned with the authors' representation of the native land

– though attention is inevitably paid to the host country, given that the two do not occupy hermetic spaces in the diasporic subject's consciousness.

In Curdella Forbes's A Permanent Freedom, the ability to traverse and even to appropriate radically different spaces while remaining culturally intact is memorably represented by the fact that several of her travellers hold on to objects which function as tactile evidence of a sort of rooted-ness – objects like the "big conch with pink inside markings and, deep in its whorls, the sound of the sea",[21] brought from Jamaica, after a last visit to the beach, as a gift for the reluctant migrant grandfather, or the small pot of "home soil" carefully tended and transported throughout his wanderings by an unorthodox, uprooted priest:

> The pot of earth he had brought from home. He had nurtured in it a gera-nium, which bloomed bright red every year, like foaming blood. . . . Carefully, he wrapped the original pot of earth in mesh and paper for safe travel in his carry-on luggage. He planned to pour it back in its own place, one day, when he got back to his own country, whenever that would be.[22]

This acceptance of a duality of location and even, possibly, of allegiance is quite different, of course, from the assumptions implicit in the comfort-ing "melting pot" metaphor (no longer current in the discourse of cultural identity) according to which one might hope for the final arrival of the migrant at a position free of angst. Visual or auditory reminders of home are hardly fail-safe remedies for existential unease. I shall argue that the writers considered here all interrogate comfortable notions of national and transnational belonging, as all portray diasporic subjects forced to nego-tiate complex identities after the initial upheaval of relocation (whether their own or that of their parents). Of relevance in this regard is J. Michael Dash's assessment of the place of Haitian American Edwidge Danticat and her compatriot Dany Laferrière vis-à-vis an earlier tradition of explicitly nationalistic Haitian literature, highlighting a broadened perspective: "Con-ceivably, both Danticat and Laferrière are using literature to rethink the idea of Haitianness and citizenship in a globalized context."[23]

This study addresses the complex and diverse identities of five Caribbean writers who are indeed functioning in that "globalized context", who have all experienced "crossings" and "recrossings". My focus is on relatively new literary texts by the writers Maryse Condé, Edwidge Danticat, Junot Díaz, Curdella Forbes and Caryl Phillips, most of them published in the first years of the twenty-first century.[24] These authors sometimes give voice to a nostalgia or even regret which many of the region's emigrants carry with them as both burden and gauge of belonging. The relation of Caribbean "exiles" to the land of origin – a little-known, near-mythical destination for some second-generation migrants who are really heirs to their *parents'* sense of dislocation – may be ambiguous and even troubled. Such migrants might share the disquiet related by Caryl Phillips, in *The Atlantic Sound*, when confronted with a question which is germane to the topic of the present analysis: "Where are you from? . . . *The* question. The problem question for those of us who have grown up in societies which define themselves by excluding others. Usually us. A coded question. Are you one of us? Are you one of ours? Where are you from? Where are you *really* from?"[25] To different extents, and with more or less certainty, these texts adumbrate responses to the deceptively simple question, "Where are you from?" As early as 1939, Aimé Césaire, the pioneering poet of Négritude, had introduced an important note of ambiguity into the discourse of national and racial belonging with the provocatively imprecise title of the epic poem which launched the movement: *Cahier d'un retour au pays natal (Notebook of a Return to the Native Land)*. Scholars of Négritude have been able to explore the connotative resonance of the term *"pays natal"*, which for Césaire might include the lost or imagined African homeland as well as the tiny island of Martinique. And the young poet had already raised the possibility of ambivalence vis-à-vis his island origin, avoiding the romanticizing homesickness one might excuse in an Antillean student writing from Paris in 1939; for the first pages of the epic poem place in cruel focus not the exotic island of colonialist discourse but a wretched colonial Martinique, locked into its alienation but also into its overwhelming *"misère"*.

For the authors considered in the present study, the term "native land" remains as emotionally charged as it was for Césaire, but its inherent ambiguity lies elsewhere: in the late twentieth-century reality of what Edwidge Danticat has theorized as "bi-culturalism",[26] the conflict not between ancestral mother/fatherland and Antillean island, but between different but overlapping identities resulting from the *choice* of migration:

> When I became a writer and started having debates with the characters in the stories I was writing, the characters would often have readjustment issues that touched on "bi-cultural life". The upside of a bi-cultural life, they would tell me, is that you are exposed to two or many realities. You have a broadening of experiences as one shadows the other. You have plantains with your Thanksgiving dinner. The proverbs of your language peek through the veil of the English you speak. You see the world with two eyes that do not always look in the same direction.
>
> The downside, they would tell me, are the struggles between many worlds, different values, different means of survival.[27]

The United States (specifically New York) is, for Danticat and her fictional travellers, the site of this process of struggle and survival. Given the chronological frame of the study – that is, essentially the first years of the twenty-first century – it is not surprising that most of the five writers reside and work in North America, reflecting a historical shift in migration patterns away from a European metropolis or "motherland". The fact that the writers considered relate migration experiences in the United States and not in Canada does not reflect a marginalization of novelists resident in the latter nation, but rather the fear of oversimplification and the difficulties inherent in the attempt to be "comprehensive"; there would clearly be a rich corpus of Caribbean-Canadian texts to include in another study (focusing, for example, on the work of writers like Austin Clarke, Dany Laferrière and Dionne Brand).

Urban space and, in particular, the city of New York – which Maryse Condé has described as "the hybrid city par excellence"[28] – loom large in much of the writing (Condé's *The Story of the Cannibal Woman*, set in Cape Town, provides an interesting variation). In this respect, my perspective is, however, different from that implicit in *Creolising the Metropole: Migrant Caribbean Identities in Literature and Film*, H. Adlai Murdoch's study of the impact of Caribbean migration in the capital cities of England and particularly France; *Creolising the Metropole* addresses "the situation of the DOM (départements d'outre mer) or French overseas departments and examines the migratory ramifications of presumptive integration into the national framework of the former colonial power".[29] The concern informing my analysis is rather the possibility of *reintegration* of the migrant character and/or writer into the land of origin and the *reimagining* of home, even in the absence of physical return.

The texts chosen are mainly fictional or autobiographical narratives, but consideration is also given to essays and to interviews; perhaps it is not coincidental that all these writers have contributed substantially to the areas of literary and cultural criticism – an activity not unusual in the Caribbean, where the creative writer often assumes the role of cultural critic and does not hesitate to give voice to a political engagement or to participate in political discourse (notable examples are Danticat, *Create Dangerously: The Immigrant Artist at Work*, and Forbes, *From Nation to Diaspora: Samuel Selvon, George Lamming and the Cultural Performance of Gender*). Art and activism go hand in hand for at least two of the authors considered, Edwidge Danticat and Junot Díaz, who, ironically perhaps, originate from nations which share the island known as Hispaniola but which have had a historically adversarial relationship. Thus, in October 2015, the two writers travelled to Washington, DC, to address congressional leaders on the injustice of the recent measure that left Dominicans of Haitian descent without a nationality. As a result of this initiative, Díaz was labelled anti-Dominican and, extraordinarily, stripped of the Juan Pablo Order of Merit, the national honour awarded him in 2009 for his writing.[30]

Such (re)actions/interactions on the part of writers forced to negotiate the shifting worlds which they inhabit are revealing, illustrating the ongoing, but sometimes necessarily conflicted, relation to the "native land", from which it is tempting, but I think simplistic, to say that they are exiled. While the term "exile" is frequently – and emotively – used in literary criticism to evoke the homesickness that is commonly the lot of the traveller, it is often an inadequate rendering of the feelings of dislocation and loss inherent in the prolonged absence from homeland *coupled with* the need to adapt to a new way of life. Odile Ferly has argued that there is validity in describing economic migrants as exiles, in part "because the borderline between economic and political emigration is often tenuous, since economic hardship usually increases for the poor under oppressive regimes, as has occurred in Haiti and the Dominican Republic".[31] While this issue of nomenclature is obviously subject to debate and controversy, it is useful to inject as much nuance as possible into the discussion of diasporic literature; certainly, in the case of most Caribbean writers, and specifically of the authors considered in this study, the inevitability of nostalgia should not be confused with the impossibility of return. Edward Said has reminded us, in "The Mind of Winter", of the finality of *real* exile: "Exile is the unhealable rift forced between a human being and a native place, between the self and its true home. The essential sadness of the break can never be surmounted."[32] This is a point worth underscoring in addressing contemporary Caribbean diasporic literature, and in explaining my own reluctance to generalize the use of the word "exile" in this context. For compelling though the memory of the more or less painful separation from land of origin may be for the descendants of uprooted Africans, destined for centuries of enslavement in the New World, contemporary journeying to locations where Caribbean peoples assume temporary or even permanent residence cannot always be best understood as a *déracinement* or "banishment" to "the rivers of Babylon".[33] Nor are these travellers usually "homeless" in the sense of the term applicable to black South Africans uprooted from familial lands and consigned to the squalor and anonymity of peripheral "townships" under the apartheid regime. Yet the land left behind frequently continues to hold sway in the imagination of the Caribbean émigré – even in part as mirage, even when the designation of a distant island as "home" might be problematic, and even when the expected reverence towards the "native land" is diluted or absent.

In the essay quoted above, Edward Said memorably articulates one of the possible "pleasures of exile"[34] in terms which are relevant to the migrant experience, and which recall Danticat's definition of the "bi-cultural" perspective: "Most people are principally aware of one culture, one setting, one home: exiles are aware of at least two, and this plurality of vision gives rise to an awareness of simultaneous dimensions, an awareness that – to borrow a phrase from music – is *contrapuntal*."[35] For the writers considered in this study, separation from birthplace is not quite the "unhealable rift" evoked by Said, and a contrapuntal awareness of the mother(land) and the other land is ineluctable and at times fruitful. Indeed, the return journey – if not home, at least *back* to the region of origin – is evoked by all the authors: sometimes as a frequent occurrence, sometimes as one meriting joy and exuberance, and most often as a momentous event. The relation is in each case an intense, visceral one. It is almost a commonplace that Caribbean writers who have lived abroad should foreground in their creative work the dazzling moment of return, demonstrating fidelity to a familiar, and even spectacular, landscape. This dream of return to a beloved island is memorably recounted, in the volume *Rights of Passage*, by a celebrated member of the first generation of West Indian intellectuals who had the opportunity to travel far from the region; in "South", Kamau Brathwaite, whose early journeys were not only to former metropole but also to continent of origin, poignantly envisages the moment of "glad reunion" with the islands of the archipelago:

> But today I recapture the islands'
> bright beaches: blue mist from the ocean
> rolling into the fishermen's houses.
> By these shores I was born: sound of the sea
> came in at my window . . .
> Since then I have travelled: moved far from the beaches:
> sojourned in stoniest cities, walking the lands of the north
> in sharp slanting sleet and the hail[36]

Writing several decades after Brathwaite, the manifestly more cynical Dominican-born Junot Díaz expresses, in the 2012 collection *This Is How You Lose Her*, a similar exuberance at the moment of rediscovery of his island and its surrounding waters; but he nevertheless compels the reader to *also* contemplate less seductive aspects of the picture he paints – with an unforgiving attention to the gritty reality into which *he* was born:

> Let me confess: I love Santo Domingo. . . . Love the plane landing, everybody clapping when the wheels kiss the runway. . . .
> If this was another kind of story, I'd tell you about the sea. What it looks like after it's been forced into the sky through a blowhole. How when I'm driving in from the airport and see it like this, like shredded silver, I know I'm back for real. I'd tell you how many poor motherfuckers there are . . . I'd tell you about the shanties and our no-running water faucets and the sambos on the billboards and the fact that my family house comes equipped with an ever-reliable latrine . . . and I'd tell you about the street where I was born, Calle XXI, how it hasn't decided yet if it wants to be a slum or not and how it's been in this state of indecision for years.[37]

While one is tempted to attribute the difference in tone between Díaz and Brathwaite to the singularity of each writer's experience of absence from home, and also more simply to temperament, to sensibility, it is interesting to note that elsewhere in the same volume, Brathwaite is much less nostalgic about the West Indies. In a poem apparently inspired by his return home from Ghana in the 1960s, he contemplates a region different from what he had hoped for/imagined:

> But I returned to find Jack
> Kennedy invading Cuba
>
> black riots in Aruba
> and Trinidad.[38]

The poem ends with a sombre scenario dominated by ambitious, self-seeking politicians and the omnipresent, victimized poor:

> while the
>
> supporting poor, famished upon their simple
> politics of fish and broken bread,
>
> begin to catch their royal asses.[39]

For Caribbean writers who have "sojourned in stoniest cities", home is therefore sometimes a lost Eden – sometimes, as for the young Aimé Césaire, a site/sight evoking pain and disenchantment. While Brathwaite first left his island of birth as a young man who would pursue tertiary studies abroad, Díaz, Danticat and Phillips travelled as children to a strange land, and would never again return permanently to the region. And yet despite the brevity of his sojourn in the Dominican Republic (his family moved to New Jersey when he was six years old), Díaz's tongue-in-cheek description of the landing in Santo Domingo of his protagonist/alter ego Yunior illustrates the complex need, frequently observed in migrant literature, to delineate and even to *claim* the "homeland" – a need which does not preclude ambivalence or even antagonism. Attitudes to the land of origin may vary from veiled hostility and harsh criticism (of which the fiction and life writing of Jamaica Kincaid offer an extreme example[40]) to the less jarring wish to redefine and to nuance one's identity, while eschewing the blind allegiance resulting from unfulfilled nostalgia. And, more happily, some writers achieve the simple, hoped for pleasure of rediscovery and reunion. It is this multifaceted relationship with homeland and its role in the shaping of a new diasporic identity that lies at the heart of this study.

The Dominican American writer Julia Alvarez has affirmed memorably in her collection of essays *Something to Declare* that reductive labels cannot adequately render or capture her complex identity. In an essay responding to the firm reminder from Doña Aida, a Dominican *grande dame*, of her *real* national belonging, Alvarez retorts: "No, I am not a Dominican writer or really a Dominican in the traditional sense. I don't live on the Island, breathing its daily smells, enduring its particular burdens, speaking its special dominicano. . . . But, you're right, Doña Aida, I'm also not una norteamericana. . . . I don't hear the same rhythms in English as a native speaker of English."[41] Alvarez's disclaimer foregrounds the dilemma faced by several migrant writers, particularly those who move outside of a familiar language space, of living in between worlds. Thus, the issue and challenge of language is both a compelling trope for that of identity and a literal element of the processes of adaptation and compromise inherent in settling into an "alien" community.

The Guadeloupean Maryse Condé, a relatively privileged "migrant" and perhaps the true itinerant of the selected writers, has lived for many decades far away from a Caribbean "home".[42] Condé frequently goes countercurrent in her utterances about her relation to the island of origin, and most of her fictional heroines replicate that restlessness in their own trajectories. She has challenged the apparent bias, in the provocative and influential text *Eloge de la créolité* (*In Praise of Creoleness*),[43] in favour of the writer who is truly "*natif-natal*" (born and bred) and who has remained at home; she has also interrogated the notion of a normative Caribbeanness, *including* the obligatory use of the Creole language: "N'y a-t-il pas des versions multiples de l'antillanité? Des acceptions nouvelles de la créolité?" (Are there not multiple versions of Caribbeanness? New ways of understanding Creoleness?)[44] Perhaps Condé's interrogation of essentialist concepts of Caribbean identity may be compared to Homi Bhabha's emphasis on the danger of representing any culture as pure: "Cultures are never unitary in themselves, nor simply dualistic in the relation of Self to Other."[45]

Maryse Condé's insistence on the heterogeneity of Caribbean culture and thought is useful to our discussion, and "postcolonial" diasporic literature, like the region's peoples, is certainly marked by diversity, contradiction and openness to multiple perspectives and preoccupations. Condé's lifetime of errancy is clearly a far cry from the modest journeying of Curdella Forbes, who has resided in the United States for over a decade. Variables such as the age at which the writer left the region are not irrelevant to the analysis of a literature coloured by differences of both sensibility and circumstance, and one resistant to simple classifications. An example of the singularity sometimes sacrificed in the impulse towards generalization is the case of the celebrated Paule Marshall, born in Brooklyn to Barbadian parents, described by some critics as African American, by others as Barbadian, while in fact neither label captures her irreducible selfhood. One of the five authors considered in the study left the Caribbean for England as an infant, two migrated to the United States with their families during childhood, one left Guadeloupe to study in France at age sixteen and only one left the Caribbean (to teach at the tertiary level) in adulthood. Four of the writers currently reside in the United States (Danticat, Díaz, Forbes and Phillips), though not all on a permanent basis. And while the fictional texts discussed are situated mainly in North America and in the Caribbean, two authors explore transatlantic locations, including Britain (represented as an alternative homeland by Phillips) and, even more interesting, due to it being a less obvious destination for travel or migration, Africa (Phillips and Condé).

Oscar Hijuelos, the celebrated Cuban American novelist (and the first Hispanic American to win the Pulitzer Prize[46]), acknowledged, in a 2011 essay, a lingering regret at the loss of familiarity with his parents' mother tongue – a loss perhaps more piercing because in his first four years, he was totally immersed in the Spanish language. Then, life's unpredictability intervened in the form of a serious illness (contracted at the end of an extended visit to Cuba): after a year of hospitalization in Connecticut, the young Oscar returned to his parents' Cuban-flavoured Harlem apartment, transformed into an English speaker – though he would grow up to lyrically chronicle the experience of the Cuban American diaspora:

It was during that long separation from my family that I became estranged from the Spanish language and, therefore, my roots. I recall returning home from the hospital to the apartment and being only vaguely aware of just who my father, mother and older brother were; and Spanish, the language I had so glibly spoken not so long before, suddenly seemed like a foreign tongue.[47]

But with the passage of time, things changed, and the adult Hijuelos acknowledged the tenacity of this first "forgotten" language: "Despite the strange baggage that I carried about my upbringing, and despite the relative loss of my first language, I eventually came to the point that, when I heard Spanish, I found my heart warming."[48] I found this poignant tale of an unusual "immigrant" childhood both moving for its own sake and suggestive of the complicated and sometimes unpredictable role played by language in our self-identification: reluctant to overdramatize his situation, the Cuban American qualifies his loss as "relative", and yet it haunts him for years. Of course, Hijuelos's linguistic situation is quite different from that of Edwidge Danticat and Junot Díaz in that he was born in New York. Danticat and Díaz, who arrived in the United States as native speakers of Kreyol and Spanish, respectively, may be considered translingual, choosing English instead of their mother tongue as their language of literary expression. Though they may both be termed "American", theirs is no simple multiculturalism. These two writers offer remarkable examples of the political and cultural implications of linguistic choices; some attention is necessarily paid, in the chapters which follow, to the importance of language as an integral part of the discourse of identity. One notes, in this regard, the incorporation in literary texts of elements of Creole/Kreyol (where the linguistic situation of the homeland is one of diglossia) or, in the case of Díaz, of the sort of mélange which has come to be known as "Spanglish".

Paule Marshall's groundbreaking novel of migration, *Brown Girl, Brownstones*, first published in 1959, offers an early example of the nexus between language and identity for travellers from what was then the British West Indies. Describing as the "poets in the kitchen" the Barbadian women who assembled regularly in her mother's kitchen to share culinary tastes, but also the vernacular language which constituted a marker of difference in the midst of American values threatening their cultural identity, Marshall quotes Czeslaw Milosz's memorable affirmation that "language is the only homeland".[49] This concern is not dissimilar to that expressed by a Caribbean writer who *did* remain at home, the Martinican Patrick Chamoiseau, celebrated author of *Texaco* and theoretician of *Créolité*, the literary movement seen as successor to Glissant's *Antillanité*. Chamoiseau has emphasized the centrality of language in his novelistic practice in a largely positive reading of Maryse Condé's *Traversée de la mangrove* (*Crossing the Mangrove*). Commenting on a book which he sees as marking the writer's homecoming to the Caribbean, the Creolist identifies and celebrates examples of her manipulation of the French language to reflect the *spirit* of Guadeloupean Creole: "My final reflexion concerns language. . . . People don't age, their age mounts them; people don't walk, they push their bodies ahead, people don't chat, they *fait-un-causer* . . . ants are not *folles* they are *tok-tok* . . . those words suit me. They ring true to my ear and echo loudly in my heart."[50]

What is noteworthy here is that although Chamoiseau's words are translated from the French, the translator leaves some of the lexical items on which the novelist is commenting unchanged, though italicized – perhaps acknowledging the necessary *limits* of translation, and also implicitly conveying the Creolophone writer's confidence in self, a confidence that renders detailed explanation gratuitous. It is significant also that Chamoiseau goes on to point to what he sees as less felicitous practice, specifically to Condé's extensive use of "the footnotes that explain what we already know", adding that "our task is to speak to ourselves, for ourselves, with an authenticity acquired from inside".[51] These controversial words are of course related to the debate/polemic in the francophone Caribbean that has tended to situate those who migrated and those who remain at home in opposite, even adversarial, camps. Their pertinence in the context of the present study is that even diasporic writers who have spent most of their lives out of the Caribbean are sensitive, in their work, to the liberatory power of "speak[ing] to ourselves, for ourselves". Such a concern is indeed at the core of Caribbean postcolonial literature, a literature which, by its very existence, rectifies and redeems the silences and misrepresentations born of the presumed subalternity of the colonial subject.

Most of the writers considered in the present analysis recognize and even honour, in unique ways, the language of their homeland, sometimes deployed in their texts as a banner of difference. The most original of these

is arguably the Dominican American Díaz, whose idiosyncratic or even revolutionary use of Spanish in all his narratives undermines the hegemony
of English, a language he nevertheless embraces: "By keeping the Spanish
as normative in a predominantly English text, I wanted to remind readers
of the fluidity of languages, the mutability of languages. And to mark how
steadily English is transforming Spanish, and Spanish is transforming
English."[52] The primacy of voice in her fiction is more directly addressed by
Edwidge Danticat, in response to a journalist's question about her translation of the words of characters speaking Haitian Creole: "Part of it has to do
with the bilingualism/trilingualism of my life. The characters are speaking
Creole in my mind. I can hear just what they're saying, and I'm the translator. Some things I leave in Creole, for readers who are bilingual and who
may have another interpretation."[53] Danticat is clearly less radical than Díaz
in her deployment of the two languages, which reveal a dual identity (she
has referred to English as her "stepmother tongue"[54]), but she also disturbs
the notion that she is an "anglophone" author by writing a brand of English in which she quietly incorporates Creolisms and the syntax, if not the
lexicon, of French. Curdella Forbes, whose gift for literary code-switching
was manifest in her first collection of short stories, *Songs of Silence*, uses
less Jamaican Creole in *A Permanent Freedom*, precisely because most of the
narratives in this later volume are set in the United States, and the adjust-
ments to the new context made by some – though not all – of her fictional
characters have spilled over into their language usage.

Although one might argue that the linguistic fluidity apparent in the
writing of Danticat, Díaz and Forbes cannot be equated with the larger
problematic with which this study is concerned – that of the *reconfiguring*
of home in the context of an evolving identity – the notion is nevertheless
suggestive of the reality for all these migrant writers, of inhabiting diasporic spaces which are neither impregnable nor immutable. Their work
exemplifies the concept of cultural identity as "process", theorized by Stuart
Hall and implicit in his observation, in the essay "Negotiating Caribbean
Identities", that "identity is not in the past to be found, but in the future to
be constructed."[55] Hall explains: "I say that not because I think therefore
that a Caribbean people can ever give up the symbolic activity of trying
to know more about the past from which they come, for only in that way

can they discover and rediscover the resources through which identity can be constructed."[56] This observation, which in the context of Hall's essay refers particularly to Caribbean people living at home, offers insight into the concern of migrants similarly impelled to explore the past – the land and culture of origin – in order to (re)construct their identity in the present.

Like Maryse Condé, the Haitian writer Edwidge Danticat is from the "francophone" Caribbean, though it is worth underscoring, as an example of the uniqueness of each Caribbean territory, that while Haiti and Guadeloupe share a not dissimilar Creole language, they are historically and culturally quite distinct. Indeed, the two nations represent what one might consider two extremes in the Antillean colonial experience: one – rebel and trailblazer – achieving sovereignty in the early nineteenth century, and the other, even now in the twenty-first century, linked and bound to France by the perhaps anachronistic but not easily surrendered status of *département d'outre-mer*. The singularity of Haiti, the tale not adequately understood in the region of its exemplary and also troubled past, its people's repeated trials at home and the burden of stereotype borne by Haitians abroad are all concerns explored in Danticat's oeuvre. Chapter 1 highlights the importance of voice in her work, with particular reference to three texts spanning different genres: the collection of stories *The Dew Breaker*, the memoir *Brother, I'm Dying* and the volume of essays *Create Dangerously: The Immigrant Artist at Work*. The chapter also briefly discusses the novel *Claire of the Sea Light*, which Danticat had already begun before the earthquake of 12 January 2011. It is instructive to note the writer's response, after that catastrophic event, to the question (posed by a reader of the *New Yorker*), "Has the tragedy in any way strengthened your Haitian identity?"[57] In her assertion that she has "always felt very strongly Haitian",[58] Danticat – who came to join her parents in New York at the age of twelve – is of course affirming an allegiance undiluted by distance, which is already manifest in her creative work. Indeed, the author consistently represents the land of her birth as central both to her artistic project and to her self-identification.

This study seeks, however, to highlight the tensions and contradictions inherent in the situation of a writer who occupies a privileged insider/outsider position in American society, and who attempts to communicate the experience of a plurality of Haitian migrants (as Danticat does through the polyphony of voices heard in the remarkable text *The Dew Breaker*). Thus, Danticat's various perspectives – as Haitian patriot, as loving family member, as black woman and as creative artist who feels an obligation to illuminate painful histories – combine to make each of the works studied multilayered, compelling and sometimes disturbing.

The second chapter, devoted to the work of Junot Díaz, demonstrates the extent to which the Dominican American shares with Danticat a commitment to both art and activism. It is Díaz, of all the writers studied, whose tone demonstrates most dramatically the tension which may inhere in the writer's wish to view the homeland through a lens that, while admittedly coloured by longing, is clear enough to allow for criticism. The chapter offers a reading of the acclaimed novel *The Brief Wondrous Life of Oscar Wao*, which won Díaz the Pulitzer Prize in 2008, as well as the 2012 collection of short stories, *This Is How You Lose Her*. In a 2015 study, Christopher González rightly signals the originality of Díaz's novel, which he considers a non-typical "Latino" narrative, an originality which does not reside exclusively in the author's memorable deployment of Spanglish: "Along with its engagements with race and history, another defining feature of Díaz's novel is its relationship to comic books, science fiction, and fantasy literature."[59] The narrative structure swings between two very different worlds, New Jersey and "the Island", seen as the source of an evolving *dominicanidad*. In the analysis of *The Brief Wondrous Life of Oscar Wao*, particular attention is paid to Díaz's concern with history as he traces the trajectories of earlier Dominican migrants, forced to leave the Island because of the brutality of its government, as well as the socio-economic concerns fuelling the departure of the families of those who, like the writer, came of age in the late twentieth century. Both the novel and the collection of stories focus on familial and societal issues such as the absence of the father and the related challenges of masculinity faced by young men of the Afro-Dominican diaspora – young men like the narrator Yunior, whose original voice animates and holds together the various episodes of *Oscar Wao*, as well as the linked stories of *This Is How You Lose Her*. As in the writing of Danticat, voice is of paramount importance in the representation of the complex belonging/unbelonging of individuals and communities in motion.

Like that of Danticat and Díaz, Caryl Phillips's work is characterized by an absence of triumphalism, perhaps born of a consciousness of the tensions inherent in a hyphenated identity: having travelled to England via boat with his parents as an infant, the novelist has never resided in St Kitts, and, after the early fiction of displacement *The Final Passage*, has written little, in a prodigious body of work, about "the islands" (with the exception of the 1986 novel *A State of Independence*). Claimed by some critics as British or "black British" (a label even more troubling than the title "African American", inasmuch as it erases origin and simplifies belonging), Phillips has documented in *The Atlantic Sound* his own difficulty with rigid classification of identity.

The present study teases out the complexities inherent in Phillips's self-representation and in his sustained commentary on the condition of "exile", including both *Color Me English: Migration and Belonging Before and After 9/11* (2011) and the 2009 novel *In the Falling Snow*, in which the writer confronts the dilemma of a second-generation West Indian emigrant and his relation to a barely known Caribbean "home". While the novel might seem far removed from Caribbean reality, in the last pages of *In the Falling Snow*, the focus shifts to an island which forms the backdrop for a surprising oral narrative, a *cri de coeur* in which the writer attempts to incorporate the rhythm, if not the actual diction, of a vernacular language – and which the protagonist Keith's dying father leaves imprinted on his son's consciousness. It is the story of a *sort* of home.

Certainly, home is more elusive for some diasporic writers than for others: in this regard, Maryse Condé, the doyenne of the five writers to be discussed, is closest to the black British Caryl Phillips. Born in 1937, Condé left Guadeloupe to study in Paris at the age of sixteen; she would subsequently live in Guinea, Ghana, Senegal, Paris and New York before resettling in Guadeloupe in 1986 – a homecoming described in a 1989 interview under the suggestive title "Je me suis réconciliée avec mon île" ("I Have Been Reconciled with My Island").[60] In the late 1980s, patently wounded by African criticisms of the historical novel *Ségou*, and seeming to turn away from the hazards of reimagining the African past, Maryse Condé appeared to signal homecoming to the Caribbean with the novels *La vie scélérate* (*Tree of Life*) (1987) and *Traversée de la mangrove* (*Crossing the Mangrove*) (1989).The latter text won her the recognition of the influential Patrick Chamoiseau, who lauded the return of the prodigal daughter after decades of a peripatetic life spent far from the Antilles. But one might well ask what is "home" for a novelist who, in her creative work, consistently problematizes the comforting certainty inherent in the term, and whose non-fictional writing has affirmed her right to embrace a transnational identity.

In *The Last of the African Kings*, Condé begins with a fictionalized account of the historical exile in Martinique of the Dahomean King Behanzin; she then shifts the narrative to Charleston, South Carolina, the adopted home of the king's Martinican great-grandson Spéro, whose American-born daughter, in turn, by the end of the novel, plans her own subversive journey "back" to Benin. The voyages chronicled in *The Story of the Cannibal Woman* are certainly less convoluted, but the Guadeloupean protagonist – whose partner, Stephen, is an Englishman with whom she has shared homes in N'Dossou (a fictional African state), New York and finally Cape Town – articulates in compelling fashion the fear of homelessness afflicting several Condéan protagonists.

The study turns finally to a "new migrant", the Jamaican Curdella Forbes, who has spent much of her adult life in Jamaica, though she has now resided and taught in the United States for more than a decade. Chapter 5 focuses on the 2008 collection *A Permanent Freedom*, which, through Forbes's vivid characterization, brings to life the challenges of separation, homesickness and reintegration evoked in much of Caribbean migrant literature. Forbes's inclusion in the study serves to confirm the range represented by this body of literature: her travellers tend to fit less easily into the familiar mould (that of migrants leaving home for financial advancement), and, indeed, one wonders, in the case of the recurring character Jeremy, the pastor who travels light but always holds on to the home soil he brought north with him, exactly *why* he left Jamaica.

The transplanted individuals who dominate *A Permanent Freedom* are mainly, but not all, Jamaican. Indeed, Forbes's characters appear to embody the notion of a plural Caribbean/African diasporic identity, a notion closer to the trope of the rhizome associated with Edouard Glissant than to the concept of an exclusive rootedness. The newly relocated family of "Macóné Macóné" can easily summon up the image of their home in Brown's Town, Jamaica, as repository of an identity to which they cling. But their Jamaicanness is not fixed or essentialized. *A Permanent Freedom* generously opens the door to spaces other than the island sites revered in so many texts, though the volume of loosely linked narratives is given structural coherence by the fact that it ends where it began, on a sparsely populated mountainside on a beloved island – presumably but not explicitly Jamaica.

Maryse Condé posited in the 1998 essay "O Brave New World" that both the Négritude movement and pan-Africanism were forms of globalization: "What was Negritude, what was Pan-africanism if not forms of globalization, the implied project of a complete identity and an active solidarity among the black peoples? At the time, all voices were unanimous. The only dissenting one was Fanon's."[61] Condé's qualifying sentence about the near unanimity of those early voices is important. The voices heard in the narratives considered in the present study are far from unanimous about matters of race, or ethnicity, or gender (and the list goes on). Yet what is striking for the contemporary reader is this bold assertion by the Guadeloupean writer of a *sort* of globalization based on "active solidarity among the black peoples". This characterization of these transnational manifestations of racial affinity brings to mind the later elaboration by Brent Hayes Edwards of "the practice of diaspora" in the powerful text bearing that name.[62] Edwards points not just to the influential role played by Paris in the early twentieth century in bridging gaps between various communities of colour, but also to the importance of translation, allowing anglophone and francophone blacks to go beyond the limits of their language of expression. This analysis of the fertile relations, in that period, between black writers of the diaspora – specifically between English-speaking writers from the United States and francophone African or Antillean writers based in Paris – highlights the role of translation in allowing transcultural exchanges between intellectuals of the African diaspora; thus, Edwards arrives at the memorable conclusion that "diasporic reciprocity is above all a call to translate".[63]

Like the intellectuals referred to in *The Practice of Diaspora*, the US-based Caribbean writers included in the present study have been able to transcend the national and to embrace a diasporan identity, but without necessarily having recourse to translation or to the insertion of glossaries in their texts: the vernacular/non-English languages incorporated in their work are employed without explanation or translation, as the phenomenon of inhabiting two idioms, as one inhabits two worlds, becomes less remarkable in contemporary multicultural societies. Of course, such duality does not preclude the potential for regret, as Julia Alvarez reminds us in the poem "Bilingual Sestina", in which she recalls – or imagines – a simpler time of childhood in the Dominican Republic before her family moved northwards. The persona evokes a lost intimacy with her mother tongue, as she remembers being sung to in Spanish:

> *Estas son las mañanitas* and listening in bed, no English
> yet in my head to confuse me with translations, no English
> doubling the world with synonyms, no dizzying array of words
> – the world was simple and intact in Spanish –
> *luna, sol, casa, luz, flor*, as if the *nombres*
> were the outer skin of things, as if words were so close
> one left a mist of breath on things by saying
>
> their names, an intimacy I now yearn for in English –
> words so close to what I mean that I almost hear my Spanish
> heart beating, beating inside what I say *en inglés*.[64]

Notwithstanding the challenge of negotiating a "doubled" world, the writers considered in this study assert a distinct and yet non-monolithic Caribbeanness within the body of postcolonial diasporic literature. One should note that writers like Condé, Danticat and Díaz, who have, to varying extents, benefited from the practice of translation, and from an increasingly multicultural readership, have imposed/mediated a Caribbean presence within the North American host land, while at the same time contributing to the elimination of boundaries in their once-balkanized region. Discussing the impact of Haitian and Hispanic Caribbean authors writing in English, Odile Ferly points out that "by encouraging comparative criticism, their fiction helps to eradicate the old but persistent colonial fragmentation of the Caribbean that has so far invariably resulted in literary insularism".[65] Certainly, the corpus of texts examined in the chapters which follow encourages a generous vision of a "moveable" and open Caribbeanness that does not preclude difference.

While all these writers were born in the region (though one might say in the case of Caryl Phillips, just barely so), they would hardly locate themselves in the category of "transients" described by Elizabeth Thomas-Hope in a recent study of Caribbean migration: "At the migration destinations, the initial migrants, in contrast to the subsequent generations born abroad, tend to see themselves as transient, still with a sense of belonging to their country of birth."[66] Yet to varying degrees, they manifestly remain connected to their island of birth. In sharing memories of the assassinated Haitian journalist, her friend Jean Dominique,[67] Edwidge Danticat quotes his comforting words on the dilemma of Haitian Americans who are subjected, on returning home, to the disparaging Creole label *"Dyaspora"*: "The *Dyaspora* are people with their feet planted in both worlds. . . . There is no reason to be ashamed of being *Dyaspora*."[68] Though Jean Dominique's metaphor elides the competing and even intractable factors which may sometimes pull Haitian Americans in one direction rather than the other, the inherently paradoxical concept of being rooted "in both worlds" is an interesting, hopeful variant of the notion of "in-betweenity" applied to the situation of postcolonial subjects negotiating complex identities. It is a useful *point de départ* in approaching the work of the writers considered in this analysis, all characterized by a certain liminality, as they struggle to respect old allegiances but also to *reimagine* and *reconfigure* the homeland.

CHAPTER 1

EDWIDGE DANTICAT

The Immigrant Writer as "Witness from Afar"

IN "BLACK BODIES IN MOTION AND IN PAIN", an essay published in the *New Yorker* on 22 June 2015, Edwidge Danticat uses the group of paintings the "Migration Series", by the African American Jacob Lawrence, to make an unexpected linkage between two groups of victims: on the one hand, the Dominicans of Haitian descent rendered "stateless" by a discriminatory Constitutional Court in 2013, and on the other, the churchgoers of Charleston killed by a bigot's gun on 17 June 2015. What is particularly compelling about this piece is that it exemplifies the breadth of vision which characterizes Danticat's oeuvre, in which the creative writer/cultural critic focuses on several categories of "black bodies in motion". In the 2015 essay, Danticat articulates, as poignantly as she ever has, her sometimes painful relation to the notion of "home". While the piece is a response to the trauma experienced by Dominicans of Haitian descent since the 2013 judicial ruling which deprived them of citizenship, its haunting title alludes not only to the dilemma of soon-to-be deported Haitians, but also to that of African Americans, confronting a problematic underdog status in their supposed "homeland" (one should note that the Jacob Lawrence paintings trace the migration of millions of African Americans from rural to urban areas in the United States):

> Human beings have been migrating since the beginning of time. We have always travelled from place to place looking for better opportunities, where they exist. We are not always welcomed, especially if we are viewed as different and dangerous, or if we end up, as the novelist Toni Morrison described in her

Nobel lecture, on the edges of towns that cannot bear our company. Will we ever have a home in this place, or will we always be set adrift from the home we knew? Or the home we have never known.[1]

Though Edwidge Danticat, like Junot Díaz and also like Caryl Phillips, left the Caribbean while still a child, she is not "set adrift" from her native Haiti, though she is clearly sensitive to the spectre of homelessness. Her generation, her almost second generation of Caribbean migrants, might in theory be somewhat detached, if not alienated, from the "old, familiar ways" of homeland wistfully celebrated in the 1920s by the Jamaican poet Claude McKay:

> Bananas ripe and green, and ginger-root
> Cocoa in pods and alligator pears . . .
> My eyes grew dim, and I could no more gaze;
> A wave of longing through my body swept,
> And, hungry for the old, familiar ways,
> I turned aside and bowed my head and wept.[2]

But I will argue in this chapter that as "immigrant artist", Danticat, who has been living in North America since the age of twelve, does in fact habitually look southward, to the island of origin. It is worth underlining, in this context, the validity of Alison Donnell's warning that diasporic criticism may tend to represent migrant writers in such a way that "the Caribbean nation, place and region becomes the dispossessed centre from which literal and intellectual trajectories take their point of departure but make no return".[3] For Haiti is not "dispossessed" in this sense in Danticat's work: the Haitian American writer demonstrates a persistent preoccupation with a land neither truly native or other. Her commitment to Haiti is manifest not only in a prodigious body of literary texts, but in her activism: for example, Danticat and Díaz were two of four writers, including another Dominican American, Julia Alvarez, who protested through an op-ed published in the New York Times against the legal marginalization of Dominicans of Haitian descent.[4] More recently, in May 2017, Danticat published an essay advocating for the approximately fifty thousand Haitians in danger of losing the "temporary protected status" they received after the 2010 earthquake in an essay entitled "A Harrowing Turning Point for Haitian Immigrants".[5]

While lacking a shared ethnicity or a common national identity, Danticat and Díaz (whose work will be discussed in chapter 2) both embody an inclusive and sometimes militant Caribbeanness. It is Danticat who has more self-consciously articulated the responsibilities of a group on whom she confers the imperative to "create dangerously" in the 2010 collection of semi-autobiographical texts entitled *Create Dangerously: The Immigrant Artist at Work*. At the same time, the *New Yorker* essay cited at the beginning of this chapter underscores what emerges elsewhere in Danticat's writing – her acceptance of the United States as more than "host country", as a location with whose political and social realities she engages as if born there. Like Junot Díaz, with whom she has enjoyed a real friendship as well as a literary alliance, Danticat cannot claim the malaise of the political refugee, irrevocably banished from homeland; nor – at the other extreme of the continuum of migrant experiences – does she exhibit the complacency of one who has accepted a comfortable hybridity. Both writers, as well as several of their fictional characters, are keenly conscious of difference, of *their* difference, and both, while manifestly rejecting the messianism of those who would seek to speak for *all* their compatriots, seem committed to advocating for inhabitants of these new North American diasporas, as well as for compatriots still in the Caribbean. While the Haitian American does to some extent assume in her fiction the role of interpreter for a people largely misunderstood in North America (and even in the Caribbean region), she does not mask the sociopolitical conditions which motivate migrancy – and which contributed to her beloved uncle's exile and death (in *Brother, I'm Dying*). It is clear, then, that to label Edwidge Danticat as either an American or a Haitian writer would be to ignore a complex identity of which language is one vital component, as demonstrated by her choice of English as language of literary creation, as the now familiar and even productive "stepmother tongue".[6] In a 1995 lecture/essay, "Haiti: A Bi-cultural Experience", Danticat used as a compelling metaphor for a divided self a memorable culinary image, claiming that according to her characters, one of the positives of a "bi-cultural life" is that "you have plantains with your Thanksgiving dinner. The proverbs of your language peek through the veil of the English you speak."[7]

The allusion to the plantain, a Caribbean favourite which knows no nationality, might appear to suggest that Danticat revels in the multiplicity of influences which the migration experience may offer. However, in the fictional and non-fictional texts on which the present chapter focuses – *The Dew Breaker*; *Brother, I'm Dying*; and *Create Dangerously* – the writer undermines comforting assumptions of a *fruitful* transnationalism or bi-culturalism, making it clear that her duality of vision and experience may also generate angst. It is important to note that for one who, like Danticat, left the Caribbean as a child, identity is not a monolithic entity, frozen in time: rather, the relation to the United States is a changing, growing thing, as revealed in these lines from "Haiti", which relate to the spring of 1981, the year Danticat and her brother arrived in New York: "None of us at that time considered ourselves anything but Haitians, even though there were many youngsters who denied it any chance they got. . . . In the eyes of our young friends, no amount of chic clothes, or modern hairstyles could hide who we were."[8] That certainty of the newly arrived would inevitably give way to a more nuanced form of self-identification, as the now-adult Edwidge acknowledges in the 1995 lecture that "our identities expand" – after quoting the theorists of Créolité who deploy another compelling trope by affirming that "our history is a braid of histories".[9]

This chapter will discuss the writer's treatment and negotiation of that sometimes painful relationship with Haiti *and* with the United States, paying particular attention to the issue of voice, which is, I believe, central to an understanding of Danticat's creative project – for several reasons. The first point of relevance to Danticat's fascination with the voice springs from what might seem a truism: the primacy of orality in Haitian culture. Danticat, by her insistence in her creative work on the potency and persuasiveness of the voice, on the resonance of words spoken whether in intimacy to a beloved listener or with authority to a group, dismantles any perceived hierarchy valuing the scribal over the oral (or vice versa). The unique position of Haiti among Caribbean nations in terms of the status given to the vernacular language is certainly worth noting here: Article 5 of the Constitution names the two official languages of that nation as Creole and French, thereby appearing to valorize the popular language: "Tous les Haïtiens sont unis par une Langue commune: le Créole. Le Créole et le Français sont les langues officielles de la République." (All Haitians are united by a common language: Creole. Creole and French are the official languages of the Republic.)[10] But the situation is perhaps more complex than that simple parity between the European language and the Creole tongue, since 100 per cent of Haitians are *créolophones*, while the number of individuals fluent in French is significantly less. Thus, the author, who herself writes English with mastery and with lyricism, and who speaks it with the faintest of accents, is certainly sensitive to the function of language in her society of origin, both in practical terms and as a symbol of an inalienable identity (despite the linguistic challenges offered by Spanish, due to the proximity of the Dominican Republic, and by English, as a result of the vast migration to the United States). As underlined by Marie-Hélène Laforest in *Diasporic Encounters: Remapping the Caribbean*, "Though Danticat relates to Haitian literature, she is also outside of it. Her dislocation to the U.S. has led her to produce a new language: behind her lyrical English, Kreyòl, another language, breathes."[11]

Danticat's thoughtful attention to the dynamic of speech and silence is also informed by her consciousness of the imperative – and the attendant difficulty – of articulating the experience of the historically silenced. In her first novel, *Breath, Eyes, Memory*, the storytelling grandmother is confident and subversive; listening to her daughter and granddaughter slip unknowingly into English, she disparages the "master tongue" as follows with a harsh, aurally unpleasant epithet: "Oh that *cling-clang* talk. . . . It sounds like glass breaking."[12] The figure of the powerful, eloquent storyteller fulfils a multiplicity of roles in the work of this Haitian American Creole/French/English speaker: that of historian and genealogist who speaks for the supposedly illiterate, as well as that of beloved elder who roots a younger generation in "exile" in the dense terrain of the homeland. And behind the figure of the storyteller, one cannot help but glimpse that of the writer herself, weaver of tales, cautious *porte-parole* (though not *griote*), whose unique voice speaks for her remarkable people, never wavering, never drowned by the different timbre of other/alien tongues which surround her.

On a more personal level, Danticat's near reverence for the sound and nuances of the human voice appears connected to her experience as a child of "doubly interpreting" for her beloved Uncle Joseph, rendered mute by cancer, an experience which of course can be seen as metaphorically related to her vocation, to her role as writer. In response to my question,[13] Danticat agreed that there was a connection between her uncle's situation and her own sensitivity to the condition of those who cannot speak, going on to cite Maya Angelou's *I Know Why the Caged Bird Sings*: "I am very intrigued by that kind of voicelessness as much as I am by the type that is imposed on people by circumstances, when you don't know how to speak another language for example and you suddenly land in another country, for all intents and purposes, mute. . . . So yes, my uncle's condition made me a close observer of all kinds of voicelessness."

At the same time, Danticat has emphasized, in response to a simplification of her role based on the assumption that one individual can speak for a heterogeneous people, that she is not *the* voice of Haiti; one notes particularly the writer's expressed reluctance to be locked into the role of spokesperson/advocate for all Haitians of the North American diaspora: "I don't really see myself as the voice for the Haitian-American experience. . . . There are many. I'm just one."[14] This acknowledgement of plurality – and implicitly, therefore, of the potential for contradiction – is inherent in the several linked narratives which make up *The Dew Breaker*, a volume consisting of texts loosely and yet carefully assembled, separate and yet capable of being read as a whole, most of them relating the experiences of Haitian migrants to North America, specifically to New York. In considering Danticat's representation of the Haitian diaspora in the United States, I find it useful to begin with two stories from that collection before examining the memoir, *Brother, I'm Dying*, to which *The Dew Breaker* is thematically linked. The uneasy or even melancholy mood of some of the narratives in the collection may be attributed to the implicit connection of many of the fictional characters to the notorious "dew breaker" of the title, the cruel henchman (also known as *tonton macoute*) of the Duvalier regime who attempts to hide from his past, having fled Haiti for New York. In discussing her translation of Creole terms incorporated in her writing, Danticat has explained the genesis of this title: "The term 'dew breaker' . . . was 'chouket laroze'. That could be translated as 'dew shaker' or 'dew smasher'. But 'dew breaker' is much more poetic, so that's how I translated it."[15] Danticat's explanation not only reinforces her self-assigned latitude as creative writer to impose her viewpoint even as translator, but also underscores the author's sense of the tragic, a sense which pervades the collection – for the verb "to break," juxtaposed against "dew", obviously connotes, in this context, a shocking and wilful violence.

Several of the stories constitute, however, more everyday – if not banal – narratives of migration, foregrounding human beings whose absence from Haiti is not obviously the outcome of political turmoil. One such text is the story "Seven", which poignantly relates the reunion of a young couple, married seven years previously, just before the husband's departure for New York. As the narrative develops, we learn that both have been unfaithful as a result of the temptations of long separation. At the beginning of the tale, however, the mood is one of high expectancy, as the husband prepares for his wife's arrival; one of the rare light-hearted moments of the narrative relates to the husband's insistence that each of his two flatmates wear a specially bought though ludicrous pink satin robe (for decorum's sake!). Yet the notion of secrecy and disguise, which constitutes a motif in this short story, is a warning that one should not expect a Hollywood-type resolution of the couple's loss of intimacy; for, as Mary Gallagher has pointed out, "*The Dew Breaker* traces, both formally and thematically, the secrets and failures, the cracks and short circuits, that undermine authentic connection in relationships":[16]

> He told Dany not to mention those nights out again. His wife wasn't to know that he'd ever done anything but work his two jobs, as a night janitor at Medgar Evers College and a day janitor at Kings' County Hospital. . . . Gone were the early-evening domino games. Gone was the phone number he'd had for the last five years, ever since he'd had a telephone. (He didn't need other women calling him now.)[17]

In addition, despite these frenetic preparations, the reunion begins under the shadow of a troubling scene at the airport, which may symbolically point to the gaps in a relationship lacking in the substance seven years of marriage would normally represent. The young woman is stripped of her carefully assembled gift packages by a customs officer who "barked questions at her in mangled Creole" (39) – the linguistic detail suggesting a superficial but unrewarding awareness on the part of officialdom of the existence of the Haitian diaspora and its vernacular language. One might be tempted to label this functionary culturally intolerant if he were not simply following a bureaucratic code based on the assumption of illegality, a code unknown to the traveller. So she must finally present herself to her husband as if she had travelled light (a near impossibility for Caribbean migrants!): "The customs man unwrapped all her gifts – the mangoes, sugarcane, avocados, the grapefruit-peel preserves, the peanut, cashew, and coconut confections, the coffee beans, which he threw into a green bin decorated with fruits and vegetables with red lines across them" (40). The gifts are diverse, some more succulent than others, but all evocative of her perceived otherness, of customs and tastes peculiar to an "alien" region and people.

This text is particularly interesting if read with "Walk Straight", one of the chapters of *Create Dangerously*, in which the narrator-author finally admits to her parents about having been forced to jettison the coffee beans so carefully bestowed on her as a gift for them during a visit to her aunt in the hills of Beauséjour. That coffee had acquired, in the writer's imagination, something of the magical abilities claimed of it by Tante Ilyana, her father's sister: "'When he has a taste of this coffee,' she says, 'it will bring him home.'"[18] But the understated, even terse, fashion in which Danticat will relate the confiscation of the precious coffee further on in the narrative conveys the writer's tacit obedience, as sophisticated traveller/insider, to the dictates of customs officers which frequently confound first-time Caribbean visitors: "I tell my father that on the last day of my visit to Beauséjour, Tante Ilyana had given me three pounds of coffee for him, coffee that had been confiscated as 'illegal agricultural transport' by customs officers at John F. Kennedy Airport in New York."[19]

In "Seven", however, the narrative point of view is quite different: Danticat stands discreetly on the periphery of the scene so that the reader is free to sympathize fully with the disappointment of the first-time traveller who must greet her husband almost empty-handed: "By the time he was done with her luggage, she had little left. The suitcase was so light now that she could walk very quickly as she carried it in one hand" (40). So she walks out to her excited husband to navigate an initially exuberant reunion which will soon give way to a mixed reality. Despite the troubling revelation, conveyed to the reader in fragmentary detail, that the husband has made another, illicit, life, which he must conceal from his wife, the narrative portrays a diasporan existence that still embraces community, where Haitian voices are regularly in dialogue with each other through the virtual relationships facilitated by the medium of radio. The lonely days spent by the wife in the confinement of her new home are relieved by the power and comfort of recognizable voices – even if the news from home and from within the diasporic community is not always good:

> At noon the phone rang. It was him. He asked her what she was doing. She lied and told him she was cooking, making herself something to eat. . . . When she hung up, she turned on the radio. She scrolled between the stations he had pointed out to her and was glad to hear people speaking Creole. There was music playing too, konpa, by a group named Top Vice. She switched to a station with a talk show and sat up to listen as some callers talked about a Haitian American man named Patrick Dorismond who'd been killed. (45)

While the Haitian tenants who share the accommodation with the young couple are obviously charmed by the wife's ability to cook "home food", reference is also made to a different lifestyle which is not without its appeal – the easily accessible comforts of cosmopolitan New York: "They seemed happy, eating for pleasure as well as sustenance, chewing more slowly than they ever had before. Usually they ate standing up, Chinese or Jamaican takeout from places down the street" (46).

Thus, the host land is not crudely drawn as a sort of Babylon, and the coexistence of a variety of culinary options hints at the excitement and convenience of the big city. A notable example of Danticat's refusal to idealize the homeland, even in a narrative undoubtedly tinged with nostalgia, is the oblique critique of the class-bound society from which these young men came/fled to the United States, a critique evident in the protagonist's irritation with himself at what he clearly deems his excessive politeness to the (Haitian) landlady: "'Thank you very much, Madame,' he said" (37). The husband immediately regrets his use of the polite term "Madame" – a courtesy which implicitly places his landlady in a stratum superior to his – and questions why he had "acted like a manservant who'd just been dismissed" (37). Subtly, then, Danticat indicates that memories of Haiti are not all positive. And perhaps the problems for this couple lie as much within their fragile union as within the society to which they must adapt.

For the young man and woman who had initially found in physical intimacy a simple way to bridge the years (on the night of the reunion, they make passionate love seven times, giving rise to the husband's whimsical notion that this corresponds to – or perhaps wipes out – the seven years of their separation) are unable to reach out to each other with words. The open-ended text does not make it clear whether there is any chance of real (re)connection between these two. In the final scene of "Seven", they take a bus ride through New York, thinking back to the street carnival in Haiti where they first met. Ironically, seven years ago, they had acted the parts, in the role playing inherent in the spirit of carnival, of a young couple addressing strangers, "looking for someone to marry them" (52). Now, however, they both wear an invisible but heavier mask, hiding the changes and losses wrought by years of separation behind a façade which impedes genuine communication: "Since she didn't know the language, they wouldn't have to speak or ask any questions of the stony-faced people around them. They could carry out their public wedding march in silence, a temporary silence, unlike the one that had come over them now" (52). These lines may be read as evocative of Danticat's wider concern with language as repository of a culture, as a necessary means of everyday communication but also, importantly, as a metaphor for and condition of intimacy; and the "stony-faced people" might well refer to an unwelcoming community in which migrants feel excluded. But as is often the case with Danticat, the narrative cannot be reduced to the sum of its political concerns; it is also the account of a real relational challenge, an account of human yearning and misunderstanding. Indeed, in this uncertain conclusion of "Seven", the personal and political themes coalesce: the husband can no more turn his back on this little-known wife than he can forget his *pays natal*. Perhaps the most striking "message" lingering at the end of this enigmatic narrative is that change of a kind neither wanted nor anticipated, perhaps inevitable in all relationships, is an ineluctable consequence of migration, both within the communities of origin and in the new groupings/alliances formed up north.

Emblematic of the threat of alienation from the homeland which haunts the husband of "Seven", as well as several migrants in Danticat's semi-fictional world – however grounded they may appear – are the unanswered letters and the silent telephone forming the disconcerting backdrop to the story "Water Child". In this title, and in that of the French version of this text, "L'Enfant d'eau",[20] one hears an echo of the earlier story "Children of the Sea" (from the 1991 collection *Krik? Krak!*). But the two narratives are quite different: the latter text was on epic scale, relating the odyssey of "boat people" perhaps condemned to death in the unwelcoming waters between Haiti and Florida, yet strangely formidable because united ("L'union fait la force" is, after all, the Haitian national motto). One might be tempted to retitle the new story "Child of the Sea" if such simplification or neat correspondence would not be antithetical to the spirit of a writer who accepts contradiction and complexity as part of her artistic birthright. "Water Child" presents a solitary protagonist living in the United States in hardly brutal circumstances, equipped with the relative comfort of resident status and remuneration, surrounded by technological aids to communication, but strangely taciturn. In the earlier narrative, the group of travellers found comfort in the spoken word, in the songs of their beloved Haiti: "Some of the women sing and tell stories to each other to appease the vomiting. . . . We spent most of yesterday telling stories. Someone says, Krik? You answer, Krak! And they say, I have many stories I could tell you, and then they go on and tell these stories to you, but mostly to themselves."[21] The ritual "Krik? Krak!" is of course the call and response formula used in several Caribbean territories[22] to punctuate the oral narrative and, importantly, to confirm the bond of familiarity and of *interest* between storyteller and audience.

Nadine, the nurse who is the main character of "Water Child", seems to have undergone a sea change in her years away from home: this Haitian's story is hers alone, unshared with those who work with her, unknown to the loving parents left at home – whose letter appears on the first page and whose voices are heard on an answering machine. Nadine is certainly not one of the category of voyagers reductively dubbed "boat people", and perhaps Danticat is highlighting here the danger inherent in seeing migrants as a faceless group. (We are reminded of the need to differentiate between economic migrants, privileged/provisional travellers and asylum seekers, distinctions sometimes glossed over by conflating all such migrants under the category of "exiles".) Yet despite her position of relative privilege, Nadine's story is imbued with melancholy, a melancholy which in fact pervades the entire collection *The Dew Breaker*, of which most of the narratives are set in the United States. That melancholy might be associated with the negative memories which many of the characters carry with them from Haiti; Aitor Ibarrola-Armendariz argues that "not even those who have abandoned the country or were only tangentially touched by the torturers' cruelties, such as the protagonists of 'Seven' or 'Water Child', seem totally free from that violent legacy that impedes their rehabilitation and reintegration into society".[23] It is not clear that the unhappiness of the main character of "Water Child" is linked to that legacy, however. Nadine seems irremediably separated, if not from family, then at least from a dream of a better life, and the journey home – mentioned tentatively by the anxious mother – is clearly deferred to a time not known: "Ten years ago her parents had sold everything they owned and moved from what passed for a lower-middle-class neighbourhood to one on the edge of a slum, in order to send her to nursing school abroad. Ten years ago she'd dreamed of seeing the world, of making her own way in it" (62–63). The painful isolation of this Haitian nurse is complex in origin, and Danticat is too nuanced a writer to attribute her problems, in Manichean style, to the mere condition of migrancy: while homeland and parents are clearly sorely missed, Nadine seems to have deliberately chosen to separate herself from other Haitians working in the same hospital. In addition, she is mourning a lost – aborted – baby, the water child of the title, and also the loss of Eric, the lover, a shadowy figure in the narrative (perhaps the unhappy husband of "Seven"), the reasons for whose defection and betrayal remain sketchy. To the easy complicity reflected in the formula "Krik? Krak!" this story opposes the unrelenting silence of a telephone unanswered, of letters apparently unanswerable.

The narrative begins, however, with a semblance of calm, of predictability: "The letter came on the first of the month, as usual" (53). But this apparent regularity does not impart on the protagonist's life the comfort of rhythm, the security of structure; rather, the text of the letter[24] betrays and produces uncertainty and even angst: "We have not heard your voice in a while and our ears long for it. Please telephone us" (53). Despite this insistence suggestive of reproach – this subtle emphasis on the inadequacy of scribal communication – the reader senses that this is no recalcitrant, no prodigal daughter: Nadine remembers, in her "exile", her duty to those who sacrificed all so that she should come to the United States to study nursing. Nor is her devotion unreciprocated; the concluding formula of this rather formal elliptical letter brings into sharp focus the reservoir of tenderness still available to her: "It was signed, 'Your mother and father who embrace you very tightly'" (53). In this ending, extravagant to anglophone ears, the francophone reader would hear a near-literal translation of a standard French formula for ending a letter to loved ones, "*Je t'embrasse très fort*," a formula which could perhaps less literally and at the same time more prosaically be translated as "with lots of love" or "with all my/our love". This avoidance by Danticat of the predictable, "normal" English expression is a striking example of her ability to exploit the resources of at least two and sometimes three languages to foreground her Haitianness while writing in English, to tap the emotion or sensibility of one language while apparently respecting the linguistic structures of the other.

The impression of coldness created by Nadine's failure to call or reply is belied by her daily rereading of a flimsy letter held close to her body, and by her expression of the rather melodramatic fear that the letter will soon disintegrate. The importance of this letter may be linked to the notion of the "remittance text", and of the remittance itself, articulated by Kezia Page in *Transnational Negotiations in Caribbean Diasporic Literature: Remitting the Text* (2010). In "Water Child", the letter creates a virtual though imperfect intimacy between the migrant and those left behind: "How had the postal workers in both Port-au-Prince and Brooklyn not lacerated the thin page and envelope? And how had the letter not turned to dust in her purse during her bus ride to and from work?" (54). Yet Nadine remains inexplicably mute, unresponsive if not impervious to the appeal made in another letter received four weeks after the first: "We have tried to telephone you, but we are always greeted by your répondeur [answering-machine], which will not accept collect calls. In any case, we wait to hear from you" (58).

The silence resulting from Nadine's inability to write back is replicated in the stillness of an apartment in which the only voices heard are, on the one hand, disembodied sounds emanating from the television and, on the other, the more troubling voice of Eric, the former lover who tries to communicate via *répondeur*: "'Alo, allo, hello', he stammered, creating his own odd pauses between Creole, French and English, like the electively mute, newly arrived immigrant children whose worried parents brought them to the ward for consultations, even though there was nothing wrong with their vocal cords" (56). However imperfect his facility in English, the reference to Eric's familiarity with three languages – in sharp contrast to the painful, self-inflicted muteness which Danticat clearly attributes to the trauma of migration – is a suggestion that Nadine's wilful silence is, in the Haitian community, an aberration. The sustaining ritual of communication integral to her culture of origin is broken, and contradictions and questions abound. Nadine's tacit rejection of Eric is countered by the fact that she saves all his messages, as the apparent distancing of her parents is contradicted by what appears to be a rare outburst of emotion: "She'd almost called many times in the last three months, but had lost her nerve, thinking her voice might betray all that she could not say. She nearly dialed the whole thing this time. There were only a few numbers left when she put the phone down, tore the letter into two, then four, then eight, then countless pieces, collapsed among her old magazines and newspapers, and wept" (57).

This intensity is conspicuously absent from Nadine's interactions with colleagues, and even the presumably beloved Eric, in a narrative that presents a life lived – or barely hinted at – in discrete scenes played out on separate stages, occupied by characters and realities which appear not to intersect. We do hear Nadine's voice, finally, on another stage, in the hospital where she works as an ENT nurse, although even here, her exchanges with compatriots are guarded; thus, she declines to make a friend of Josette, who is "one of the younger Haitian RNs, one of those who had come to Brooklyn in early childhood and spoke English with no accent at all", and who "liked to throw in a Creole word here and there in conversation to flaunt her origins" (55). Danticat is laconic, to a provocative extent, about the reasons for Nadine's own refusal to use – if not flaunt – those shared origins, if only to overcome solitude. One is tempted, on the basis of these awkward interactions, to extrapolate from this individual scenario, to imagine a divided community, in which some willingly stay away from the homeland while others "flaunt" their Haitianness. Danticat, whose straightforward narrative style sometimes conceals a fundamental opacity, leaves the reader to complete the gaps in the story of Nadine's isolation; and the short story format allows that enigma to thrive, so that the reader must infer motivations in this complex, compelling tale. One such inference has to do with Nadine's capacity to communicate creatively with, and to express empathy for, the only one of her patients with whom we see her interacting: Ms Hinds, a young woman, a teacher by profession, who has just experienced the trauma of a total laryngectomy – a literal loss of voice. It is Nadine who brings a sort of calm to the devastated patient in a particularly gruelling scene, as Danticat compels the reader to imagine a mute hysteria, an affliction even more compelling than an outpouring of words; it is Nadine who forces pen and paper on Ms Hinds, thus freeing her to state the obvious, "I'm a teacher", and then to express her rage, in capital letters which approximate a shout: "WHY SEND ME HOME LIKE THIS?" (61).

Perhaps the reason for Nadine's ability to open up to one imprisoned in a new world of wordlessness is that she senses a parallel to her own self-inflicted condition: she imagines (but refrains from) warning Ms Hinds of a time "when she would awake from dreams in which she'd spoken to find that she had no voice, or when she would see something alarming and realize that she couldn't scream for help" (66). The focus of the long sentence from which these words are taken shifts almost imperceptibly from the dilemma of the newly mute patient to the less obvious predicament of the protagonist herself, a shift barely accentuated by the disruption of the sequence of subject pronouns ("she") with the intrusion of the emphatic "she herself": "or when she would see something alarming and realize that she couldn't scream for help, or even when she would realize that she herself was slowly forgetting, without the help of old audio or videocassettes or answering-machine greetings, what her own voice used to sound like" (66). The reference to the audiocassettes reminds us of the fondness of migrant Haitians for simulating/recovering the immediacy of face-to-face conversation through oral messages consigned to cassettes.[25] Here, the voice evidently denotes the medium of communication on which human beings rely (especially those like teachers and preachers who depend on its resources daily as a means of persuasion). But one may also interpret the author's insistence on the dynamic of speech and silence as a wider concern with the unique personality and the culture which distinguish each immigrant, and the dread of dilution or loss of that identity – the other side of the positive evolution that some critical discourses have ascribed to terms such as "integration" or "hybridity".

In Edwidge Danticat's 2007 memoir *Brother, I'm Dying*, the issue of voicelessness, both literal and figurative, is accorded primacy as the writer-narrator remembers the singularly expressive voice of her uncle (who was also surrogate father to her) as "being crisp and distinct".[26] While the trope of silence is widely used in Caribbean literature *and* literary criticism, for Danticat, the condition of one whose larynx has been removed is patently more than metaphor. A few years after the publication of *The Dew Breaker*, the disturbing memoir revealed to her readers[27] the ordeal of her beloved uncle, a pastor who lost his voice after an operation similar to that of the fictional Ms Hinds, and for whom Edwidge functioned, in a part of her childhood, as spokesperson. For her uncle, denied the privilege of self-representation, and for her fellow Haitians, Danticat is both witness and advocate in *Brother, I'm Dying*, using the fluid genre of autobiography as a fertile space, in a narrative which may be read as a tale of personal *and* collective loss.

Brother, I'm Dying honours the writer's father, who lived and worked for several decades in North America, and above all the uncle who remained at home until a final visit to the United States which would have tragic conse-quences. So creative writing is shaped and in fact inspired by lived experi-ence; and so, in *Brother, I'm Dying*, autobiography must contain and not be overwhelmed by emotion, that of the outrage felt by the author whose Uncle Joseph died a lonely death in the custody of US immigration authorities in 2004. Of all Danticat's writing, it is this explicitly autobiographical text that most powerfully conveys her painful sense of being Haitian and yet also beneficiary of a sort of Americanness. Here, the tone is palpably less serene than in the early essay "Haiti: A Bi-cultural Experience", in which the writer accepted her uncle's assurance that her shadow remained in Haiti: "This reassures me that my shadow is in places I can't be. And when I am there I step in its place."[28] The account of her relationship with Joseph Dantica, to whom her parents entrusted the task of taking care of the author and her brother while they sought a better life in New York, could be read as a bitter tale, a tragic story. It is a narrative which has ultimately troubling undercurrents for many who, like Danticat, and like several of the fictional characters in *Krik? Krak!* as well as in the *The Dew Breaker*, can hardly claim to be resident aliens in the United States. Yet *Brother* is also emblematic of the possibility of resilience; it is also a story of birth and renewal: the birth of the novelist's first child, whom she is able to present to her father shortly before his death, and to whom she gives his name, Mira. It is also the story of words offered and shared against the odds: it tells the tale of an eloquent pastor who lost his vocal facility, but discovered new ways (assisted by technology) to speak powerfully from the heart. Like the teacher Ms Hinds, Uncle Joseph had depended on his voice – on its persuasive nuances, on its compelling resonance – to perform his chosen vocation.

The section of the narrative telling of the uncle's operation, in New York, after the diagnosis of throat cancer – by American doctors visiting Haiti – is striking in its economical, almost bare style: "My uncle had his radical laryngectomy the next day. When he came out, he was never able to use his own voice again. He was fifty-five years old" (42). The enormity of the loss is only appreciated by comparison to the earlier, much less terse description of a man who had converted from political activism to being a Baptist minister, whose voice was an essential part of his mission as preacher. In the narrator's reminiscence of her uncle during the years she spent with him, one notes a close attention to the uniqueness of the voice, of this voice, its modulations, its variations, its capacity to rivet congregants and family members alike: "As a child living in his house from the time I was four until I was twelve years old, I remember my uncle's voice being crisp and distinct: deep and resolute, breathy and jingly when he was angry, steely and muted when he was sad" (34).

But even after the loss of a voice, life goes on, even for this passionate, gifted preacher – but a life that is different, truncated. Perhaps in her wish to privilege above all the dignity of this suddenly mute man whom she loved, Danticat sketches out more than she details: but the adult narrator of *Brother* does remember that although Uncle hired two associate preachers to keep his church going, he could not so easily resolve the suffering of his imposed silence. In a chapter exuberantly entitled "Brother, I Can Speak", we learn that, remarkably, Uncle Joseph will regain some measure of speech, though never the full breadth of his rhetorical skills, after another visit to the United States and the acquisition of a mechanical voice box which he must hold to his neck. From this point of the narrative, the image of this awkward instrument, reminiscent of but never equivalent to the human larynx, serves to underscore that speech and self-expression should never be taken for granted; and at a different level, one is reminded of the reverence in many African and Caribbean cultures for those who speak *well*, a reverence predicated on an understanding that mastery of the spoken word is at once a prodigious gift sanctioned and applauded by the community and a reflection of one's individuality. In accessing this technological miracle, Edwidge is both companion and interpreter: "My father decided it was best that I take my uncle to his appointment at Kings County Hospital the next day. Unlike anyone else, I could now doubly interpret my uncle, both from silence to voice and Creole to English" (129).

From that point onward, Uncle Joseph will benefit from what the narrator frequently refers to as his "motorized voice". But he will finally be silenced, ironically in the United States, the site and to some extent the agent of his return to voice. This episode of the memoir, which occupies some forty pages near the end, leaves the reader with a keen sense that the label "Haitian American" is inadequate to translate the ambivalence of the insider-outsider, sensitive to the gap separating privileged bearer of a green card from semi-mendicant traveller without status. Incarcerated in the notorious Krome Detention Center, an unwelcome asylum seeker in the land to which he had fled, Uncle Joseph no longer has Edwidge as his interpreter, and for all her eloquence and celebrity, she is unable to persuade the authorities to let her even visit him. So all she will have to remember his final visit is one phone call, marked by this sharing of *words* – words both nurturing and inadequate. Here, as elsewhere in Danticat's writing, several languages coexist, and while she translates – without emphasis on a complex linguistic situation – the few words in Creole and in French appearing in this final exchange with her *créolophone* uncle, their place in this moment of high emotion gives them an affective value greater than that of the "standard" English of the narration.

> That night at around six o'clock, my uncle called me from Krome.
> "Bon dye," I shouted, so overjoyed to hear that motorized voice. "My God. It's so good to hear you."

"Oh, I can't tell you how good it is to hear you," he said.

Then I slipped into a repartee I had fallen into with my father in the last weeks or so as he'd grown sicker. I called him cher, amour, mon coeur, darling, my love, my heart.

"How are you, my heart?"

"M nan prizon," he said. I'm in jail. (228–29)

So Joseph Dantica dies alone, stripped of agency, deprived of the medicines he needs, his attempts to speak for himself – literally and figuratively – misunderstood by officialdom. Though he arrived by plane, with a perfectly legitimate, previously used US visa, he is reduced to the level of "boat person"; and were it not for the identity of his writer niece, his lot would have been the anonymity which is often the portion of such undocumented migrants; from cherished uncle and visitor, he is transformed suddenly, finally, into one of an undistinguished mass. A remark by Sandra Pouchet Paquet in *Caribbean Autobiography* is, I think, germane to Danticat's project in writing a story which is as much her uncle's as her own, the story he was unable to tell on his own behalf: "Despite great variation in modes of representation, the consistent expressive need in autobiography is the representation of individual identity and its concomitant burden of difference."[29] For in the end, Uncle's Haitianness, his ability to express himself in Creole but not in English, is both a burden and the source of a unique selfhood to which the writer clearly attaches great value.

It is striking the extent to which the author-narrator, in her account of her uncle's ordeal, avoids personalizing the carefully researched details she provides, which sound as though taken from the official record[30] – though one must assume that they are filtered and ordered by her creative lens. Hers is a challenging task, and one feels the tension between emotion and an apparent objectivity. A passionate authorial involvement is, I believe, discernible beneath the surface of the sometimes understated text; in one revealing section, from which an extract appears below, the almost clinical nature of the narrative is disturbed by an elegiac tone created by the repetition of the words "my uncle":

At 7.00 p.m., after more than twenty hours of no food and sugarless IV fluids, my uncle was sweating profusely and complained of weakness. He was found to be hypoglycemic, with a lower than normal blood sugar level of 42 mg/dl.

The doctor on duty prescribed a 5 percent dextrose drip and twenty minutes later, my uncle's blood glucose stabilized at 121 mg/dl. It was then noted that he was awake and alert and his mental response "appropriate". (239)

In the irony of the final adjective, and above all in the quotation marks which problematize it, lies the sting of this meticulously detailed account of the treatment of an eighty-one-year-old man who would be pronounced dead by 8:46 p.m., no longer able to communicate through his voice box, and who was not allowed the presence of relatives who might have mediated his dealings with medical personnel whose assumptions about race and illiteracy made them ill-equipped to judge whether his responses were in fact "appropriate".

Rage might seem then to be the "appropriate" response for the narrator who is also niece; yet, while these final pages suggest an anger barely reined in, the mood of condemnation is accompanied – though not necessarily tempered – by Danticat's sense that villains exist both at home and abroad. The novelist Evelyne Trouillot has written the following of her country-woman: "Edwidge Danticat's gaze rests upon Haitian society with no indulgence."[31] This comment, intended to be complimentary, is to some extent troubling in that it indirectly emphasizes the burden that Haitian writers (especially those living abroad) are called upon to bear, as if the stories they tell are inherently sombre, and as if their role is similar to that of the journalist or the historian. Danticat is further described by Trouillot as having "a truth-seeking eye",[32] and in her portrayal of the indignities to which her uncle was subjected, such commitment to truth-telling – even in this case, in the midst of great pain – is apparent. For the author is not partial in her exposure (in chapters entitled "Beating the Darkness" and, simply, "Hell") of the political turmoil which led to Uncle's unplanned departure from Haiti, or of the gang violence directed at him and his family, which he sought to escape by fleeing to the generous embrace of foreign relatives, only to find American soil to be no safe haven. His is a much more dramatic version of Nadine's homelessness – his banishment, in shackles, to Krome a real solitary confinement in comparison to her isolation by choice. Danticat's grief is patent, though at times, in the last pages of the memoir, her language, usually fluid even when unembellished, seems remarkably colourless, as if her own voice is faltering.

Towards the end of *Brother, I'm Dying*, Danticat goes back, as she often does in the non-linear narrative, to the cultural heritage which is the well-spring of her creative work. She inscribes a poignant folk tale: a story of familial loss learned from Granmè Melina, Uncle Joseph's eloquent mother-in-law, of a daughter reluctant to hold the traditional wake at the death of her beloved father. In the oral narrative, one of the elders reproaches the bereaved daughter, underscoring the story's didacticism from the start: "'Daughter . . . let the wake be held. Your father is now in the land beneath the waters. It is not our way to let our grief silence us'" (266). And one page further on, the daughter finally takes up the refrain, elaborating on the moral in these concluding words: "'We will eat. We will sing. We will dance and tell stories. But most importantly, we will speak of my father. For it is not our way to let our grief silence us'" (267).

After the inconceivable tragedy that befell the Haitian people on 12 January 2010, I heard in these words something of the same resolute endurance and grace manifested, in the aftermath of the earthquake, by so many Haitians: celebrated artists like Wyclef Jean,[33] Dany Laferrière, Evelyne Trouillot and Edwidge Danticat, and, above all, by the many so-called ordinary people who refused to retreat into the abdication of silence. What the 2010 volume of essays *Create Dangerously: The Immigrant Artist at Work* shares with the memoir *Brother, I'm Dying* is the writer's willingness to confront and to represent the complexity of a people often defined on the basis of uninformed stereotypes. In responding to my question, "How would you describe your people?",[34] Danticat underscored the extent to which Haitians are often misunderstood: "That sense of ingenuity and creativity and self pride is very strong in Haitians. The rest of the world doesn't see that. People want to either pity or idealise Haitians, especially now, but we are a very proud and complicated people." In *Create Dangerously*, the author self-consciously embraces that complex reality as *one* of the voices of Haiti. She is frequently, as all interpreters/translators try to be, preoccupied with *fidélité* – with accuracy in rendering someone else's story; but as creative writer, as passionate witness to a cruel history, both collective and familial, she is compelled to speak in her own voice.

Danticat's perception of her role vis-à-vis this battered but still not prostrate people, implicit in *Brother*, emerges more clearly in the essays comprising

Create Dangerously. The book is framed by two devastating moments in Haitian history, both of which the author involves herself in, as witness and scribe. The text begins with the account of the massacre of two political activists – which the writer relates in graphic detail, as if she had actually witnessed it – and ends with a chapter titled "Our Guernica", which memorializes those lost in the earthquake of 2010, a disaster of epic proportions, and one having personal implications for the Danticat family. The first of the two events – which, chronologically, are more than forty years apart – is a chronicle of brutality wrought on Haitians by fellow Haitians; the second evokes random natural violence, triggering the death of hundreds of thousands of victims (evoked elliptically in the dedication of *Create Dangerously*: "two hundred thousand and more"). The significance of Danticat's interest in the 1964 (when she was not yet born) execution of two young Haitian patriots, Marcel Numa and Louis Drouin, is the bond she establishes with these two men on both public and personal levels: regarding the former, the author adumbrates in the first chapter of *Create Dangerously* the importance for artists of "several stories – one might call them creation myths – that haunt and obsess them".[35] That she claims this terrible episode in Haitian history as part of the *raison d'être* of her own work is revealing of the very *public* nature of Danticat's writing and of its inextricable connection with Haiti's past, as well as with collective memory. At the same time, the young writer feels a link to the two men, whom she describes as "patriots who died so that other Haitians could live" because they were "also immigrants, like me" (7). Importantly, they too suffered the sting of a challenge to their nationhood, for Duvalier "labelled them not Haitian, but foreign rebels, good-for-nothing *blans* [whites]" (7). In a 2011 interview with *Guernica*, Danticat elaborates on the significance for her and for many other émigrés of these two brutal deaths: "For me, and a lot of people I talked to, their deaths signalled a more brutal dictatorship and created a new reality that drove a lot of Haitians away from their homeland. That connection between this very brutal act and the further migrations it inspired has always intrigued me."[36]

It is certainly no coincidence that in the section immediately following the description of Numa and Drouin's deaths, Danticat shifts narrative focus from the national – from the large event – to the local – to the story of her parents, whose decision to relocate their young family would have such far-reaching consequences. Here, as frequently occurs in such semi-autobiographical texts, the personal and the collective stories are juxta-posed, if not inextricably entangled: "At the time of the execution of Marcel Numa and Louis Drouin my recently married, twenty-nine-year old parents lived in Haiti, in a neighbourhood called Bel Air, about a thirty-minute walk from the cemetery" (7).

Not all of the essays comprising *Create Dangerously* are as explicitly politi-cal as either the first chapter, which tells the story of the public execution of activists, or the final text, "Our Guernica", devoted to the earthquake and its aftermath. One of the most haunting of the narratives, "Walk Straight", relates what at first appears to be an individual journey – that of the author, who, on a visit to Haiti, makes the trek uphill to the home of her elderly aunt. In "Walk Straight", multiple journeys and their complex significance are encapsulated in the writer's account of what becomes a sort of pilgrim-age into the heartland of Haiti in the company of her cousin Nick. Here, Danticat's concern with genealogy may be read as an individual, *intimate* story. But readers familiar with other narratives by the writer also recognize its epic dimension, as she articulates her engagement with the story of the tribe, whether home or abroad:

> It is the summer of 1999 and I have come to revisit these mountains from which our family has sprung and which have released us to different types of migrations. . . .
>
> After a brief rest, I reclaim my mountain legs and continue on. Along the way, Nick and I retell each other fragmented stories about my great-grand-parents – his great-great-grandparents – the furthest that memory and history go back in our family, vague tales that we've gathered from older family members. (22)

The verb "to release" in the first sentence above is unexpected: one might read it to mean "to liberate", as if from a prison, with the inescapable nega-tive connotations of confinement preceding escape; or, more optimistically, "to release" as plants send pollen into the air, evoking the possibility for growth, which some migrations offer. Equally suggestive is the image of "mountain legs", which conjures up the figure of a valiant walker, tested but undefeated by the obstacles confronted on a lengthy odyssey. And the fragmented tales with which the travellers pass the time might signify not simply the bits and pieces or even debris of family lore to which the cousins cling, and which they try to reassemble, but also Danticat's vocation as historian and storyteller.

It is, I believe, noteworthy that the brief but therapeutic visit to Aunt Ilyana's home in the serene hills of Beauséjour is not represented by the writer as an idyllic interlude – though of course one cannot ignore the multiple biblical and fictional allusions which come to mind, evoking the mountain as sanctuary; nor can one forget its resonance in Caribbean culture as the historical site of *marronage*.[37] In this respect, as in several others, the autobiographical essay echoes and overlaps with "Night Talkers", the only chapter of *The Dew Breaker* set entirely in Haiti. "Night Talkers" tells the story of the orphaned migrant Dany, who on a visit to Haiti made the arduous journey to a nurturing Haitian mountaintop, where a sort of healing awaited the weary traveller in the home of his elderly aunt. In an article entitled "Home Is Where the Heart Is: Danticat's Landscapes of Return", Elizabeth Walcott-Hackshaw points to Danticat's ambiguous representation of the mountain sojourn: "At first glance Danticat's treatment of this rural landscape in 'Night Talkers' seems ideal and edenic, but it is complicated by Dany's tensions and desires."[38] Similarly, in "Walk Straight", the episode of the narrator's visit to her aunt seems to present in microcosm, or even to sharpen, several of Danticat's anxieties and concerns as "immigrant" and as writer. It is on one such visit to Beauséjour, for example, that the novelist penned what became the explicatory afterword to a new edition of her first novel, *Breath, Eyes, Memory*, affirming to her readers and, perhaps above all, to her Haitian critics that she did not seek to represent the troubled protagonist Sophie as typical of Haitian women as a group.

It is here too that Danticat experiences that dread of future loss which makes it impossible to fully "seize" the present day. Towards the end of her stay, words begin to fail her: "Uncle Joseph and Nick lose themselves in the details of the school while Tante Ilyana and I talk less and less, to avoid, I suspect, speaking of separation. There are already so many separations in our family, constant departures and returns" (35). On her last night at Beauséjour, she suffers a sort of emotional hypersensitivity; unable to sleep, the visitor is distracted in this peaceful spot not only by nature's sounds, but also by sounds within: "It is the mountains maybe, it being so quiet here at night that you hear everything, the swing of every tree branch. . . . And I listen for everything because I know it won't always be so. I listen too closely and sometimes the listening gets too loud" (36). Is this not the archetypal malaise of the returning traveller who must live each moment differently, more intensely, more self-consciously than if no journey back to the adopted home loomed on the horizon? Perhaps this is why the reader feels a certain dissatisfaction, a sense of the *unfinished*, as Edwidge returns to the plain; and in the last pages of the text, we learn of Aunt Ilyana's death a year later, news that seems to magnify for the migrant family, who will not even be able to attend her funeral, the difficulty, if not the impossibility, of return; for it was Ilyana's mission "to guard a very small house in the ancestral village, to sustain a faraway world to which we could return, if we wanted to, and find traces, however remote and faint, of who we are" (38).

While "Walk Straight" purports to tell one traveller's story – though the narrative has something of the appeal of allegory – most of the essays of the collection have a more obvious resonance for "immigrant artists" as a group. The earthquake of January 2010, related in the final chapter, is obviously the most memorable of such stories. Questioned by a reader of the *New Yorker* after the tragedy as to how she viewed her relation to that experience, Danticat spoke, with characteristic refusal of self-aggrandizement, of the limitations of her role as writer from abroad, clearly not impervious to the angst of distance; and also, importantly, she articulated a compensatory sense of vocation: "The artist, I think, is a witness. I am trying to be a witness from afar, which is hard and makes me feel really ineffective sometimes, but there is something worth witnessing here as well, this lesser side of the tragedy."[39]

This comment foreshadows a less tentative affirmation of vocation which forms the subject of *Create Dangerously*, whose provocative subtitle, *The Immigrant Artist at Work*, calls attention to the imperative to write with a sense of purpose. That consciousness of mission is also inscribed in the title of the final essay, "Our Guernica", which constitutes a revision of the original wording (the piece had previously appeared in the *New Yorker* under the more enigmatic title "A Little While"). The revised title, in its allusion to Picasso's famous piece created to honour victims of the Spanish

Civil War, expresses the writer's preoccupation with her craft. But this final essay also shifts movingly and sometimes unpredictably from the story of the group to *her* story; more than a travel narrative, more than an artist's manifesto, it is, first of all, an act of familial homage, as, twenty-three days after the earthquake, Danticat visits the home and burial place of her beloved cousin Maxo. The voices heard are several, but none is more potent than that of Maxo, son of a preacher father – the revered uncle of *Brother, I'm Dying*, fierce advocate for his people. In her memories of Maxo, Danticat seems to reach for a tone that dedramatizes – as if aware that emotion could overwhelm her, and overwhelm her writing. Narrative point of view is particularly intriguing here – as it was in her recounting of Uncle Joseph's death – given the familial relationship at the core of what struggles to sound like matter-of-fact narration:

> Two days after a 7.0 degree earthquake struck Haiti, on January 12, 2010, I was still telling my brothers that one night, as we were watching the television news, Maxo would pop up behind one of the news anchors and take over his job.
>
> Maxo was a hustler. He could get whatever he wanted, whether money or kind words, simply by saying, "You know I love you. I love you. I love you." (154)

But the reference to news anchors brings the narrative's focus back, for the time being, to an issue beyond that of personal loss: to an imperious concern that Haiti's story not be told only on and by CNN, to the issue of self-representation. The link between the private and the collective is clearly not gratuitous, given the passions which characterized Danticat's cousin; for Maxo, the lover of literature, was also informal journalist, social worker and storyteller. On this pilgrimage, Danticat brings with her, and is haunted by, a text he valued, *The Blacks*,[40] by French playwright Jean Genet – a choice which underscores both cousins' preoccupation with their "great black country":

> He felt it was a perfect play for Haiti, one that could easily have been written by a Haitian.
>
> In light of Maxo's death, these lines from the play now haunt me: "Your song was very beautiful, and your sadness does me honor. I'm going to start

life in a new world. If I ever return, I'll tell you what it's like there. Great black country, I bid thee farewell." (154)

Genet's imagining of a "new world" is strikingly poignant here, and one might read these words, appropriated by the grieving emigrant cousin, as evocative of the aspirations of thousands of Haitian travellers heading for North America by sea or air, or of Maxo's final journey to another, better, place.

While highlighting the importance of activism and community work in "Our Guernica" through the example of her cousin, the writer also privileges the role of the artist, adumbrating, in *Create Dangerously*, an inclusive vision of the arts in the Caribbean and its North American diasporas. Her affinity for the work of artists in domains other than the scribal is manifest in an episode which widens the implications of the essay's title: accompanied by an artist friend on a visit to areas of Haiti where family members have suffered losses, Danticat shares his sense of wonder that creativity, stubborn and imperious, survives:

> While driving through Léogane one morning, Jhon and I spot, past a cardboard sign with a plea for food in the entryway of a makeshift refugee camp, a large white tent with a striking image painted on it: a stunningly beautiful chocolate angel with her face turned up toward an indigo sky as she floats over a pile of muddied corpses.
>
> Jhon leaps out of the car to have a better look.
>
> Misty-eyed, he whispers, "Like Picasso and *Guernica* after the Spanish Civil War. We will have our Guernica."
>
> "Or thousands of them," I concur. (169–70)

It is hardly coincidental that each of the three essays in the collection preceding "Our Guernica" pays tribute to an immigrant artist with a Caribbean affiliation. While the second of these memorializes the controversial Haitian/Puerto Rican/American Basquiat, the third tells the story of celebrated Haitian photojournalist Daniel Morel, obsessed – like Danticat – with the tragic ending of the two activists whose killing she describes in the first chapter. The first narrative, entitled "Flying Home", pays tribute to Michael Richards, Jamaican American sculptor who died in his studio on the ninety-second floor of the World Trade Centre on September 11. This last story is especially poignant, as Danticat recalls the obsession with flight which she shared with the sculptor, ending with the whimsical and haunting notion that perhaps, like Toni Morrison's Milkman,[41] Michael Richards was able to embrace flight in his final, potentially terrifying, moments: "maybe he had enough time to stop and whisper, 'I will take off . . . and fly away on my own wings'" (126).

Structurally, then, the collection reinforces the writer's patent affinity with fellow artists, specifically with immigrant artists. The three essays just mentioned lead almost seamlessly into a final assertion, in "Our Guernica", of the need to write, to paint, to create, even after disaster: "Daring again to speak for the collective, I will venture to say that perhaps we will write with the same fervor and intensity (or even more) as before. Perhaps we will write with the same sense of fearlessness or hope. Perhaps we will continue to create as dangerously as possible, but our muse has been irreparably altered" (162). In this account of a visit home, the writer is not as tentative about her ambiguous status as she is elsewhere in the volume, and her confident use of the first-person plural in this meditation on the role of the artist is instructive. Danticat makes it clear also, even in this elegiac narrative, that there is room, in Haitian artistic expression, for a diversity of moods, and also for laughter. Quoting the Haitian novelist Lyonel Trouillot (writing for a French publication a few days after the earthquake), she is reminded that, like him, she needs to laugh – and, importantly, sometimes observer though not voyeur, she too is drawn to the group:

> Last night . . . I heard the drums from a Vodou ceremony. . . . I didn't have enough energy to go and find out if they were praising or rebuking the gods. I started heading there anyway, but came across a group of people playing dominoes by moonlight. I listened to the jokes being told by the players, about both the living and the dead. . . . I know that like them, at the end of the day, both to forget the darkness and to not curse the dawn, I need to laugh. (160)

And Danticat herself is attentive to the need "to not curse the dawn": "I too needed to laugh, so I began reading my friend Dany Laferrière again" (160). By referring to her brother writer Dany Laferrière, famously known for his irreverence,[42] Danticat seems to acknowledge that melancholy cannot be a lasting response – for her or for the Haitian people – to tragedy. And the traveller does receive from her loved ones, on this first pilgrimage home after the earthquake, the gift of laughter, in response to her feeble attempt at an insider joke: "They laugh and their laughter fills me with more hope than the moment deserves. But this is really all I have come for. I have come to embrace them, the living, and I have come to honor the dead" (168).

But even in this moment of reintegration with community, the narrator is keenly aware of the American passport she holds, and which is metonymic of her legal status and evocative of her situation as member of the diaspora – or, from a Haitian perspective, the often disparaged "dyaspora" (a label frequently used as a taunt by Haitian residents on the island for those coming "home" from the United States). For another home, another life awaits her up north. One of the most moving sections of "Our Guernica", and perhaps of the entire collection, is found on the last page of *Create Dangerously*, as the author finally gives primacy to her own speaking voice, relating a verbal outburst particularly compelling from one whose prose is so often understated. Danticat has returned, at the end of "Our Guernica", to the motif of flight underpinning the essay "Flying Home". On the plane that is taking the writer back to the United States, the stewardess offers the passengers, mainly American medical volunteers, the precious bounty of ice, and utters the ritual phrase of the patriotic American: "God bless America." Danticat, though conscious of her "Americanness", a status which has made possible her departure from Haiti at this time, surprises her readers with a loss of composure, shown in an impetuous response:

> Feeling overly protective of an already battered Haiti, I hear myself cry out, "God bless Haiti, too," drawing a few stares from my fellow passengers.
>
> The man in the seat behind me taps me on the shoulder and says, "Really. God bless both America and Haiti." (173)

We are reminded here that the identity of this immigrant artist cannot be reduced to an angst-free transnationalism/cosmopolitanism/hybridity, that Danticat, insistent on nuance and painfully conscious of contradiction, will always testify in her own voice – though at the same time creating space in her work for other and sometimes dissonant voices. It is clear that the writer has little in common with Nadine, the solitary protagonist of "Water Child", whose relationship with home fluctuates between unease and distance. Despite the absence of Tante Ilyana, of Uncle Joseph and now of Maxo, Danticat will always be much more than a "witness from afar".

And so, at the very end of the essay, after the episode just cited, it is hardly surprising that Danticat should finally, fully, give voice to her mourning of Maxo. Here, we have a powerful example of the quality that Dany Laferrière has highlighted in noting that his first impression, as he began to read Danticat's work, was one of composure and serenity. Laferrière goes on to nuance this judgment: "But this sense of calm does not eliminate anxiety."[43] Despite an underlying and even fundamental anxiety, "Our Guernica" ends on a note which demonstrates Danticat's singular deftness in negotiating a virtual swamp of emotions, in telling a painful story which is both public and personal without falling into the maudlin or sensational. She continues the appropriation inherent in Maxo's reading practice with a pointed addition to Genet's words – taken out of context – which now translate her own mournful assertion of fidelity: "Great black country, I too bid thee farewell, I think. At least for now" (173). The ambiguity inherent in these, the final words of *Create Dangerously*, is fruitful: perhaps even more than a gauge of fidelity spoken by the traveller to those left behind, they express the hope that the once "great black country", so long a victim of natural and man-made violence, will stand up again as Césaire saw it in the *Cahier*: "Haiti où la négritude se mit debout pour la premiere fois et dit qu'elle croyait à son humanité." (Haiti, where Négritude stood up for the first time and said that it believed in its humanity.)[44] "At least for now", the writer will use her American passport to leave, but not to flee, the beleaguered birthplace which will continue to orient her writing.

At the time of the earthquake, Danticat was working on a new novel, *Claire of the Sea Light*, which would be published in 2013. This narrative stands out in the body of her fiction by its near-complete focus on the native land, so that the migration story which usually preoccupies the writer appears as a faint – though not insignificant – thread in the intricate fabric of the text. The novel is reminiscent of *The Dew Breaker* in its juxtaposition of several different but related life stories (though the linkages are much clearer and the characters fewer in the more recent work); in several important ways, however, *Claire of the Sea Light* is dramatically singular. In *Brother, I'm Dying*, the final paragraphs seem to return wistfully to the dream of reintegration with the land of origin, but it remains a dream. The two brothers, both Haitian patriots in their different ways, are denied the return journey which many émigrés long for, and the autobiographical text ends in New York, the metropolitan city where most of the stories of *The Dew Breaker* are set. In the final pages of *Brother*, the tone is undoubtedly nostalgic, as the author relieves her disquiet by imagining the two men reunited in the hills of Beauséjour (the same mountain refuge to which the narrator of "Walk Straight" struggled to ascend):

> I wish I could fully make sense of the fact that they're now sharing a gravesite and a tombstone in Queens, New York, after living apart for more than thirty years.
>
> In any case, every now and then I try to imagine them on a walk through the mountains of Beauséjour. It's dawn, a dazzling morning over the green hills. . . . And in my imagining, whenever they lose track of one another, one or the other calls out in a voice that echoes throughout the hills, "Kote w ye frè m?" Brother, where are you?
>
> And the other one quickly answers, "Mwen la. Right here, brother. I'm right here." (268–69)

In *The Dew Breaker*, as mentioned earlier, only one story takes the reader "home" to Haiti. Valerie Kaussen rightly underscores the structural significance of "Night Talkers" vis-à-vis the wider narrative: "Its setting, the lush mountain village in Haiti, is the imagined 'home' that binds together the fragmented episodes and characters of *The Dew Breaker*."[45]

Conversely, *Claire of the Sea Light* is firmly located in various sites of Haiti: first, the sea, where the young protagonist's father, Nozias, tries to make a living, and where his fellow fisherman loses his life in the opening scene; the hills to which Claire flees in the final pages of the novel; and, more prosaically, the sprawling urban space of the fictional town of Ville Rose, with its slums, its gang violence and its few lavish dwellings. One hears of characters who migrated to the United States, but with little detail about their lives there; the real drama plays out on Haitian soil. There is also reference to migration as a *possibility*, especially for Nozias, Claire's father, who contemplates giving up his motherless daughter so that he can make it "elsewhere". In fact, the bilingual phrase "chèche lavi, looking for a better life" or a slight variation thereof becomes a quiet but troubling refrain, appearing several times in the narrative, and framing the strange story of Nozias's attempt to "give away" a beloved daughter. He explains his motivation to the vendor whom he has chosen as surrogate mother: "'I'm going away,' Nozias said. 'Pou chèche lavi, to look for a better life.'"[46] But Claire's strong resistance to her father's project serves as a comment on the undesirability of what therefore appears as a radical option. In one of the child's lyrical inner monologues on her fear of losing her father, she displays a precocious understanding of the pain or even the futility of flight for those who must leave loved ones behind: "But what if there was no better life? How could he not know this? How could granmoun, grown people, not understand such things?"[47] And perhaps happily, Nozias's plan to travel remains nebulous, though one reference is made to the possibility of working in the neighbouring Dominican Republic.

Towards the end of the narrative, the reader may dare to hope, with his daughter, that the gentle fisherman will remain at home: "At least she would be staying here, and if her father didn't leave, if he gave up on chèche lavi elsewhere and stayed in Ville Rose, she could visit with him now and then".[48] Despite the enormous hardships the author scrupulously relates, those caused by a harsh sociopolitical context as well as the several private sorrows memorably recounted, Haiti then remains, for most of the characters of *Claire of the Sea Light*, the land to live in, the land to die in. Danticat's intriguing comment in a 2014 interview on the nature of nostalgia is instructive, even as it leaves room for a nuanced position regarding her own attitude to her homeland:

> Even though I am not in Haiti all the time, Haiti is always with me. . . . For me, Haiti is more than memory. I am not stuck in the nostalgia of the past. Few writers are anymore. . . . That issue of nostalgia is often not as simple as some folks make it out to be. Diaspora writers are not all nostalgic and the ones who seem to be are not the only ones who are.[49]

Claire of the Sea Light exemplifies the compulsion to return inherent in all of Danticat's work, a compulsion not based on a romanticizing nostalgia, but also not excluding a remembered love of country and heritage. This recent novel, in which the author narrows her canvas to focus on the uneven ter-

rain of homeland, reminds us of her commitment both to looking contemporary – and sometimes harrowing – Haitian reality in the face and to
honouring "the great black country".[50]

CHAPTER 2

JUNOT DÍAZ

"Soy dominicano, dominicano soy"

EDWIDGE DANTICAT AND JUNOT DÍAZ ARE both fundamentally allied and radically different: they tell the stories of Caribbean immigrants in the United States, struggling with economic difficulty as well as identity issues born of racial and national stereotyping. Their keen sense of place should not be simplified, however, by reference to the coincidence of their birth on the same land mass, Hispaniola: though Haiti and the Dominican Republic have the common experience of brutal dictatorship and persistent political unrest, these two nations awkwardly conjoined as neighbours on Hispaniola display singular differences. These of course include one of the most obvious markers of identity: language – a difference complicated by racial disparities. While most Haitians are conspicuously of African origin, dark-skinned nationals of the Dominican Republic would have experienced some of the racism often associated with migrant relocation in their land of origin – a home-grown racism highlighted by Díaz in his fiction. One tragic connection between the two countries, not unrelated to a melanin-based discrimination, continues to loom large in the consciousness of those who cannot forget a terrible history: the execution of thousands of Haitian workers in the Dominican Republic in the 1930s at the command of the dictator Trujillo. And in the past few years, and specifically at the time of writing, these long-standing tensions between the two nations have been brought into painful focus with the legal marginalization in the Spanish-speaking country of thousands of Dominicans of Haitian descent, now denied citizen status.

Against this background, I have found intriguing and provocative the friendship and solidarity manifest in the art and activism[1] of Edwidge Danticat and Junot Díaz, but also patent in interviews with these two writers: Díaz, for example, with characteristic exuberance, has said of Danticat that "her words will break your bones",[2] and includes her among the friends and relatives acknowledged at the end of *The Brief Wondrous Life of Oscar Wao*, labelling the Haitian writer his *"querida hermana"* (dear sister). Not only have they on several occasions shared the same stage as readers;[3] they have also each chosen the other's work to introduce in a podcast series focusing on writers from the *New Yorker's* archive. In 2007, Danticat selected "How to Date a Browngirl, Blackgirl, Whitegirl, or Halfie", a story that seems an incongruous, even jarring, choice, when one contrasts the quiet elegance and sobriety of Danticat's prose to Díaz's sometimes bawdy irreverence. In the discussion with Deborah Treisman, the *New Yorker* fiction editor, Danticat referred to the fact that they are often invited to speak at the same events, laughingly referring to their shared status as "Hispaniolans". But on a serious note, the two have in common that they both write from the liminal position of migrant: privileged though they have become (both are graduates of creative writing programs of Ivy League American universities; both have been recipients of several major literary prizes[4]), in their fiction, they retrieve, from the undifferentiated mass of non-native residents of New York/New Jersey, the experience of "ordinary" Haitians or Dominicans still tied to, or at least marked by, the land of origin.

Díaz read and commented on the narrative "Water Child" for the literary podcast in 2015. In an article entitled "Caribbean Collusion: Junot Díaz, Edwidge Danticat and the *New Yorker* Fiction Podcast", Anne Margaret Castro approaches this and the 2007 podcast from the perspective of translation studies, describing both writers as cultural translators. Citing the important work of Brent Edwards on black transnationalism,[5] Castro concludes her article by locating Danticat and Díaz as participants in the digital humanities and members of an inclusive literary community: "By framing the two authors and their works through the digital medium of the podcast, this article challenges scholars to consider new zones of inquiry regarding cultural translation and international literary communities."[6] That participation in an international community of writers is underscored by the fact that having already read "Water Child" in 2015, Díaz went on in February 2017 to single out "Seven", another of Danticat's early short stories, for attention on the podcast. It is particularly striking that the Dominican writer should choose to foreground a text that addresses even more explicitly the condition of the "ordinary migrant", a category to which neither author can be said to currently belong. Explaining his attraction (the word he uses is actually "devotion") to his fellow writer's work, Díaz makes it clear, without any of the sardonic humour one finds in much of his fiction and of course throughout *The Brief Wondrous Life of Oscar Wao*, that he admires the effort and sacrifices of migrants in general; he poignantly compares the challenge confronting the young wife in "Seven" to that facing many new and not so new migrants: "How do we reconstitute ourself on this new land?"[7]

His tone in this 2017 conversation, taped in the aftermath of the 2016 US elections – on the very day of the new president's inauguration – and manifestly affected by the fear of a wave of anti-immigrant sentiment in the post-Obama era, is thoughtful, understated and at times sombre. The writer describes the historical moment as characterized by a "hysterical anti-immigrant xenophobic atmosphere". Yet there seems to be a glimmer of light even in this bleak scenario as Díaz affirms that "home is vast" while insisting on the necessity, both for the female protagonist of "Seven" and for migrants like her, irrespective of nationality, of re-creating a self in the new land: "I think home is vast . . . and I think that home is very near to the immigrant. . . . What are we bringing from home? What is going to help hold us together here?"[8]

One may argue that this is an existential challenge pervading all of Díaz's fiction, whether his characters are American-born or belong to the first generation of migrants. My analysis, in this chapter, necessarily includes the celebrated novel *The Brief Wondrous Life of Oscar Wao*,[9] which has been the subject of much critical discussion, but also pays considerable attention to Díaz's short stories, especially those contained in the recent *This Is How You Lose Her* (2012), confirming the thematic and stylistic range evident in the novel. I argue that this body of work, shaped and influenced by the idioms and lifestyle of urban America, specifically of New Jersey, where Díaz himself grew up, appears at times critical or dismissive of "the Island", with its tyranny, its prejudices and its poverty, and yet remains stubbornly, self-consciously *dominicano*. Unlike that of Danticat, Díaz's prose suggests – or affects – a resolute lack of emotionalism about the "homeland": the writer has expressed his awareness of being neither a "real" Dominican nor an unhyphenated American in an interview with the provocative title "Fiction Is the Poor Man's Cinema". He asserts a complex belonging in a nuanced and superficially contradictory formulation: "I definitely would never try to pass for an island person. But I know that I'm Dominican."[10] And in that respect, he is, like Danticat, an "immigrant artist".

Yet despite the recurring themes of mobility and the quest for identity which link Díaz to Danticat – and, in fact, to several other migrant writers – his work is a powerful reminder that thematic correspondence and overlap do not make diasporic literature a neatly packaged whole. Díaz's work is undeniably stamped with a strong sense of *dominicanidad*, as well as with a unique personality that transcends race and nation. In the riveting and yet painful story of *Oscar Wao*, the reader is immediately struck by Díaz's singular style – including his fondness for expletive and for sexually explicit detail, coupled with a biting and often contagious sense of humour, even in the description of the gravest of situations. But what is also compelling is the narrative's function as archive: the dizzyingly rich novel tells the story of both first- and second-generation migrants from the Dominican Republic, beginning with the younger members of the De León family, with whom the narrator – the character Yunior, who recurs in Díaz's fiction (and who first makes himself manifest on page 167) – has had a lengthy if turbulent friendship. In the initial pages, their mother is portrayed as a harsh, unlovable and apparently unloving figure: in the section of the narrative related from Lola's point of view, Belicia's tale of woe is clearly not one which engenders much sympathy in a sceptical American-born daughter: "She had raised me and my brother by herself, she had worked three jobs until she could buy this house . . . she had come from Santo Domingo all by herself and as a young girl she claimed to have been beaten, set on fire, left for dead."[11]

It is only in the third section that we learn of a childhood of abuse, and of the circumstances related to the Trujillo regime which led to Belicia's departure from Santo Domingo. Díaz is attentive both to the element of fantasy, which he admits frankly colours his narrative, and to the factual history of Dominican migration before and after the bloody *Trujillato*, which he documents in prodigious and unforgiving detail. More memorable than the somewhat dreary urban landscape of Paterson where the family has made a new home is the formidable and colourful *presence*, throughout the long text with its polyphonic narration, of Santo Domingo. The frequency with which the word *"dominicano"* or *"dominicana"* – sometimes deployed in conjunction with "nigger", another often-used and obviously provocative label – appears, even in the many pages chronicling the lives of the characters in the city of Paterson, New Jersey, is conspicuous. Also striking is the repetition of epithets in Spanish denoting racial origin, such as *"moreno"* (black man) and *"morena"* (black woman), making it clear that Díaz aligns himself with the dark-skinned Dominicans sometimes elided in representations of the national identity. Christopher González argues convincingly in his comprehensive study of Díaz's work that what the author does in this novel is to shed light on the African origin of Dominicans of colour, thereby implicitly valorizing not only migrants in the North American diaspora but also the disparaged black minority in the homeland: "Díaz places an Afro-Dominican family at the center of his novel, simultaneously foregrounding their African heritage while vilifying the Negrophobia they experience, which reflects the political and ideological power structures in the Dominican Republic, the nexus of which is the Trujillato."[12]

What is particularly interesting here is that in his many published interviews, Díaz, whom many West Indians would describe, in the strange inherited taxonomy of shade, as "a brown man",[13] implicitly self-identifies as a person of colour – as does the fictional character Yunior. In a discussion of the possibility of solidarity between African Americans and other ethnic minorities in the United States, Tommy L. Lott points to the "practice of ethnic switching".[14] Specifically, he suggests reasons why Hispanics of Caribbean and Latin American origin, including Dominicans,[15] might seek to avoid the racial classification of "black" by choosing to be subsumed instead under labels based on cultural affiliation: "The need to maintain a distinct identity and garner institutional recognition as a distinct ethnic group often inclines Afro-Latinos, such as Dominicans, to opt to *escape* anti-black racism by occupying a de-racinated 'Latino' status."[16]

Race is manifestly integral to Díaz's self-identification, however, and so is nation of origin. At various points in the narrative, the Dominican Republic is referred to simply as "the Island" – its *dominance* in the consciousness of both narrator and characters removing the need that the uninitiated (reader) might have for greater precision. For the brother and sister Oscar and Lola de León, it is the land where their mother was born, but to which they travelled first as children at her insistence, and later on of their own free will. Early in the novel, the Dominican Republic is represented as the distant spot to which recalcitrant children are banished, presumably in the hope that they will be cured of their "American" ways; and for Oscar's sister, it functions initially as an island prison: "And that is how I ended up in Santo Domingo. I guess my mother thought it would be harder for me to run away from an island where I knew no one, and in a way she was right" (70). Lola, having run away from home and above all from a mother who appears incapable of tenderness, lands first in the Jersey Shore, in the arms of Aldo, an undesirable nineteen-year-old boyfriend. But after the prodigal daughter is discovered and brought back to un-nurturing Paterson, she is summarily shipped off to the "homeland". Despite an initial resistance, she embraces the life of a "real Dominican girl" (71) on the island, becoming close to La Inca, a grandmother figure (who is in fact her mother's aunt) whose affection compensates, to some extent, for the void in her relationship with Beli. It is in Santo Domingo too that she confronts the reality of her mother's early suffering: the reality that Beli will always be marked by "the fact that her long-gone parents had died when she was one, the whispers that Trujillo had done it, those first years of her life when she'd been an orphan, the horrible scars from that time, her own despised black skin" (80). Thus, the Dominican Republic, hardly a tropical paradise, emerges in this section of the novel as central to illuminating the past of those born on the Island, but also as capable of influencing the trajectories of the Americanized second generation.

Lola's mother left Santo Domingo at the age of sixteen, and despite the brutal memories, the last two pages of chapter 3 (rather ominously entitled "The Three Heartbreaks of Belicia Cabral 1955–1962") are tinged with a strange nostalgia, documenting, as many narratives of migration do, a poignant scene at the airport – a scene continued on board the plane which is to take the travellers to a new world. What makes this episode of leave-taking particularly memorable is the narrator's ability to remain grounded in the harrowing present but also, almost simultaneously, to leap forward to a future in which Belí becomes wife and mother. So the no longer innocent but still hopeful young woman leaves home, mercifully ignorant of the disappointments lying ahead, carrying with her a simple dream: "Her fiercest hope? That she will find a man. What she doesn't yet know: the cold, the backbreaking drudgery of the factorías, the loneliness of Diaspora, that she will never again live in Santo Domingo, her own heart" (164). Most striking here are the final three words, appended to the sentence without fanfare and yet, for the reader, impossible to ignore. The description of Santo Domingo as "her own heart" is a surprising outburst of something akin to patriotism from a character already too familiar with the cruelty of Dominican society during and after the Trujillo era.

Some pages further on, when it is Lola's time to bid farewell after a forced stay in Santo Domingo, which has become, unexpectedly, a fruitful return to roots, the writer revisits the migrant difficulty of separation from the Island. Devastated by the parting from her beloved Abuela La Inca, as well as by the tragic death of her new boyfriend, Max, the young woman is sobbing on the plane. Yet Díaz complicates the predictable scenario by hinting that Lola is not the typical departing émigré who should command the reader's sympathy – and certainly, her mother's caustic response to an old man's reminder that "Santo Domingo will always be there" undercuts what might have been seen as the sentimentalism of this farewell to an "island in the sun":[17] "For God's sake, my mother muttered, and then closed her eyes and went to sleep" (210).

For a teenager like Lola, forced to go to school there, the Dominican Republic is the place where girls on rival track teams taunted her with the label *"gringa"*,[18] but it is also represented in the novel as a land almost magnetic in appeal for its roaming offspring who suddenly feel – or are made to feel – the call of home: "Every summer Santo Domingo slaps the Diaspora engine into reverse, yanks back as many of its expelled children as it can; airports choke with the overdressed. . . . Like someone had sounded a general reverse evacuation order: Back home, everybody! Back home!" (271).

Yet the almost ritual homecoming is sometimes undermined by brutal reality; the section quoted above occurs shortly before the news that Oscar, a young adult recently graduated from college but still lacking in direction, has agreed, almost perversely, to go home with his family for the summer – the first time in seven years. For Oscar, of course, a return to Santo Domingo could never have been simple, suffering as he has, from childhood, from being that apparently strange combination of Dominican and "nerd", accustomed to having his origin questioned because he fails to perform masculinity in the manner prescribed for his male compatriots. When he arrived at Rutgers, aspiring to at last find favour with the opposite sex – to find "someone like him" – his hopes were dashed by the reductive force of stereotype: "The white kids looked at his black skin and his afro and treated him with inhuman cheeriness. The kids of color, upon hearing him speak and seeing him move his body, shook their heads. You're not Dominican. And he said, over and over again, But I am. Soy dominicano. Dominicano soy" (49).

Dominican though he aspires to be, on his return, the still displaced protagonist confronts an intimidating reality. In a section sardonically entitled "Oscar Goes Native", he encounters conditions of squalor described in detail and summed up in a refrain as "the mind-boggling poverty". These words recur throughout a three-page-long sentence that gives unsettling snapshots of multiple conflicting experiences: "After his initial homecoming week, after he'd been taken to a bunch of sights by his cousins . . . after he refused to succumb to that whisper that all long-term immigrants carry inside themselves, the whisper that says *You do not belong* . . . after he'd watched shirtless shoeless seven-year-olds fighting each other for the scraps he'd left on his plate at an outdoor café" (276).

The title of a preceding section, "The Condensed Notebook of a Return to a Native Land", obviously gestures to the long narrative poem which first established the singular voice of the Martinican poet of Négritude, Aimé Césaire;[19] and although the words are used ironically here, Díaz has in common with Césaire that he foregrounds details which shatter the stereotype of the "fortunate isle" inscribed in colonialist discourse. Oscar finds unchanged aspects of the island remembered from earlier visits, including "the air pollution and the thousands of motos and cars and dilapidated trucks on the roads and the clusters of peddlers at every traffic light" (273).

But Santo Domingo will also become, for Oscar, more than the destination in which he confronts a familiar squalor and then departs: it will be the site of a final disastrous attempt at an intimate sexual relationship, the place where he encounters the wrath of his new love's policeman boyfriend – a character as ominous and as cruel as any of the dreaded Duvalierist Tontons Macoutes who hover over Danticat's fiction. It is here that Oscar comes to the end – an end, to some extent, self-inflicted – of his short life; and the power of the narrative – the empathy that the reader feels for this complex character, faithful friend and would-be lover, consumer of science fiction, immersed in American popular culture and yet resolutely *dominicano* – is such that after reading of Oscar's death, one assumes that the narrator of the story will never again set foot on the island. But in the last pages, we discover that this is not so, despite Yunior's patent and prolonged grief – that one does not cease to be Dominican even after falling prey to the reputed curse, the *fukú* supposedly afflicting the de León family, or after experiencing first-hand the cruelty of Trujillo's successors. After Oscar's death, Lola had been adamant in turning her back on the island where they had travelled to recover his body: "Lola swore she would never return to that terrible country. On one of our last nights as novios [boyfriend and girlfriend] she said, Ten million Trujillos is all we are" (324).

But even for the grieving, home is not so easily written off. Near the end of *Oscar Wao*, the narrator refers casually to a subsequent trip to Santo Domingo; and in a condensed account of ten years of falling apart and gradually recovering after Oscar's death, Yunior imagines that one day he will have a chance to share with Lola's daughter Isis her uncle's treasure house of writing and other prized possessions (stored improbably in four refrigerators!), that one day he will have a chance to talk about the past. And in a 2007 interview with Edwidge Danticat, Díaz seems to endorse Danticat's optimistic reading of the ending of the novel: "In spite of Oscar's brief life, the narrator's life – writing-wise – ends on a happy note."[20] Indeed, we learn in the last pages of *Oscar Wao* that while Yunior apparently regrets that Lola is happily married to someone else, he himself appears to have settled down – still in New Jersey, now married and teaching at a community college, but never forgetting the adventures of the displaced Dominican nerd who insisted on returning "home", and paid with his life.

In the 2012 collection *This Is How You Lose Her*, Díaz takes us back to the Island in several stories about the homeland – and something akin to heartbreak, though the word might be disdained by the ostentatiously cynical narrator. These stories are told from various perspectives: that of the child narrator Yunior (whom some would see as Díaz's alter ego) in "Invierno"; that of the fickle young man in "The Sun, the Moon, the Stars" who attempts to mend a broken relationship by taking his girlfriend on vacation to Santo Domingo; and, finally, that of the jaded near middle-aged protagonist of the pithily, defiantly titled "The Cheater's Guide to Love". That the impulsively undertaken journey to Santo Domingo in "The Sun, the Moon, the Stars" (the first story of the collection) ends badly may be read as emblematic of the protagonist's profound ambivalence about home – although the primary concern of the narrator seems to be with his own serial infidelity. Yunior had initially seen the trip to the Dominican Republic as a sort of magic potion strong enough to distract his Cuban-born girlfriend from his failures: "Deep down, where my boys don't know me, I'm an optimist. I thought, Me and her on the Island. What couldn't this cure?"[21]

And, indeed, the flight to Santo Domingo does seem to reinforce Yunior's sometimes conflicted connection with home, according him temporary insider status based on his understanding of his fellow passengers and his acceptance of their Third World rituals (including clapping when the plane lands safely[22]). Yet *This Is How You Lose Her* is more than a collection of migration narratives: it is a volume resistant to categorization, one that, though prone to ellipses, highlights the primacy in Díaz's oeuvre of a concern with interpersonal relationships. His choice of Danticat's "Seven" for the *New Yorker* podcast mentioned earlier is suggestive, underlining a thematic affinity between the two writers which transcends the preoccupation with diaspora; one may argue that in Díaz's fiction, the search for love and genuine friendship is never a subplot – that the personal and the political are given equal billing. The outcome of the relationships portrayed in *This Is How You Lose Her* is sometimes daunting: the reader may arrive at the pessimistic conclusion that Díaz's male protagonists are irredeemable, repetitively and relentlessly "messing up" in the same way, chasing too hard after the sort of woman who would embellish their reputation as hypermasculine Dominicans and, in the process, betraying those who love them.

While all of these narratives tease out the complexities of the male-female relationship, two of the stories in the collection stand alone in their central concern with the experience of new migrants, with those who, unlike Yunior, have not had the time to assimilate the culture of the host land. One is "Invierno" (Winter), a narrative quite distinct – in its historical sweep, its generally formal register and its often sombre tone – from the stories recounting Yunior's womanizing exploits and failures. It seems thematically linked to "Negocios" (Business), the final text of the 1996 volume *Drown*,[23] which focuses on the experiences of recent travellers. In the latter story, a couple affected by the husband's pursuit of the American dream must face an even more dramatic erosion of intimacy than the Haitian characters of "Seven". Although the story is told from the point of view of Yunior, it is less of an indictment of the absent father than most of the previous texts in *Drown*. One forgets at times that given the age of the child when his father leaves, much of this narrative, filtered through the consciousness of Yunior, is in fact based on Ramón's own tales – consigned to the oral familial archive – of his first years in the United States. "Negocios" recounts the (mis)adventures of the narrator's father in the host land; structurally, it is underpinned by the motif of the journey, beginning with flight from the Dominican Republic: "My father, Ramón de las Casas, left Santo Domingo just before my fourth birthday. Papi had been planning to leave for months, hustling and borrowing from his friends, from anyone he could put the bite on."[24]

The father's trajectory commences in Miami, but his objective is the city which mesmerizes so many voyagers – and to which he ultimately journeys, after unrewarding months in Florida, hitchhiking and even on his own two feet: "The ticket to Miami had saved him money but he intended to continue on to Nueva York as soon as he could. Nueva York was the city of jobs, the city that had first called the Cubanos and their cigar industry, then the Bootstrap Puerto Ricans and now him."[25] New York, though initially as unwelcoming as Miami for a penniless foreigner ("His first year in Nueva York he lived in Washington Heights, in a roachy flat"[26]), will also be the site of his integration into a diasporic community. After losing hundreds of dollars in a failed attempt to buy his way into legal status by marrying an American, Ramón does make a marriage that is part business, part affair of the heart, as in Nilda he finds a nurturing woman who speaks excellent English, owns part of a house in Brooklyn and – importantly – has her citizenship. And he also forms a friendship with Jo-Jo, a Dominican businessman, who both urges him to take advantage of his situation and reminds him, ad nauseam, of the imperative of loyalty to his neglected family back home: "Now that you have a place and papers, Jo-Jo told Papi, you need to use these things to your advantage. . . . Save some money and buy yourself a little business. . . . Then you get your familia over here and buy yourself a nice house and start branching out. That's the American way."[27] There is a striking correspondence, in this narrative, between the migrant's ambivalence about the two women to whom he owes allegiance and the visceral pull of homeland,[28] only equalled by the compulsion to exploit the opportunities of the host land. That Yunior's father finally seems to choose his two sons and his legal wife, whose accusatory letters during a period of his neglect are imaged as "corrosive slaps in the face", is certainly not a simple happy ending, though the last words of "Negocios" portray the prodigal finally "flying south to get us".[29]

The reader senses, at the end of "Negocios", that Ramón's welcome in the Dominican Republic could not be taken for granted; and "Invierno", from the later collection *This Is How You Lose Her*, will confirm that no patient Penelope awaited this wandering husband. The latter story represents the dislocation of the transplanted mother and two sons, having to make do with their own company during a brutal winter, respecting but resenting the father's injunction that they stay inside. After five years in the United States, Ramón seems indifferent to the rigours of winter; for the newcomers, however, snow is at times fascinating, but often alien and threatening. They are cold even indoors: "I was watching the snow sift over itself, terrified, and my brother was cracking his knuckles. This was our first day in the States. The world was frozen solid" (121). The trope of snow, familiar in Caribbean migration novels, is metonymic here of the physical difference of the New Jersey area where the family is virtually dumped; it also evokes the emotional distance between the father and his children and, particularly, his wife, left behind for years in the Dominican Republic. Yunior's matter-of-fact voice, often bare of affect, states this simply and powerfully: "I didn't know him; he'd spent the last five years in the States working, and we'd spent the last five years in Santo Domingo waiting" (122). One may see the unrelieved pallor of the landscape as symbolic, too, of the monotony of their days; the father has forbidden the family from going out in the snow, promising that when winter is finally over, he will show them the ocean – which the narrator informs us at the start of the narrative was barely visible from "the top of Westminster, our main strip" (121):

> How much longer does winter last?
>
> Not long, he promised. You'll see. In a few months none of you will remember this and by then I won't have to work too much. We'll be able to travel in spring and see everything.
>
> I hope so, Mami said. (138)

The mother seems dangerously fragile, separated from friends and extended family (even more so than the young wife in Danticat's "Seven"), and almost from reason. Experiencing a loss that domesticity cannot assuage, she craves an absent community, wanting to "talk about unimportant matters, to speak to someone who wasn't her child or her spouse" (139). Finally, near the end of the story, Mami terrifies her children by going outside in a snowstorm. Ramón had phoned from work to say that he would not be able to return until the next day, and the mother initially occupied herself with the semblance of normalcy, adjusting the thermostat and generally keeping things going as a "good woman" should. But after an unrelenting snowfall, she ventures out when she thinks the boys are sleeping, and they follow her, amazed that she is "standing on the edge of the parking lot, ready to cross Westminster. . . . The snow was gusting" (144).

This powerful scene is ultimately an allegory of challenge and survival; for, holding on to the mother, who commands the children to "go straight. . . . That way we don't get lost" (145), they explore the neighbourhood – even arriving at the vista which the father had so far denied them, the point at which the sea becomes visible: "We even saw the ocean, up there at the top of Westminster, like the blade of a long, curved knife. Mami was crying but we pretended not to notice. We threw snowballs at the sliding cars" (145). The mother's tears, juxtaposed against the image of snowballs thrown by exuberant children, encapsulate the duality of this new land for the displaced Caribbean family – an experience both painful and magical.

In fact, the boys had already been tempted by the dazzling strangeness of the snow, and the mood of the sombre narrative is lightened by the appearance of *"gringo"* children. They had seen a brother and sister from the neighbouring apartment go out to play, and it is Yunior who takes the initiative to follow them outside, introducing himself and his brother and yelling, "I want to play with you" (132). It is Yunior who gives his name and, in two separate encounters, elicits the knowledge that the boy is called Eric and the girl Elaine. Thus, to the seductive novelty of snow is added the natural appeal of other children, perhaps the writer's way of prefiguring the adaptation to this newest of worlds which the young arrivants, like Edwidge Danticat and Díaz himself, must negotiate: "I stopped and we faced each other, our white breath nearly reaching across the distance between us. The world was ice and the ice burned with sunlight. This was my first real encounter with Americans and I felt loose and capable. I motioned with my mittens and smiled" (133). This exhilarating feeling of being "loose and capable" is not, of course, characteristic of the attitude of all the migrant subjects portrayed by Díaz. And the possibility that the newest arrivals will be separated from Eric and his sister by an impenetrable wall of racial difference is an underlying complication in this understated narrative; for, after all, "in less than a year they would be gone. All the white people would be. All that would be left would be us colored folks" (137–38). But I think the words "loose and capable", following the startling image of ice which "burned with sunlight", hint at a certain migrant audacity, a liberating fluidity, the prodigious and sometimes fertile openness to change which some of these fictional characters demonstrate; and the ability of both mother and sons to venture into the hostile snow, to cope with this unfamiliar, potentially harmful element, may prefigure the migrant's successful immersion/ incursion into an initially forbidding space.

A very different narrative is the story "Otravida, Otravez" (Another Life, Another Time), offering a remarkable example of Díaz's deftness in varying narrative point of view: this tale of a Dominican woman, Yasmin, working as a supervisor in the laundry of a Paterson, New Jersey, hospital, is far removed in tone from the various texts in which the adult Yunior is narrator, and in which the language is sometimes vulgar and the tempo rapid. Here, through a first-person narrative, the reader instead enters into the muted pain of a woman who is accustomed to little, an "ordinary migrant" who wears protective gloves indoors every day as she sorts through soiled sheets, deciding which ones are too badly stained to be restored by the washing machine. It is a task the squeamish might refuse; and the friend who told her of the hospital job signalled that difficulty by the succinct warning that "there'll be blood" (62). But the description of the faithful daily discharge of this responsibility is the writer's quiet tribute to migrant workers who do the jobs citizens might disdain – and it is noteworthy that Díaz offers a gendered version of the migration narrative, creating a female protagonist who, though not dependent, appears much more vulnerable than her partner. Twenty-eight-year-old Yasmin is seen by the young women whom she directs as the *"veterana"*; she shares their homesickness, feeling compassion for the youngest member of the team, the newly arrived Samantha, who at the age of fifteen has already mothered a child, a child now left behind in the Dominican Republic. What binds Yasmin to Samantha is a common experience of loneliness in displacement: "Most of the people I know in the States have no friends here; they're crowded together in apartments. They're cold, they're lonely, they're worn. I've seen the lines at the phone places, the men who sell stolen card numbers, the cuarto they carry in their pockets" (60). Like the newly relocated family of "Invierno", the Dominican characters in the story, including the "veteran" Yasmin, share an intolerance for the biting cold of winter, an image which recurs several times in "Otravida, Otravez". When Samantha shows up at the laundry for the first time, she "cannot believe the cold"; and she is represented further on as a victim of winter's ravages, a woman stripped of her youthful appearance and arguably of her femininity: "Winter has dried her out, left her with reptile hands and lips so chapped they look like they might at any moment split" (72).

But as always in Díaz's fiction, there are no heroes here, no conspicuous paragons of virtue; Yasmin lends Samantha eight hundred dollars, half of her savings – but when the young girl abruptly leaves the job, she does so without informing her mentor and without repaying the loan. The narrator makes little of this, as if normalizing the imperfections and rifts within the diasporic community of which the group of laundry workers may be a microcosm. The young woman must also make compromises in her personal life, sharing accommodation with several women but also "entertaining", in limited space, a lover, Ramón, whose wife left in the Dominican Republic communicates regularly with him through written letters: an intimate correspondence on which Yasmin eavesdrops by reading the stack of letters that Ramón keeps in her lodgings. She is moved and yet perversely made more secure of her status by the desperation conveyed in the wife's letters, by the tone of supplication and the signs of unwanted solitude: "*Please, please, mi querido husband, tell me what it is. How long did it take before your wife stopped mattering?*" (59). And Yasmin feels guilt about that "*otravida*", the "other life", the other/legal wife that Ramón has left behind – a guilt compounded by the fact that he and Virta share the grief of the death of a son.

In his many narratives about couples, whether married or not, Díaz reveals a thoughtful and at times pessimistic concern with the challenge of fidelity – a concern which to some extent disturbs the superficial nonchalance of his male narrator. It is the challenge experienced by Danticat's young married couple in "Seven", and of course by Yunior's parents in "Negocios" – and obviously a challenge not restricted to migrants, but made more poignant as the betrayal cuts sharper when one partner has already experienced the first "desertion" of being left behind on the Island. Responding, in a 2016 interview, to questions from the audience about "Otravida, Otravez", Díaz confirms the linkage between this story and the earlier "Negocios": "This is a second iteration of the story, told from the point of view of the woman whom his father almost leaves the family for."[30] But "Otravida, Otravez" is not simply a tale of woe or of betrayal; the lovers, though clearly not ideally paired, experience together an aspiration familiar to migrants accustomed to precarity, a yearning reminiscent of that which divided the Barbadian couple in Paule Marshall's *Brown Girl, Brownstones*.[31] It is the dream of permanency, the lust for home ownership – in this case, a dream pursued by the male partner: "Do you know how long I've waited for this? To own a house in this country is to begin to live" (69).

But when will Yasmin "begin to live"? In the last scene of the story, she pays a visit to her close friend and former roommate Ana Iris, who has left her three children behind in Santo Domingo, who "understands what has to be sacrificed on a voyage" (54), and who had told her, on the day they met,

"We are not here for fun" (59). The episode troubles the relative predictability of this migrant journey, highlighting the possibility that any traveller may change course, even when apparently gripped by the all-consuming quest for material advancement: Yasmin is pregnant, a condition about which she appears ambivalent – and at the same time, Ana Iris tells her that she has been speaking to her children by phone. Though Díaz deprives us of a wished-for certainty that Ramón and Yasmin will work their way through their challenges, there remains the hope that they will honour the responsibility of parenting together, especially juxtaposed against Ana Iris's pain at being separated from her children. Some readers may see this text as inextricably tied to "Negocios" and may imagine an ending in which Ramón returns to Virta, the sympathetic mother figure of the earlier story. I prefer, however, to be guided by the author's apparent predilection for ambiguity over closure, mindful of Díaz's assertion, in discussing the outcome of Danticat's migrant narrative "Seven", of the power of hopeful uncertainty: "A reader could take it either way . . . it is explicitly open to multiple readings."[32]

Such a *possibility* of a happy ending might seem to counter the bleak representation of sexual relationships in several of the narratives in this volume, especially in the title story, "The Sun, the Moon and the Stars", and the final text, "The Cheater's Guide to Love". For readers who have followed the narrator Yunior from boyhood to brash young adulthood, this last story is both memorable and disquieting, in part because linked to the protagonist's still furious Don Juanism is a tacit longing for a sort of rootedness and, in fact, for fatherhood. In her explanation of her choice of story for the *New Yorker* podcast, Danticat indicated that she was attracted, in "How to Date a Browngirl, Blackgirl, Whitegirl, or Halfie", to "the mix of both bravado . . . this machismo and this kind of vulnerability that this character shows". It is a comment which is equally pertinent to "The Cheater's Guide to Love". Much of the latter narrative describes the womanizing protagonist's struggle to get over his "real love", the girlfriend/fiancée whose place in his life is established at the very start of the story: "Your girl catches you cheating. (Well, actually she's your fiancée, but hey, in a bit it *so* won't matter)" (175). His recovery from the break-up is prolonged and difficult, and it is after he acknowledges that it is truly over that he has a fling, which will prove decisive, with a "young morena from the Harvard Law School": "You no longer have fantasies that the ex will be waiting for you in front of your apartment, though every now and then you still call her and let the phone ring to the in-box" (189). The brief affair will end with Yunior spending months hosting the law student, in an atmosphere of near hostility, after she arrives at his doorsteps with all her possessions, pregnant and claiming that he is the father. He pays all her medical bills and rushes to the hospital when her labour begins, only to find himself strangely devastated when she tells another story, with cruel bluntness, on the verge of childbirth: "but as soon as you walk into the birthing room the law student shrieks: *I don't want him in here. I don't want him in here. He's not the father*" (200–201).

This muted yearning for paternity is also, ironically, evident in the episode in which Yunior accompanies his best friend Elvis to Santo Domingo to meet the son who is allegedly the fruit of a brief illicit relationship far away from the safe permanency of his life in Paterson. While it is at Yunior's insistence that Elvis initiates the DNA investigation which will confirm that the child is not his, one senses in the former's interaction with the boy a longing for his own child: "Elvis Jr. watches you with considerable gravitas. He is a piercingly cute carajito [kid]" (205). It is not a happy journey for either character: in this final story, the two returning émigrés are, despite their flaunted machismo, vulnerable figures whom the locals do not hesitate to exploit, and the narrative focuses to an unsettling extent on the squalor of the neighbourhood in which they visit Elvis's presumed son. The attention paid to the ghetto-like conditions of life for many Dominicans recalls the sharp sense of injustice of the protagonist of the earlier story, "The Sun, the Moon, the Stars" – forced, in order to placate his girlfriend, to spend part of his visit to the Dominican Republic in a luxurious resort where he knows many people originating, as he does, from the harsh streets of the city would not be welcome: "Has its own airport, thirty-six holes of golf, beaches so white they ache to be trampled, and the only Island Dominicans you're guaranteed to see are either caked up or changing your sheets" (14). Díaz explores and adds nuance to the politics of place, reminding us that "home" for many returning Caribbean migrants is a multilayered concept, far removed from the stereotype of the paradisal island in which the tourist industry is necessarily invested.

For Elvis and Yunior, both in their way "cheaters" in the sense alluded to in the title, an *alleged* paternity, with its implications of ownership and agency as well as productive masculinity, has ended, then, in disillusion. Yet, although Elvis's immediate reaction to the realization that he has been duped is to turn his back on both child and mother, later on in the narrative we learn that he does return to Santo Domingo, where he undertakes a futile search for the (almost) lost son. That both Elvis and Yunior move frequently between New Jersey and Santo Domingo is worth underlining, even though neither of them feels truly at home in the Dominican Republic. In an article subtitled "The Impossibility of Return in Junot Díaz", Santiago Vaquera-Vásquez begins by narrating his own personal experience of the dream of return in terms which are of interest for many whose identity is shaped by two worlds:

> I left, I saw, I returned; everything had changed. The story of migration in nine words.
>
> This is how these stories are often told.
>
> For years I grew up in a household with a mother who often said: next year we return to Mexico. . . . My mother is the classic transnational, the border girl with one half of her life on the Mexican side of *la línea* – the border – and the other half on the other side. When she returned to Mexico – returning to what she thought was home – everything had changed. And so she resumed her transnational identity as a border-crosser.[33]

In addressing the trajectories of Díaz's unsettled migrants and specifically the journeys of Yunior, Vaquera-Vásquez goes on to posit that "departures in his stories often imply an uneasy return".[34] At the conclusion of "The Cheater's Guide", the reader may assume that the two friends will continue to experience "uneasy returns" to Santo Domingo, becoming adept at navigating borders, even those less conspicuous than that separating Mexico from the United States. While there is no obvious happy outcome on the horizon for either Elvis or the childless Yunior, the final story of *This Is How You Lose Her* ends with the protagonist's return to writing, even if it is about his treacherous career as "cheater". This is an activity, indeed a vocation, which links Yunior to Oscar and, the reader is entitled to believe, to Junot Díaz himself: "In the months that follow you bend to the work, because it feels like hope, like grace" (213). Ending the collection on this self-reflexive note, to some extent tentative but emphasizing the power of story, Díaz implicitly takes us back to the dénouement of *Oscar Wao*, in which the roles of both Oscar and Yunior as storytellers are highlighted in a quietly elegiac tone: "These days I write a lot. From can't see in the morning to can't see at night. Learned that from Oscar" (326). Paul Jay's comment on the conclusion of *Oscar Wao* is pertinent in this regard: "The ending of Diaz's novel offers the tentative hope that in writing about systematic forms of injustice and brutality one might begin to undo them by weaving a counterspell that resists dominant narratives and brutalizing voices."[35] Indeed, the liberation of Dominican voices in Díaz's fiction is both boldly subversive and, for writer and for protagonist, ultimately therapeutic.

Nowhere is this emancipation more evident than in the area of linguistic expression. Christopher González has pointed to Díaz's attention to his craft, and particularly to his deployment of language, as central to the originality of his work. Throughout his fiction, it is important that Yunior's voice asserts an identity that is neither Dominican nor American, but a complex, sometimes shifting blend of the two. In the story just analysed, one of the women with whom the protagonist tries to distract himself after the big break-up, an older, "real" Dominican spending a year away from her family at business school in Boston, taunts him playfully by questioning his national identity: "At the end of the semester she returns home. My home, not your home, she says tetchily. She's always trying to prove you're not Dominican. If I'm not Dominican then no one is, you shoot back, but she laughs at that. Say that in Spanish, she challenges and of course you can't" (193). Yet what is memorable, in reading Díaz, is that he "says it" in English, and also in a sort of Spanish, in a creative, idiosyncratic and sometimes disturbing mixture, which, more than anything else perhaps, makes it clear that his identity is unique, to some extent fluid and certainly non-monolithic. At times in *Oscar Wao*, the narrator playfully stands back from his frequently hyperbolic and even surreal text, asking the reader to laugh with him at its bombastic, inflated, *wondrous* qualities. The sometimes wild, sometimes lyrical and generally irrepressible nature of his prose is a vital element of the narrative's power. Equally compelling is the constant interplay, throughout Díaz's writing, of the two languages coexisting rather than competing in his consciousness. González attributes the originality of Díaz's "Spanglish" to the absence of concessions for the non-hispanophone reader: "Díaz's use of Spanish is not in and of itself a novel innovation. Rather, his decision to use Spanish without much consideration for a reader that does not understand Spanish is key. Instead of providing a glossary or translating the Spanish he uses, Díaz allows the Spanish to stand for itself."[36]

The juxtaposition of Spanish and English words, or of sentences in the two languages, means that sometimes the non-hispanophone reader can only guess at the meaning by referring to the context, as in the example which follows, from "The Cheater's Guide" (the protagonist is in a Latin club in the States): "There's a girl who keeps bumping into you. You say to her Pero mi amor, ya. And she says: Ya yourself. She's Dominican and lithe and super tall" (211). At times, we witness a marvellously inventive fusion of the two languages. A striking example is the neologism "berserkeria" appearing in "The Cheater's Guide", a noun created by appending a Spanish suffix to the English adjective "berserk". In a conversation between the parents in "Invierno" about the mother's longing for company, the father retorts in words presumably in Spanish, but which Díaz translates, leaving only the expression *"Me da vergüenza"* (I am embarrassed") in Spanish: "None of you are ready for guests, Papi said. Look at this house. Look at your children. Me da vergüenza to see them slouching around like that" (139).

Other examples abound of the apparently unselfconscious injection of Spanish lexical items or entire sentences in Spanish into Díaz's fiction. At points in the narrative, a sentence in Spanish is inserted without explanation and without any contextual indication of its meaning, as in La Inca's simple, devastating comment on the vicious abuse of Oscar's mother as a young child, which left her back terribly scarred. Discussing the rescue of Beli "from her so-called parents", the narrator reproduces a full sentence in Spanish: "Even today La Inca rarely saying anything more than *Casi la acabaron* [They almost finished her off]" (258). The words *"guapa/guapo"* (pretty, handsome) and *"fea/feo"* (ugly) are employed liberally by the writer, the latter carrying the particular affective sting of the curse word, used for instance by Beli in commenting on her recalcitrant daughter Lola's punk hairstyle: "Que muchacha tan fea" (What an ugly girl) (54). It is as if Díaz can only convey certain extremes of emotion – and significantly of abuse – in Spanish, though he does also use "strong" language as he feels the need in the borrowed/familiar tongue of English, which he manipulates deftly and boldly. As with Creole speakers, Díaz's characters, even if apparently bilingual, rely on the mother tongue as the reservoir of expletives; thus Papi yells at Yunior: "What in carajo are you doing?" (122). And a particularly biting insult from one brother to another in "Invierno" is couched in Spanish: "You're just a little mojón [turd]" (131).

In a more positive vein, in the last pages of *Oscar Wao*, Yunior's persistent love of Lola is expressed through the combination of languages which establishes his essential, unrepentant *difference*, specifically by the insertion in a sentence in English of a single Spanish word, the term *ciguapa*, evoking a mythical woman: "she's heavier and less guileless, but she's still the ciguapa of my dreams" (327). And in a similar moment of affective intensity, the protagonist of "The Cheater's Guide" describes Elvis's reputed son as a "piercingly cute carajito" (205), offering no translation or synonym but leaving the reader to *divine* the wealth of emotion contained in the single Spanish noun.

Thus, language, for Díaz and for his characters, is a unique antidote to the dilution of identity that threatens Caribbeans in "exile". And precisely because his idiosyncratic Spanish is at times jarring, and because the reader may be disturbed by the linguistic unevenness of the text and by its occasional dissonance, it is also a subversive tool, a sign of refusal of acculturation, a negation of the sometimes comfortable concept of cultural hybridity, to the extent that the latter implies the harmonious fusion of competing elements. Despite conspicuous differences, Díaz may be usefully compared to the writer Julia Alvarez,[37] who memorably foregrounded the nexus between language and identity in *How the García Girls Lost Their Accents*. Alvarez, whose fiction suggests a greater embrace of English than that of Díaz, has eloquently theorized her identity while articulating her project as writer: "Sometimes I hear Spanish in English (and of course, vice versa). That's why I describe myself as a Dominican American writer. That's not just a term. I'm mapping a country that's not on the map, and that's why I'm trying to put it down on paper."[38]

Like Alvarez, who labels herself a "gringa-dominicana",[39] Díaz complicates his identity, liberating himself from the claustrophobia of imposed belonging. Yet in all of his fiction, one senses a profound empathy with his most memorable character, a young man born in the United States who nevertheless affirms, with defiance and with rhetorical emphasis, "Soy dominicano; dominicano soy." (I am Dominican; I *am* Dominican.) It is a sentiment which does not preclude that other conflicting fear evoked in the last pages of *Oscar Wao*, the fear of the returning traveller that reintegration is no longer possible: "that whisper that all long-term immigrants carry inside themselves, the whisper that says *You do not belong*" (276). At the same time, it is an understanding of and even empathy with both the transplanted and those left at "home", a sentiment which relieves, though it does not remove, the angst of displacement.

That same empathy with the transplanted is manifest in *Islandborn*,[40] published by Díaz in March 2018, a children's text which appears as a departure, if not an aberration, in relation to his existing body of work. In this short picture book, a Dominican American child, whose name "happens" to be Lola, seeks to draw closer to the land she left as a baby by calling on the resources of the imagination and memory, the memory of adults around her who share riveting images of the Dominican Republic. Thus, the Caribbean homeland, and the diasporic writer's connection to a land more imagined than remembered, continue to hold sway in the fiction of one who will not forget that he too is "Island-born", while also acknowledging that he can never be an "Island Dominican".

CHAPTER 3

CARYL PHILLIPS

Stories from England, Stories from Home

There is a kind of loss,
like coming home
to faces; the doors open in-
differently; they whisper,
" . . . Who/is this new traveler?"
—Dennis Scott[1]

IN THE 1995 ESSAY "HAITI: A BI-CULTURAL EXPERIENCE", Edwidge Danticat memorably theorized the condition of diasporic subjects who, like her, inhabit a
situation of liminality vis-à-vis both homeland and "host land", using an
image more startling than the common trope of double vision, an image
suggestive of roaming sight: "You see the world with two eyes that do not
always look in the same direction."[2] Yet Danticat's writing does not usually
evince discomfort with what could be an unsettling focus on two vastly
different worlds. Indeed, both her novels and her life writing exemplify and
fulfil the dual mandate assumed by so many Caribbean writers at home
and abroad: to tell stories for and of the group – which would include the
community of origin, as well as, in the case of émigrés, the new diaspora.

The situation of the St Kitts–born Caryl Phillips is, however, more complex, and less coloured with the emotion inherent in long-standing familiarity with "homeland". One would assume that this Caribbean/black Briton
would have a particularly keen sense of in-betweenness, an experience of
duality that goes far beyond the familiar and non-threatening fusion of

cultures wrought by creolization. Caryl Phillips, more radically separated from his land of birth than writers, like Danticat, who spent their formative years in the region (he travelled to England with his parents as an infant), has in his considerable oeuvre explored both his own sense of difference, as a black son of migrants who cannot forget his Caribbean origin, and also his complex, cautious sense of being English. Maryse Condé has suggested that "maybe to be a Caribbean or an African is no longer a matter of the place where one is born, the color of one's skin, and the language one speaks",[3] a provocative remark that is not irrelevant to Phillips's reluctance to circumscribe identity. Yet it would be erroneous to describe his position as "cosmopolitanist". In her study of his work, Bénédicte Ledent argues persuasively that if it were indispensable – though not necessarily desirable – to *label* Caryl Phillips, then it is the term "Caribbean" that best captures his complex identity: "Were any classification at all necessary, none of the applicable tags would come closer to describing Phillips's multifaceted identity than 'Caribbean', in itself an essentially inclusive and multicultural label, which . . . sidesteps the conceptual straitjacket of adjectives such as 'Black British' or even post-colonial."[4]

But can national identity be subsumed, perhaps even erased, under the more comfortable but sometimes imprecise notion of Caribbeanness without a corresponding ache of loss? Phillips's perspective is quite different from that of Caribbean writers who grew up in the region, and who have remained close to their country of birth while also embracing the global. The Jamaican Kei Miller, in paying tribute to Derek Walcott on the death of the great St Lucian poet, chose to emphasize the latter's connection to his homeland as central to his vision: "I always say I want to write a large literature from a small place, and it is Walcott who embodies that attitude more than anyone else."[5] Both Walcott and Miller have the advantage of intimacy with an island, of having that "small place" vividly present in their consciousness. Certainly, the poetry of Derek Walcott is inextricably bound up with his beloved St Lucia, the wellspring of his imagination, with its people, its landscape and the Caribbean sea that surrounds it. In a 2002 interview, Phillips, who first returned to his native land in his twenties, does point to the central place of St Kitts in his own personal quest for understanding of self, making clear that his is not a deterritorialized identity: "I knew, once I came here first in '80, I realized I would have to keep coming back because so much of who I was and so much of who my generation were in Britain – so many of the questions which were gnawing away and informing the anxiety – the answers were here."[6] More elliptically, he uses as epigraph to his 2001 collection of essays *A New World Order* John La Rose's poem "Not from Here", which ends with the memorable lines

> Yet what we leave
> > we carry.
> It is no mud
> > we dry
> on our boots.
>
> The saliva we swallow
> must ever dwell
> > down there.[7]

Yet *A State of Independence*[8] is the only one of Phillips's novels, after the early *The Final Passage*,[9] to focus significantly on a West Indian island from a West Indian perspective;[10] and that narrative ends with the protagonist Bertram acknowledging that "home", no longer a familiar location, is certainly not a welcoming haven for him. The entire novel conveys a profound unease, a sense of the presumably unbridgeable distance between the protagonist and his childhood friends, and perhaps even his family, as well as the acknowledgement – or fear – of being irremediably transformed into the outsider in his country of birth. However, in the final pages of *A State of Independence*, despite his scepticism at the path on which the new nation is embarking, and despite his disenchantment with its freshly minted political leaders, Bertram seems to leave the door open to reconciliation with home, and first of all with his once lover Patsy. Yet, with the refusal to hide behind platitude and political correctness which is characteristic of the author himself, he struggles for clarity about his adopted homeland and about his personal history. After twenty years in England, initially on a scholarship and subsequently on an income derived from a string of unmemorable jobs, he has returned home as his country prepares to celebrate its independence from Britain. Finding it difficult to renew ties with old friends, and finding his own family diminished, Bertram articulates vividly to Patsy an initial ambivalence about England: "English fog always used to seem to me like a grey-white blanket that would rip as easily as water, yet it was as thick as solidified coconut milk. It used to fascinate me, you know. In those first few months when I arrived in England everything was either fascinating or frustrating or both."[11]

His description of England as fundamentally alien, though fascinating in its very difference, leads Patsy to ask the obvious: "You don't feel at home there?" But Bertram's answer lacks the simplicity, the binarism that would have made this a "straightforward" anti-colonial text:

> "But I . . . " he paused. Patsy took his hand and he found the confidence to con-
> tinue. "But," he said, "I don't yet feel at home back here either." He loosened
> himself from her grip and stood. "Maybe I better go now."
>
> Patsy looked up at him. The moon caught the slight lustre on his face. "You
> coming back here again tonight?"[12]

Underlying the sexual – and emotional – tension between the couple is the narrative's attention to the difficulty for the "returning resident"[13]/prodigal son of unreservedly embracing a now unfamiliar home (and indeed, Bertram is a prodigal son, having so neglected to keep in touch with his family that he was unaware, until his return, of the death of his only brother). And in fact, the remaining pages of *A State of Independence* pivot towards the explicitly political. While the text memorializes, in these final scenes, the moment of accession to statehood that usually is remembered as a time of joy and pride, the protagonist watches as if from the point of view of the foreign journalist, intrigued by a spectacle of exotica. There is no resolution of the emotional uncertainties which match Bertram's political detachment, no distracting confirmation of what has been hinted at: that he is in fact the father of Patsy's child. Phillips does not, would not offer such a facile conclusion. Indeed, the same lack of certainty that marks the outcome of his relationship (reunion?) with Patsy surrounds the future of his now "independent" island, especially with regard to its increasing ties to the United States. In a compelling article (which attempts to account for the relative lack of critical attention to this early novel), J. Dillon Brown highlights the uncertainties inherent in the novel's conclusion: "The novel's ending underscores its insistence on a complex vision of contemporary cultural negotiation."[14]

The Jamaican Dennis Scott's poignant evocation, in the poem "Exile", of estrangement after return would seem relevant to Bertram's dilemma, whether or not the reader feels any sympathy for a migrant who has turned his back on home and family for twenty years:

> There are patterns to assure us:
> at table, familiar spices;
> the garden, hardly greener;
> but something has changed:
>   clothes we left behind;
>   the old affections hang loosely.
>   . . . To travel
>   is to return
>   to strangers.[15]

Not all West Indian travellers find their affections to "hang" so "loosely" on return, but in the figure of Bertram, Caryl Phillips memorably captures the melancholy attributable to the outsider status that may be forced on many migrants seeking reintegration into homeland.

Such outsider angst is explored from a different perspective in the 2009 text *In the Falling Snow*,[16] the first novel by Phillips since *A State of Independence* in which West Indian characters occupy centre stage (though there is no physical return to the island): Keith, the British-born protagonist, may be conflicted about his identity, but it is his father, who migrated to the north of England several decades earlier, who longs for a distant "home". Keith has never visited his parents' homeland; he has had a long marriage to a white Englishwoman; and he acknowledges that he is not "really" West Indian. Yet through the protagonist's difficult relationship with his father Earl – who arrived in England in the 1960s – and as a result of the latter's anxiety to finally claim and share a long-muted life story, the narrative ultimately takes the reader far away from the town in the north of England in which it is set.

Born in England to parents who travelled several years after the "Windrush" generation, Keith struggles both to navigate a muddled emotional life and to realize his literary ambitions, craving the fulfilment of writing a book on soul music, which would resonate with readers who, like himself, are of African origin. But his *Caribbean* origin seems almost nebulous, and he is unconvincing in his attempt to convince his son Laurie – who is third-generation black British – of the value of a trip "home". At the start of *In the Falling Snow*, the protagonist has been unhappily separated for three years from the Englishwoman whom he met at university. As in the case of *A State of Independence*, it is tempting, though not uniformly productive, to draw parallels between the protagonist's relationship with a woman he has loved and his unease about his identity vis-à-vis his homeland/host land. The difficulties in his relationship with his wife, Annabelle, cannot be attributed simply to racial difference: they met as equals, as young university students, who loved and listened to the same Grover Washington cassette (Phillips's fondness for African American music is apparent in this novel, as it is elsewhere in his writing). Her father's unabashed bigotry is certainly a source of pain to them both: for instance, in telling his daughter that the writer of an anonymous letter had accused him of having a "'nigger-lover' for a daughter", Keith's father-in-law elaborates with gusto that the letter writer in question "hoped [he] would never have the ill manners to pollute our village with my mongrel family" (24). But despite the sting of the taunt of mongrelization, the British-born Keith acknowledges the nuances inherent in racial relations in late twentieth- and twenty-first-century England. Sitting on a train on his way home to Shepherd's Bush one evening, he is aware that three teenagers opposite him are vaguely menacing – for complex reasons not necessarily to do with race:

> He can see that, like his son Laurie, all three kids are partly white, but it is clear from their baggy dress sense, and from the way that they slouch and speak, that they identify themselves as black. Gone are the days when, sitting on the tube at night, he would feel perfectly safe if a posse of black youths got into his carriage. Back then he often took silent satisfaction in seeing how their exuberance made older white people somewhat uneasy, but today's teenagers no longer respect any boundaries. Black youths, white youths, mixed race youths, to them all he is just a middle-aged man in a jacket and tie who looks like he doesn't know shit about nothing. (13–14)

But while it reflects changing racial dynamics and the apparent blurring of racial borders, Keith's encounter on the train is hardly a celebration of diversity: his bitter awareness of how alien he is to these potentially hostile youths is no doubt aggravated by the fact that he also struggles with his relationship with his teenage son.

The tension in this family's relations is all the more painful because it is intergenerational. Keith is virtually estranged from his father, who arrived in England as a young man; he has failed in his relationships, both with Keith's mother and with his long-time partner, Brenda; and he has spent years hospitalized for mental problems (during one prolonged sojourn, the son told his friends that his parents had returned to the West Indies, leaving him to complete his education in England). Keith himself has had mixed fortunes in his romantic life: separated from his wife after a single infidelity, which he chose to reveal to her, he enters into a relationship with a young colleague, who, when he decides to end the affair, accuses him with sound and fury of sexual harassment. Forced to take an indefinite break from his job as a social worker after his indiscretion becomes public, Keith must finally face the fact that his long-dreamed-of writing project – perhaps simply a pretext to give validity and direction to a drifting life – will never come to fruition.

Even more painfully, he realizes that his little-known father is in his final days, and as the son is forced to do what he can to ease the transition, he discovers that what Earl needs more than anything is to be *heard*. Even before the latter's final hospitalization, the son – and the reader – is prepared for the drama of the crucial "story within the story", first by Keith's discovery, on a visit to his ailing father, of a mysterious, carefully stowed-away cardboard box, which is "full of photographs, but they are mainly black and white shots of people that he doesn't recognise" (165). A few tantalizing bits of the puzzle that is, for Keith, his father's life in England are provided by Earl's old friend, the Jamaican-born Baron, in a moving monologue of disenchantment – the story of some first-generation migrants: "'Look at us. The sons of Empire. The men who came to this country to make life better for ourselves. . . . And look at how we're living after all these years. When your mother and father come to this country, you really think that either one of them expect to die here?" (184). Baron's rhetoric only adumbrates a more complex story, an individual and collective history which will catch and hold the attention of son and reader.

Near the end of the novel, the narrative voice changes abruptly, subversively, as the writer gives primacy not to Keith's still unfinished (perhaps unfinishable) manuscript, but to a lengthy oral account by Earl of his time in England. This intensely personal history is disruptive of what had seemed to be the predictably smooth surface of the narrative. By positioning it as he does near the end of the novel, Phillips gives power and legitimacy to a finally eloquent voice which, although close enough to standard English, recalls the rhythms, and sometimes the syntax, of a vernacular language, transporting the reader far away from what had seemed a bland town in the north of England. The father's story occupies close to fifty pages; and the possible criticism regarding the lack of *vraisemblance* of this episode – in which a gravely ill character is able to speak at such length and with such coherence – is, I think, beside the larger point. Reviewing the novel in the *Guardian*, Christopher Tayler remarks that this section of the narrative is "improbably long and writerly from a narrow point of view" but acknowledges its impact, noting that it is "also more powerful than anything else in the book".[17] Realism is certainly secondary to the emotional and narrative impact of the insertion of the voice of one who speaks passionately for himself, but also for many. In the father's narrative, the distant, sketchily delineated island in the West Indies becomes reality, not paradise, distinct in all its contours and challenges.

The father's long story begins with an imperious, even testy, question, underscoring the importance of an attentive audience familiar to all schooled in the Afro-Caribbean tradition of storytelling. Earl overcomes his habitual taciturnity about the past, and he who had previously accused his son of being "a man with such a big education [but one who] can sometimes act stupid" (164) now takes command:

> "You listening to me?"
> He looks down at his father's face.
> "I want to go home, Keith. I don't mean to some stupid English house. I mean home. Home, home." His father stares up at him. "You understanding what I mean? I'm not from here. I land in England on a cold Friday morning. It is April 15, 1960." (252)

Then follows a riveting, detailed account of the journey, that "final passage" recounted in some detail in Phillips's first novel; it is part story, part oral history/commentary on the West Indian experience at home and abroad, including an example of the insularity disguised as nationalism which leads the peoples of the region to divide themselves into sometimes anxiously guarded camps: "I remember, soon after we leave the West Indies, two Trinidadian fellars fall into the habit of sitting out on deck in the afternoon and talking all singsong about what to expect when we reach England" (252). Although the father disparages these know-it-all Trinidadians, former members of the Royal Air Force who went home after the war, the fact that he now reproduces their message at length (perhaps unconsciously editing and expanding their cautionary tales about the English) gives credence to their experience: "and they telling us that in England everything is dear . . . and English people don't like noise or any kind of trouble with the neighbours, and you must get accustom to the fact that everywhere is a sea of white faces, everywhere you turn you always looking on a sea of white faces and they don't know nothing about you, or where you from, or who you be" (253).

In his article "The Dynamic of Revelation and Concealment: *In the Falling Snow* and the Narrational Architecture of Blighted Existences", Gordon Collier rightly emphasizes the importance of the Creole syntax which informs this outpouring: "Interestingly enough, the flashback architecture employed in the main narrative line throughout the novel is also found here, but with the grammar of creole eliding the boundary between present-tense experience and past tense recollection; everything here is 'present'."[18] And indeed, Earl's memories of the distant past are remarkably vivid.

It is important to note that in this somewhat predictable though powerful account of racism and challenges faced by West Indian migrants, the storyteller does not hide the other side of the story, the conditions which led others like him to get on that banana boat. This is hardly surprising in the work of Caryl Phillips, who has emphasized (in response to the notion that *The Final Passage* might be seen as a "celebration of immigration, of difference") that "there's nothing glamorous about immigration".[19] Phillips can hardly be charged with the tendency to idealize the homeland described by Maria Antonia Oliver-Rotger in her introduction to *Identity, Diaspora and Return in American Literature*: "In the narrativization of the migrant experience, the notion of home is frequently permeated by a certain

'localism' or idealization of the country far away."²⁰ In the case of the character Earl, family fragmentation had already begun with the disappearance
of his big brother Desmond, who left more than ten years previously to pick
oranges in Florida: "once upon a time my father get a card from somewhere
in America, but my brother don't send an address so it ain't possible to write
back or anything like that" (258). Though Desmond's story is not developed – in fact, his relative absence from the family history is conspicuous,
underscored through narrative gaps which serve to highlight the emotional
cost of migration – this elliptical reference to the allure of the United States
recalls Bertram's sense, at the end of A State of Independence, of shifting
power relations in former British colonies. Earl does remember vividly the
moment of departure of the first and favourite son, Desmond; he remembers his "long-faced parents" (259) fixated on the image of the boat carrying
his brother away from home – and the reader senses a muted grievance
at Earl's father's attachment to Desmond. The loss of this brother, and its
implied impact on the sibling left behind, recalls the role of the brother
Dominic in A State of Independence: in each case, the brother who migrates
(Desmond or Bertram) maintains little contact with the family group left
at home, which is irremediably changed because of his departure. Richard
Patteson makes the valid point that Bertram himself is incomplete, his life
truncated in part because of his brother's absence, describing Dominic as
"the novel's ghost-protagonist, the other half of Bertram, the half embody-
ing the island and the past".²¹

Earl remembers an imperfect past in his land of birth, recounting to his
son the scarce opportunities on the island, his love of books and dreams of
higher education, and his unrewarding job at the sugar factory: "'The island
have only one scholarship for studying overseas at university and at least
six boys in my class have parents who can pay for extra lessons, and all of
these town boys have new textbooks'" (259). The unabashed *subjectivity* of
this account is noteworthy: the son does not interject questions or remarks
to interrupt the long sentences, nor does the narrator seek to comment on
or correct this version of history. Earl's childhood is at times painted in
chiaroscuro: memories of home are complicated by familial tensions, and
made sombre by the death of Earl's mother and, a few years later, that of
his father. And with the nuclear group painfully diminished, it is his sister

Leona, now married and with children, who urges him to take the bold step away from home, as friends have before him. It is noteworthy that here she invokes the *mythology* of England, land of opportunity, that prevailed in the "colonies" in the mid-twentieth century; at the same time, we are reminded of the gendered aspect of the migration story, of the greater freedom and perhaps of a *learned* audacity which led more young men than women to seek their fortune in a strange land: "'Look,' say Leona, 'why you don't take yourself and your books to England. I can sell the house and send you the money to pay back the price of the boat ticket. No point you staying here and feeling miserable. Me, I can't go no place with two children because England is for people without no obligations'" (263).

The flow of words constituting Earl's story begins on page 252 and continues uninterrupted until page 264, broken, perhaps logically – in a narrative not conspicuously governed by a preoccupation with chronological coherence – by the arrival of evening, and a night that Keith spends alone in his father's dreary house. There, the atmosphere is charged, marked by "the unpleasant smell of mouldy food" (264), but Keith has the company of the cardboard box of photographs – some of them now spilled on the father's abandoned tabletop – which is potent in its tacit documentation of the migrant story that the father has finally unmasked. These images, metonymic of Keith's sometimes obscure identity, form an inviting but incomplete pictorial record of Earl's history; and the son's inability to name the characters of that history explains his own need to hear the outpouring of details and anecdotes which will continue the next day: "For a moment he is tempted to gather up the photographs and toss them all into the box and then push the cardboard receptacle into a cupboard and out of sight, but unlike the pots and dishes these photographs have considerable weight. He can't bring himself to pick them up, or even touch them. Not now, not at this moment" (266).

When he returns to see his father the next morning, Earl is still loquacious, even petulant, jumping right into the continued story: "Last night I was talking to you, remember? One minute saying something to you, and the next minute you gone. You don't want to hear what I have to say?" (268). The remainder of Earl's story occupies some thirty more pages of the narrative, a narrative in which the father who was not always there explains his own losses, his lack of readiness for the responsibility thrust on him after the early death of Keith's mother. He recalls the benevolent insistence that he *father* his son by Brenda, no stereotypical wicked white stepmother (Phillips avoids racializing the relationship between Earl and Brenda, though the reader might infer her Englishness as another cause of his prolonged silence about his feelings of alienation). It is Brenda who would care for the child even after Earl was committed to a psychiatric hospital – for an illness which brings to mind other fictional migrants whom England has "sent mad", such as the memorable "Uncle" in Olive Senior's story of the Jamaican who returned with a grievance against the monarchy in "The Case against the Queen".[22] Earl's is a remarkable monologue which bridges the gap between the oral and the scribal, ending with an enigmatic statement of the schism between this migrant's expectation of England and the reality, as well as an explanation of his related reluctance to accept the charge of fatherhood: "It's not you that I don't want, son. I just don't want this life, because England already hurt me enough as it is. . . . The idea of England is fine. I can deal with the idea. You understand me, son? I can deal with the idea" (297).

The father's death, told euphemistically by a nurse to Keith, who has fallen asleep at the end of Earl's final monologue, occurs near the end of the novel. After this compelling narrative, bringing the father – and, indeed, an entire generation of migrants – centre stage, what follows in the final pages appears almost like an afterthought. Phillips makes no attempt to tie up narrative loose ends – for example, by staging a scene in which Keith might share with either Annabelle or, perhaps more logically, Earl's grandson Laurie the episode to which he has been a solitary witness. There is no smooth transition here, and certainly no resolution of the novel's central problematic of identity. Yet we sense a changed Keith, one whose personal and professional problems are unresolved, but who seems, though without enthusiasm, open to a rapprochement with Annabelle, and who is forced into a resumption of responsibility at the news that Laurie's girlfriend is pregnant. One might share Kasia Boddy's view that "Earl's deathbed narrative provides a jolt both to the book and to Keith",[23] but it is far from clear how the son will define his identity now that his closest link to his origins is gone. Certainly, returning to the Caribbean is not an option, and one wonders in what direction his literary aspirations will go, now that he has been privileged as interlocutor for his father, now that he is keeper of so much more than a box of photographs, guardian of a narrative more deeply felt than anything he has been able to write. One of Phillips's most striking achievements in this foregrounding of the father's story is that he complicates widely held assumptions about West Indian migrants to England, reminding us that they do not form a monolithic group whose reasons for leaving home may be summed up in a sentence or two. As Avtah Brah has memorably emphasized, "All diasporic journeys are composite. . . . They are embarked upon, lived and re-lived through multiple modalities: modalities, for example, of gender, 'race', class, religion, language and generation."[24]

Earl's account is linked to a particular historical period, that of the mid-twentieth century, and to a specific class experience, that of migrants who found themselves forced to do the most menial of tasks, whether or not they, like the protagonist's father, had dreams of education in the "mother country". The younger, more privileged Keith inhabits a different Britain, as does his son, Laurie. In this context, one may recall Stuart Hall's analysis of the interpenetration of cultures in a changing England where, in his opinion, young blacks have achieved a certain dominance, even while still economically disadvantaged. Hall asserts, in an essay entitled "Frontlines and Backyards: The Terms of Change", that "Black British culture is today confident beyond its own measure in its own identity".[25] Speaking specifically of young black people in the 1990s, he goes on to suggest that "their stylization of their own bodies is a remarkable feature which has made them the dominant defining force in street-oriented British youth culture. Without them white youth culture would not exist in the form it does today."[26]

Keith, though aware of the racial tensions which persist in his time, is unfamiliar with the bitter history which marked the first few decades of West Indian migration to Britain; he is thus positioned not quite on the periphery of the narrative, as attentive listener whose presence and engagement facilitate and validate the telling. It is interesting that Phillips should deploy the narrative device, after pages and pages of text which sound not unlike the author's voice, of effacing – or perhaps, more accurately, masking – his own persona[27] by creating this lengthy monologue written in a somewhat creolized English which commands the reader's attention. The section spoken in Earl's voice is all the more startling since Caryl Phillips has rarely manipulated in his writing the two tongues or, at the very least, the varying registers which most Caribbean diasporic novelists[28] claim as both resource and marker of identity. Perhaps what Phillips is doing with this narrative strategy is consonant with his declared belief in literature as "plurality in action".[29] He confronts the challenge of *representation*, for those who like Earl are frequently silenced in the official discourse, and appears to surrender the narrative to one overwhelming voice, a voice which eloquently tells an old story, a story quite different from that of the second generation of migrants to whom both Phillips and the character Keith belong – the story of leaving home, and of longing to return.

In most of the narratives which make up *The Atlantic Sound* (2000), a non-fictional account of travel through areas associated with the triangular trade, Phillips writes very much from a first-person perspective, in his own voice, and here he is more traveller than migrant – though conscious in all his trajectories of the need to explore, to reimagine and perhaps finally to accept his Englishness. In the memoir, he recounts his journeys to geographically diverse locations linked by the nefarious commerce which was the Atlantic slave trade, beginning with his attempt to replicate his parents' voyage to England by boat in the late 1950s. Phillips has noted in an interview the familial silence on this turning point in their history, in words that remind us of the function of the father's account of crossing the Atlantic in *In the Falling Snow*:

> That journey from the Caribbean to Britain that my parents undertook with me in the late fifties is a journey that they've never really talked about, and I've asked them both together and individually over the years to explain why they left, what the actual journey was like, the sense of anticipation. . . . So I thought the only way I could at least emotionally retrace it was by actually getting on a banana boat myself and going there.[30]

It is interesting, however, that the Caribbean/Latin American countries mentioned at the start of what will turn out to be a convoluted itinerary are francophone and Spanish-speaking territories (the narrator informs us in the first pages that he flew straight from the United States to Guadeloupe), as if Phillips shrinks from the pain of the particular, from the sense of "former homeland" implicit in the setting of *A State of Independence*. Perhaps, also, the writer consciously seeks to de-dramatize his departure from the islands, to avoid what might appear as a self-indulgent, convenient nostalgia at the start of this new but not final passage. Certainly, his description of Guadeloupe is suggestive of the casual interest of the tourist on a cruise, stopping at one island after another, and this location seems incidental, as if representing no more to him than the various islands of the archipelago to which Europeans rich enough to purchase secluded space retreat from time to time – exotic sites like Mustique or Necker Island. I believe that a comment by Phillips about his changing approach to the non-fiction form is instructive here: "that's very much what *The Atlantic Sound* was about – trying to reclaim, re-find, and rediscover the personal pronoun but not to lose the critical angle".[31] Indeed, he occupies the role, in this memoir/travel narrative, of both diasporic subject and cultural critic – writing with a purpose but without the confident theorizing inherent in Paul Gilroy's "Black Atlantic" model.

Importantly, the West Indian segment of *The Atlantic Sound* – the prologue entitled "Atlantic Crossing" – ends with a statement of a *sort of* belonging to England that is, though not exuberant, less muted than one might expect, and one feels here the full force of the first-person pronoun. Though sensitive to the historical resonance of the iconic cliffs of Dover, to their strangeness for the first migrants such as his parents, Phillips quietly affirms that *he* is not displaced, that the predictable images of greyness and coldness which evoke, for many West Indian writers/travellers, England's essential otherness[32] do not daunt him: "On this bleak late winter's morning, I am happy to be home. . . . I have not travelled towards Britain with a sense of hope or expectation. I have travelled towards Britain with a sense of knowledge and propriety, irrespective of what others, including my fellow passengers, might think. For one brief moment I imagine that a chapter in my own personal narrative has closed."[33] Yet the last sentence of the nuanced declaration quoted above is perhaps the most intriguing, because, typical of this author, it eschews easy certainties: the rest of *The Atlantic Sound* will make it clear that arrival in England – arrival perhaps in any other land, however familiar – is never, for this traveller who embodies but does not quite make peace with a sort of hybridity, a definitive moment, an end to the persistent temptation of mobility.

More complex in tone than the account of his arrival in England are the sections of the text in which Phillips confronts the distant, ancestral past, through his journey to Ghana, the former Gold Coast, from which in the Caribbean imaginary many of the ancestors came. In the third part of *The Atlantic Sound*, ironically titled "Homeward Bound", the writer relates his travels to Ghana and finally to Elmina, to the slave port transformed into a tourist destination but still bearing its painful history, remembered as site of incarceration and deportation, its awesome "door of no return" transformed but not sanitized by its designation as a UNESCO World Heritage Site. Here, the narrator appears to remain as detached as in the islands, but he is also troubled by the apparent compulsion of fellow travellers to pin him to a place of origin: "Where are you *really* from? . . . I make the familiar flustered attempt to answer *the* question. He listens, and then spoils it all. 'So, my friend, you are going home to Africa. To Ghana.' I say nothing. *No, I am not going* home."[34] And once in Ghana, the traveller seems unmoved by modern-day Elmina, and by the chaotic cultural event of Panafest, an event predicated and orchestrated on the assumption of commonalities among Africans and diasporic peoples. Perhaps what the narrative reflects here is something close to Stuart Hall's sense of the finality of the migrant journey, memorably articulated in the recent volume *Familiar Stranger: A Life between Two Islands*: "Migration is a Humpty Dumpty phenomenon. Once shattered, the past can never be put back together again as it once was, in all its essential identity. This is because the past has not been stranded there all the time, preserved and unchanged, waiting for us to come home."[35]

Yet the distant past hovers constantly in *The Atlantic Sound*, and Phillips is drawn to memorialize, with brutal and poignant detail, the experience of the soon-to-be enslaved who awaited deportation in the castle which functioned as a dungeon. That Elmina is central to Phillips's remembering of what preceded his ancestors' "New World" experience is further demonstrated by other references to the site in different texts. In *A New World Order*, he links it with his own origins: "All journeys have a beginning. Mine began on the west coast of Africa in a slave fortress. Perhaps it was Elmina Castle in Ghana."[36] But it is finally in North America, in Charleston, South Carolina, near Sullivan's Island, where some 40 per cent of the Africans transported to the United States as slaves disembarked, that Phillips seems to come alive, as if his compass has finally pointed him not *home* but to a place familiar because it embodies a diasporic identity connected with Africa, an identity which, even for one fleeting moment, he can embrace:

> And now the African dancing begins. Five young black women explain the origins of each dance before they dramatically twirl and throw their arms into the air. This is Shango. This is from Senegal. This means we are making a blessing, an offering, praising the sun, the moon. . . . Their sinewy bodies weave invisible threads that connect them to the imagined old life. . . .
>
> The rhythms of Africa floating over Charleston. White men and women dancing behind the United States Customs House. Somewhere in the distance, around the corner and out of sight, Sullivan's Island. And before Sullivan's Island? Africa. . . . White men and women dancing to the rhythms of Africa in the street behind the United States Customs House. History smiles. Magnolia cemetery on a bright moonlit night, some distance to the north. Home. African drums. The police looking on, guns on their hips. Ghosts walking the streets of Charleston. Ghosts dancing in the streets of Charleston.[37]

Here, Phillips, certainly not partisan of Afrocentrism and manifestly uncomfortable with performing racial belonging, appears to signal empathy with those descendants of the long dispersed, who must reimagine, if not invent, rituals. The simple celebration of origins associated with and legitimized by the Négritude generation is conspicuously absent from Phillips's travel narrative, as is the self-conscious affirmation of shared cultural values which seemed to disturb the writer at the earlier festivities in Ghana. Yet in his description of a cultural festival in Charleston, without making peace with the history of enslavement, Phillips acknowledges the survival of a people and the retention and reinvention of rituals which nourish and sustain.

The writer's consciousness of the racial tensions still endemic in the United States – and nowhere more than in the racially polarized South – is apparent in the juxtaposition of the image of African drums against the stark reference to a watchful, even ominous police presence. There is no triumphalism here, and Wendy Knepper is right in underscoring the ambivalence which inheres in this scene, as indeed it does in much of Phillips's journeying: "The present is haunted by the past with all of the ambiguity this entails. . . . Accompanying the view of America as home to integration, democracy and freedom, Phillips offers us the ambivalent image of a world haunted by ghosts where the legacy of slavery is palpable."[38] The reader is left to decipher the complex and even contradictory messages emerging from this scene in Charleston. But what is certain is that the young women participating in this "Festival of African and Caribbean Art" dance within the structure of a "New World" rhythm, a rhythm which precludes stasis or nihilism, which transcends the traumas of the Middle Passage, which calls out defiantly to the ancestral origin. And so, the writer fashions, in documenting this sojourn in Charleston, a personal cartography of remembering through which ties to a distant but essential continent, though not intact, are reimagined and given creative form.

Remembering as act of will is also manifest in a simple monument erected on Sullivan's Island on 28 July 2009 in a ceremony/invented ritual by the waters. A stone bench was installed at this location by the Toni Morrison Society[39] as one response to a comment by Morrison on the absence of monuments marking the existence of slaves: "There is no place you or I can go, to think about or not think about the presences of or perhaps the absences of slaves."[40] Similarly, Phillips's memoir, which predated the installation of that bench summoning to memory the sombre arrival of future slaves, laments the historical silence on the treatment of the Africans deposited on Sullivan's Island; in *The Atlantic Sound*, the writer describes his own solitary exploration of a site that revealed little of its shameful history: "Nobody seems to know exactly where the pest houses were located, and of course nobody has thought it necessary at least to speculate and mark a place with a monument or plaque."[41] In several sections of *The Atlantic Sound*, Caryl Phillips remedies that absence in a text structured around journeys that memorialize, forcing his readers both to visualize the unredeemable monument of Elmina and to listen to the "rhythms of Africa floating" in Charleston, South Carolina.

The Atlantic Sound tells the story of an uprooted traveller, the son of West Indian migrants locating himself within a transatlantic history of displacement. In 2011, Phillips would publish another non-fictional account of journeying, also transcontinental in its reach, though its routes are less closely linked to one overarching concern. The title of the latter work wryly conflates two discrete markers of identity – race and nationality – in order to highlight the conundrum of unbelonging often confronting those bearing EU passports in Europe but who are visibly other. Phillips's subversive title *Color Me English* may be read, ironically, as the antithesis of that of Isabelle Boni-Claverie's documentary *Trop noire pour être française? (Too Black to Be French?)*[42] – but while the latter title, in its interrogatory form, implies either doubt or bitterness, the former appears grounded in certainty or at least confident aspiration.

In the collection of essays *Color Me English*, the author elaborates on his long-standing preoccupation with origins and hybridity while formulating a generous vision of the role of the writer, exploring and indeed reaffirming his vocation as storyteller. Phillips's characteristic breadth of vision is enhanced by the experience of living both in England and in the United States, where he has taught since 1990 (the volume's subtitle is "Migration and Belonging Before and After 9/11"). One of the early sections, entitled with some irony "Homeland Security", begins with an account of the day when the New York landscape was brutally changed. In the powerful and yet understated piece "Ground Zero", the author relates his own experience of that day, as a New Yorker who saw the black cloud of destruction, who at first retreated after a long walk to his apartment and then came outdoors again – anxious spectator, not flâneur – in time to hear one of the towers crash to the ground: "I don't know how long I stood on the West Side Highway, but I know that I heard the almighty crash of World Trade Center Tower 7 as it collapsed. I stood with dozens of others as we saw the enormous mushroom cloud and heard the nerve-shattering noise of the forty-seven-storey tower coming down."[43] What is striking in this narrative is that it exposes Phillips's sense of being almost at home, but not quite belonging, in the big city. When he first realizes the gravity of the event, having taken the subway to his office at Columbia University, where he should have taught a class, he makes one phone call, to his mother in St Kitts, and it is she who informs him of the attacks on the South Tower and on the Pentagon. He recalls an attempt to contact a student recently employed in the World Trade Centre; he remembers with sympathy the palpable anxiety of a colleague unable to reach her husband – but he remains somewhat of a loner, even as he stands in a crowd which he describes as "a macabre audience witnessing this catastrophe" (24). It is in some ways his city, this mesmerizing space with which he had built an intimate connection, and yet he is fundamentally an outsider, apparently without any loved ones to call. J. Dillon Brown is, I believe, perceptive in suggesting that *Color Me English* reflects a "sense of agonized engagement with both the pleasures and peril of American affiliation".[44] Immediately after the experience of collective tragedy that was 9/11, a discussion with a diverse group of students leads the writer, in "American Tribalism", to acknowledge a truth which he had initially denied, based on his early experiences of the country, based on his imagined America: "I now understand that behind the façade of a racially and ethnically mixed society all is not well" (28–29). Yet in another essay in the collection, he will affirm that his reaction to September 11 was "fed by proprietorial anxiety" (307).

The collection is somewhat uneven in tone and thematic focus, and certainly not as cohesive as *The Atlantic Sound*; other essays in the volume take us back to its essential *point de départ*: Leeds, England. The most moving and by far the most personal of the various chapters of *Color Me English* is a piece which is manifestly autobiographical though written in the third person, entitled "A Life in Ten Chapters" (2005). In that section, Phillips chronicles, inter alia, his first visit to the United States and its empowering, life-changing effect. With compelling understatement and relatively unembellished prose, the narrative traces the evolution of a young man who, by the tenth chapter, passionately informs us that he has found his life's purpose: to be a writer. But the unnamed subject has travelled a sometimes tortuous road to arrive at that certainty. In the first, abbreviated and yet memorable, "chapter", the author highlights both the power of story and the exclusionary form of education, which threatened to marginalize this five-year-old, the only black boy at a school in Leeds: "The five-year-old boy is beginning to understand difference – in the form of *class*. The final lesson of the day is story time. The neatly dressed children sit crosslegged on the floor at the feet of their teacher, Miss Teale. She begins to read them a tale about 'Little Black Sambo'. He can feel eyes upon him" (107). The writer need not elaborate on the boy's discomfort at the expectation that he will perform blackness, nor on the impact on young migrants in Britain of such stereotypical literary images of racial identity; Phillips is adroit in avoiding explicit statements which might distract from what is first of all the account of an individual experience. At age eight, the child does not understand the racism he encounters when he discovers that the mother of neighbours from whom he borrows books "warms the Enid Blyton paperbacks in the oven when he returns them" (108), ostensibly in order to destroy germs. And the adult narrator refrains from commentary on what memory is likely to have converted into a galling episode.

Other challenges, familial rather than public, will face the boy, whose consolation amid personal troubles – such as his parents' divorce – is his immersion in the world of books. At age nine, seduced by the magic of words, he tries to share a story he has written with his father: "The story includes the words 'glistening' and 'glittering' which have a glamour that the son finds alluring. When the son eventually hands the story to his father, the father seems somewhat baffled by this offering" (108). Here, the misunderstanding between father and son recalls the difficult relationship, the *silence*, between the characters Earl and Keith in *In the Falling Snow*. The absence, in this "Life in Ten Chapters", of the first-person pronoun, which might characterize it as autobiography, is suggestive of what is perhaps at the heart of Phillips's literary project: the wish to tell not just his own story (and several biographical details make it difficult to dissociate the unnamed "boy" from the writer) but also that of many others – migrants, writers, individuals *like* him but not quite him, each on a personal quest for understanding and belonging.

Despite the young protagonist's disappointment that his father failed to appreciate his first attempts at writing, his fascination with books offers a powerful distraction and the beginning of a vocation. So, for the young boy learning to revel in the texture of words, the love of reading becomes a solitary passion, so much so that, transfixed by *Anna Karenina*, he is irritated that his family is impervious to the drama in which he is engrossed: "He stares at his brothers, at his father, at his stepmother. Do they not understand? Anna has thrown herself in front of a train" (110). The reader will remember the trauma experienced by the five-year-old forced to represent an essentialized blackness as the class read "Little Black Sambo" when the young man discovers American writers, first John Howard Griffin in *Black Like Me*. A new university student at age eighteen, he reads *Blues for Mister Charlie* and is "completely overwhelmed by Baldwin's brutal prose" (110). When the twenty-year-old leaves England for the first time (chapter 9), it is for the United States, where he discovers with excitement more of the African American canon, buying his own copy of *Native Son*. Alone on a beach in California after reading Richard Wright's novel, "he now knows what he wishes to do with his life" (111).

And yet despite the exuberance of that moment, one of the most haunting sections of this "Life in Ten Chapters" refers to a period after the young man has in fact become a published writer: it relates his return to his native St Kitts and the discovery that the first editions of each of his two novels, so carefully packaged and dispatched to his great-grandmother by his editors, had remained unread, *unreadable*, for a reason unsuspected by one brought up – in faraway Leeds – to value the scribal and to take "literacy" for granted: "He sits with his great-grandmother in the small village at the far end of St. Kitts, the island on which he was born twenty-eight years earlier. He has now published two novels, and on each publication day he has asked his editor to send a copy of the book to his great-grandmother" (111). Finally back "home", he is able to question why she has never mentioned the books, and in a response which initially sounds like a non sequitur, she begins to talk about her childhood:

> She was born in 1898 and so he realises that she is talking to him about life at the dawn of the twentieth century. "And," she continues, "I missed a lot of school for I had to do all the errands". Suddenly he understands what she means. She cannot read. . . . She looks at her great-grandson. She doted on this boy for the first four months of his life. The great-grandson who disappeared to England. The great-grandson who all these years later now sends her stories from England. (112)

"A Life in Ten Chapters" ends on this note, and Phillips is elliptical in his treatment of this apparent failure of the young writer to bridge the gap between England and his great-grandmother's very different world. It clearly raises the issue, always challenging for Caribbean writers, of audi-

ence: for whom do those whose work is published, publicized and con-
sumed in "First World" cities write? Does the use of the European official language of these former colonies inevitably mean that reading and
writing become elitist activities, inaccessible to those who, like the St Kitts
great-grandmother, born in 1898, are marginalized by their "illiteracy"? On
the one hand, the fact that the great-grandson had no idea that the sharing
of the bounty of newly published books was to some extent a futile gesture,
more meaningful to the giver than to the recipient, underscores the gaps in
communication which may inhere in the separation of families on either
side of the migrant divide. On the other, the young writer's determination
to "write home", sending "stories from England" which implicitly honour
familial and national origin, may be read as confirmation that though there
may be a shift in relationships, a lessening of intimacy, there is no irrevo-
cable rupture of bonds. His physical presence, his position, as he sits with
his great-grandmother, signify fidelity, even reverence, negating the finality
implicit in the perhaps overused notion of exile; and the materiality of the
books, carefully kept in their original cardboard packaging, refutes the idea
that he had "disappeared" from her life. Yet the young man's predicament
also recalls the sense of disconnection from Caribbean reality experienced
by the protagonist of *A State of Independence*, and perhaps also hints at Phillips's own perception of the difficulty of telling stories for a group to whom
he is fundamentally an outsider, albeit a benevolent one.

But I think one may fruitfully contrast "A Life in Ten Chapters", including both the powerful account of a coming to voice and the realization of
the limitations of that voice, to the vicissitudes of the would-be writer of *In
the Falling Snow*. For the young writer of "A Life in Ten Chapters" is clearly
resolute in his wish to inscribe a life that is not his alone, a life that has
much to do with his West Indian origins. And however understated his
tone in these non-fiction texts, Phillips, like Danticat, writes with a sense
of purpose; it is interesting to note – based on various musical allusions in
his collection of essays on migration, for example – that he shares the fictional Keith's interest in the music of the African diaspora and specifically
in African American rhythms.[45]

The title essay, "Color Me English", begins by recalling the personal
story narrated in "A Life in Ten Chapters": "I was thirteen and entering my

third year at Leeds Central High School, an all-boys grammar school in the centre of Leeds. This year marked a transition because for the first time I would no longer be the only black boy in the school" (3). That increase in numbers is, however, a modest one: all that has changed is that the writer's two brothers have joined him at school. But a page further on, the author narrates an arrival that really marks a turning point, that of Ali, a Muslim of East Asian origin, who is defined by a "palpable sense of isolation" (4). Ali, the young Phillips realizes, is more "different" than he is, and is subjected to teasing and bullying precisely because of that difference. After one unsuccessful attempt to stand up for Ali in the face of hostile schoolmates and indifferent authorities, the narrator seems to acknowledge the futility of such small rebellions and to admit his own failure as a black teenager to go beyond a token, superficial solidarity with a young Asian, conspicuously non-English. Yet the adult Phillips certainly does not accept the status quo; he does not come to terms with the painful unbelonging embodied by Ali, pushing back against the normalization of bigotry and castigating himself now for his youthful inability to befriend a newcomer, a stranger more "extravagant"[46] than himself: "although I felt some immigrant kinship with him, and had instinctively tried to help him, things between us went only so far, and no further" (6–7). What follows, after these memories of troubling schooldays, is a meditation on what it means that England is being "coloured" by migrations from black and Asian countries, and on the stubborn prejudices and nativism that survive in this "postcolonial" era.

It is a meditation that is particularly compelling now, several years after the publication of *Color Me English*, at a time when the ongoing debates about multiculturalism and the rise of ethnonationalism in Europe renew the urgency of this Caribbean/black Briton's preoccupation with the othering of racial and ethnic minorities. The narrator singles out the attack in London of 7 July 2005, emphasizing and lamenting the fact that the four young Asian "terrorists" who blew up themselves and many others in the Underground were in fact British-born, and that three of the four were, like him, from Leeds. Yet despite the sadness which pervades this section of the essay – an essay in which the writer wavers between the competing perspectives of cultural critic, transnational intellectual and Caribbean

Briton – Phillips boldly expresses the conviction that the creative writer can make a difference:

> Europe is no longer white and never will be again. . . . I believe passionately in the moral capacity of fiction to wrench us out of our ideological burrows and force us to engage with a world that is clumsily transforming itself, a world that is peopled with individuals we might otherwise never meet in our daily lives. . . . Europe needs writers to explicate this transition, for literature *is* plurality in action; it embraces and celebrates a place of no truths, it relishes ambiguity, and it deeply respects the place where everybody has the right to be understood. (16)

Perhaps Caryl Phillips's credo springs from the writer's memory of not being understood, as a young boy growing up in Leeds, and from his sharpened awareness of both the negative and positive effects of the first stories to which he was exposed, as well as the power of the canonical writers, European and African American, who first sharpened his aesthetic and political sensibilities. For him, then, literature must mediate the differences between those who must rub shoulders in a changed Britain, in a changed Europe: "As long as we have literature as a bulwark against intolerance, and as a force for change, then we have a chance" (16).

In one of the final chapters of *Color Me English*, entitled "Ghana: Border Crossings", Phillips seems to arrive at a relatively hopeful conclusion on the challenges of migrancy: "Yet human beings have a tremendous capacity to absorb the chaos and confusion that comes with migration, forced or voluntary" (310). This remark is all the more surprising since the writer is visiting Ghana, the site of his disenchantment in *The Atlantic Sound*, now finding himself befriended by a taxi driver anxious to migrate to the United States. It is noteworthy that the final section of *Color Me English*, entitled "Distant Shores", comprises six chapters, of which four are set on the African continent (one in Ghana, two in Sierra Leone and one in Tanzania, the departure point for a gruelling climb up Mount Kilimanjaro), perhaps an epilogue of sorts to the unrewarding African journey of *The Atlantic Sound* – as if in this exploration of his Englishness, Caryl Phillips has found it crucial to return to the point of origin of the Afro-Caribbean diaspora.[47]

One of the chapters documenting a journey to Sierra Leone is in fact a journey up the Sierra Leone River into the past, foregrounding once again

Phillips's preoccupation with the history of slavery. It is a solitary journey by small boat to Bunce Island, notorious in the author's mind and imagination for its role in the massive uprooting of Africans: "Bunce Island was a well-fortified holding place, a processing centre, and a place of dispatch from which tens of thousands of Africans were forcibly removed from their homeland" (334). One may infer a connection in Phillips's imagination between Bunce Island and Elmina Castle, not because the two locations have anything in common superficially but because of the symbolism of the island as isolated, secluded space, a site lending itself to incarceration, a site foreshadowing the radical separation which would be effected by the transatlantic crossing – a site reminiscent of the bleakness of South Africa's Robben Island, from which prisoners did not escape simply because of the terrors of the surrounding waters.

In "Ghana: Border Crossings", the tone is initially lighter, as the narrator recounts a request by his driver for assistance in filling in a visa form. The location of this conversation is, for Phillips, a potential source of irony – for they are in Elmina, the port from which so many unwilling travellers were shipped to the New World, "the site of one of the largest and most impressive slave forts, those troubling edifices from whose dungeons millions of Africans were shipped in conditions of unspeakable misery . . . and deposited into the new American world" (301). But his driver's gaze is not fixed on the "door of no return",[48] nor does he intend to stay indefinitely in the United States; rather, he is already planning his remittances to Ghana: "Awuje has absolutely no interest in the psychological needs of displaced Africans in the diaspora. He wishes to go to America for the same reasons that my parents decided to come to Britain, and I decided to stay in the United States. To grow. And that's just fine. . . . Displacement, whatever. He just wants a chance, that is all, and who can blame him?" (312). Here, the semantics of diasporic journeying, the notions of dislocation and *déracinement*, are implicitly called into question. The slightly mocking interrogation of the very term "displacement", and perhaps specifically of its undifferentiated application to all migrant narratives, is certainly provocative; importantly, the writer challenges the assumption that travellers across national borders easily morph into rootless wanderers or happy hybrids. Earlier in the text, Phillips had already used the word less dismissively, identifying his own connection to his parents' transatlantic journey and even to what he describes as the forced "migration" (a term I find problematic, given the difficulty of locating the cruel singularity of slavery in the continuum of migrant experiences) of the slave trade: "I have made three migrations, all of which have brought me into close proximity to this troubling word 'displacement'" (305). But the writer's account of his parents' brutal discovery of discrimination on arrival in Leeds in 1958 changes the tone of the essay, for a moment brimming with an outrage verbalized in an intense catalogue of insults, in a lengthy sentence which may be read as a synopsis of the multiple humiliations related by the fictional Earl: "For the first time in their lives my parents were called 'nigger', my mother was spat at in the street, my father punched, they were short-changed in shops, offered accommodation that you wouldn't kennel your dog in, and constantly told to go back to the jungle. I was, of course, too young to know what they endured" (305).

Despite the anger inherent in the retelling of these bruising encounters with bigotry, however, the representation in "Ghana: Border Crossings" of the aspirations of the would-be Ghanaian emigrant is a reminder that many continue to travel far from home with expectations of advancement. Thus, in the end, *Color Me English* is a testament to Phillips's fundamental belief in the possibility of negotiating dual belonging – and of writing both from and to the place(s) one calls home. Phillips, shaped by his "three migrations", does not manifest the unresolved anxiety articulated by the Guyanese author Fred D'Aguiar, who writes, in an essay entitled "Home Is Always Elsewhere": "London was spoiled for me by my belief that one day I would return to Guyana, and when that was no longer true, by a feeling that London did not belong to me, could never belong to me, on account of my race, my minority status."[49]

Perhaps Phillips's apparent optimism is akin to a view expressed by Derek Walcott in a 2014 interview that a position of duality is not without advantages; asked to respond to a question about the ambivalence of "a person who was born and raised in America by Caribbean parents", the Nobel laureate seemed dismissive of the notion that identity should be a problem for such a diasporic subject, asserting that "the ambiguities and contradictions that we deal with in our lives are good reservoirs for writers".[50] As a Caribbean/black Briton, however, Phillips's situation is obviously not without angst; in the final chapter of *A New World Order*, he suggests how this impacted his early work: "As a young boy growing up in Leeds, I was both confused by, and afraid of, the word 'home'. Fear and confusion are fertile soil in which to plant the young writer" (307). In the past two decades, Phillips has grappled creatively with the problematic of reimagining and articulating a hyphenated diasporic identity without recourse to convenient certitudes. The mature writer whose voice we hear in *In the Falling Snow* and *Color Me English* embraces both his allegiance to several "homes" and his lingering, fertile anxieties about belonging.

MARYSE CONDÉ'S ELUSIVE ORIGINS

To Africa, Again?

AUDACIOUS JOURNEYS TO STRANGE LANDS AND to imagined, elusive homelands are certainly familiar tropes in the fiction of the Guadeloupean Maryse Condé, herself a prodigious voyager, never fully nomad, never definitively rooted. Even her "reunion" with her native land asserted in a 1986 article[1] would prove tenuous in the medium term. Commitment to one site is in fact rare in Condé's fiction, as her protagonists' trajectories appear to mirror the writer's own fundamental restlessness – which one might also describe as the passionate assertion of a right to autonomy, even when this includes the unorthodox or even the transgressive.

This chapter analyses both the 1992 text *Les derniers rois mages* (*The Last of the African Kings*) and the intriguingly titled *Histoire de la femme cannibale* (*The Story of the Cannibal Woman*), published in 2005. Beginning with her first novel, the provocative and celebrated 1976 *Heremakhonon*,[2] Condé has created memorable protagonists – mainly but not exclusively female – who travel far from their "native" Antilles to Africa but also, less dramatically, to North America and to Europe. Several of these characters are privileged voyagers, for example, leaving home for study in the "*métropole*", while some economic migrants do encounter the social marginalization which is often the lot of those seeking their fortune in foreign lands. In the 1997 narrative *Desirada*, the character Ludovic, stepfather to the young Guadeloupe-born protagonist Marie-Noelle, epitomizes the rootlessness which has marked several Condéan fictions; Ludovic, whom Marie-Noelle first encounters in

Paris, is originally from Haiti, but that origin is problematized by a history of migration and remigration:

> Ludovic always hesitated a moment when asked where he was from. His father had left Haiti for Ciego de Avila in Cuba, where the caneworkers' pay was much better. Then he had had three boys with a woman who also broke her back working in the canefields. He had lived some time in Santo Domingo, where he fathered other children. Then he went back to Haiti, for he was homesick for the acrid smell of its burnt earth. As soon as he turned eighteen Ludovic began to wander in his father's footsteps. He put far behind him the bottomless despair of Haiti, tried his luck in the United States of America, Canada, Germany, and Africa before ending up in Belgium and striding across the border to Paris.[3]

The journey of Ludovic's father and, even more so, the travels of Ludovic himself sound like the odyssey of mythical heroes crossing vast oceans; and yet paradoxically, they encapsulate a Caribbean reality, a history of both intra-regional and external migration, the story of the relentless search of the poorest travellers for a better life, a search which hardly diminishes the yearning for the "rock" – in this Haitian's case, for a less than exotic but necessary smell of "burnt earth". It is worth noting that of the Caribbean countries portrayed in her fiction, Maryse Condé seems especially drawn to Haiti, foregrounding that nation's glory and misfortunes through characters appearing in several narratives.[4] It is particularly interesting that Condé, in the 2010 novel *En attendant la montée des eaux*, should return to the adventures of a male traveller – this time part African, part Antillean – linked to Haiti. The title of course is reminiscent of *En attendant le bonheur*,[5] the renamed edition of *Heremakhonon*, in which Guadeloupean Veronica, after studies in Paris, seeks legitimacy and prestige in Africa and from an African lover with royal antecedents. In the 2010 novel, the journey is, at first glance, less circuitous, from Guadeloupe to Haiti, where Babakar searches for the relatives of a little girl whose mother, living as an undocumented immigrant in Guadeloupe, has died in childbirth. But as Condé herself suggests, the composition of the disparate group of friends who join in the benevolent mission on Haitian soil highlights ethnic and national plurality: Movar, who accompanies Babakar from Guadeloupe, is Haitian, while Fouad, with whom they form an alliance, is of Palestinian origin. The author explains: "*En attendant la montée des eaux* takes us back to Ségu. The main character, Babakar, is one of the last of the famous Traorés. He is of mixed blood since his mother is Guadeloupean. . . . Finally he ends up in Haiti, a place for living dangerously."[6]

In *Desirada*, Ludovic's trajectory, taking him away from the Caribbean, is grandiose, encompassing, as it does, three continents, and the character is figured as the hero of a sort of marathon, overcoming all hurdles before striding (improbably) across the French border and finally into Paris. In the 2003 novel *Histoire de la femme cannibale*, on the other hand, Condé once again takes the leap of imagination back to the continent of origin, though this time to southern Africa. The novelist had decided, with the passion of the rejected "outside child", that she would "never write about Africa again"[7] as a reaction to the negative response of African critics to the bestselling 1984–85 *Ségou* (a historical fiction in which the Guadeloupean novelist boldly writes about an African society without the obvious mediating lens of a West Indian spectator). Condé would nevertheless continue to be haunted by a journey which I think confirms her as rightful heir to the Négritude pioneer Aimé Césaire[8] (however conflicted the filial relationship may be). The seduction of a distant fatherland and the concomitant uneasiness with the familiar place of origin persist in her work, connecting characters as different as the Barbadian protagonist of *Moi, Tituba sorcière . . . noire de Salem* (*I, Tituba, Black Witch of Salem*) (1986), and Anita, the American-born descendant of an African king in *Les derniers rois mages* (1992). Even Marie-Noelle, the more cautious voyager of the 1997 *Desirada*, though brought up in the suburbs of Paris and focusing much of her own quest on the tiny island of Désirade where her grandmother still lives, experiences vicariously, through the adventures of West Indian and African American friends, the possibility of "return" to ancestral sites.

The reader familiar with this oeuvre of displacement and provisional homecoming(s) is therefore hardly surprised at the response of the character Rosélie, in *The Story of the Cannibal Woman* (*Histoire de la femme cannibal*), to the question "'Aren't you going to return home?'": "Home? If only I knew where home was. Chance had it I was born in Guadeloupe. But nobody in my family is interested in me."[9] One might be tempted, then, to feel a weariness at this prolonged literary journey to and through unrewarding destinations, tempted to wish for at least *one* of Condé's travellers a cure for a debilitating wanderlust. And yet, such stability would be surprising in the work of the tenuously rooted Condé; the latter's sense of the elusiveness of "home" and her continuing interrogation of comfortable notions of national and racial belonging are reminiscent of "black British" Caryl Phillips's expressed difficulty with labelling himself in accordance with rigid, exclusive categories.[10]

The francophone Caribbean has generated more discrete ideological camps than the rest of the region – from the trailblazing and globally resonant Négritude movement, through the concept of Antillanité associated with Edouard Glissant, to the Créolité movement of the late twentieth century of which Patrick Chamoiseau and Raphael Confiant are eloquent champions. Maryse Condé has resolutely stood apart from such ideologically focused, and sometimes divisive, discourses of identity, and has in fact been the subject of critical controversies about what represents real "Creoleness", especially since the ideology introduced in the resounding 1993 manifesto *Eloge de la créolité* (*In Praise of Creoleness*) privileges the vernacular language as a condition sine qua non of French Caribbean belonging – and literary practice. She does celebrate the unique voice of a writer whose English is indelibly marked by the Haitian Creole which she spoke almost exclusively for the first twelve years of her life, saying of Danticat, "Between the words in English, the Creole rears up like a stubborn and rebellious memory."[11] And from time to time, Condé herself incorporates in the French text Creole terms – usually italicized in *Les derniers rois mages*, for example, in the following reflection by the Guadeloupean protagonist, on his arrival on Crocker Island (the island near Charleston where he and his wife Debbie finally settle), on the similarity of his situation to that of his ancestor, the exiled king of Dahomey: "A son arrivée à Crocker Island, Spéro n'avait pu s'empêcher de penser à l'ancêtre, qui, au terme de son voyage sur la mer, avait débarqué à la Martinique. . . . Quoi! C'est sur cette *krazur* de terre qu'il allait finir son existence?"[12] Richard Philcox, Condé's habitual translator, uses the same word *"krazur"* (also italicized) without explanation in his translation of the novel: "When he had first arrived on Crocker Island, Spero could not help thinking of the ancestor, who, at the end of his journey by sea, had landed in Martinique. . . . What! He was going to finish his life on this *krazur* of land?"[13] While Condé hardly deploys the vernacular language with the confidence of the Creolists, in this case and elsewhere, her narrative reflects the *untranslatability* of Kreyol on occasions when it most eloquently expresses strong sentiment – in this instance, a sentiment of intense frustration with limited island space. Yet she remains a writer difficult to define as *créolophone*, and her frequent and sometimes polemical affirmations of a reluctance to be limited by ideology or national origin are in fact consonant with her propensity to create "migrant" characters in thrall to a compulsion to wander.

The present chapter foregrounds the journeying impulse, in two of Condé's novels, of West Indian characters who have sojourned in North America but who, either through the imagination or in reality, are ultimately drawn "back" to Africa. In both these texts, the writer, celebrated for the formidable historical narrative *Ségou* (dedicated to the novelist's imaginary "Bambara ancestress"), returns to the African continent, but significantly, in *The Story of the Cannibal Woman*, to South Africa, a region not associated with French colonialism. In *Les derniers rois mages*, translated as *The Last of the African Kings*, Condé creatively rewrites a fascinating historical saga. King Behanzin of Dahomey, defeated after a heroic resistance against the European invader, did experience an enforced "relocation" to Martinique in 1894, though under circumstances different from the shipment of Africans to a life of servitude in the New World several centuries earlier. But what Condé does in *The Last of the African Kings* is create for the displaced monarch a fictional Antillean family, born of his relationship with the Guadeloupean maid Hosannah, who bears him a child, Djéré. This New World son resents, with the bitterness of the unclaimed "bastard" child, the *genuine* African father who abandoned him – but Djéré will nevertheless initiate, and pass on to his own son, a "cult of the ancestor". The first page of the text foregrounds both the exotic, unforgettable spectacle of the king and his entourage and the devastation wrought years later by his departure from the Antilles: "His great-grandfather had brought with him into exile five of the Leopard wives, his daughter the princess Kpotasse, his son Ouanilo, and his *honton*, his alter ego, the prince Adandejan" (5).

In the photograph that the fourteen-year-old protagonist Spero Jules-Juliette, already a painter, would transform into a portrait, the young Djéré is a cherished member of the imposing family group. But we learn a few lines further on that "this blissful, apparently beloved illegitimate son, however, would be left behind by the family together with other relics when they returned to Africa" (5). It is that schism, that assumed betrayal,[14] that lends the poignancy of unfulfilled yearning to the relation of Djéré and his descendants to an *imagined* Africa. Long after Behanzin was sent back to the African continent, but not to his homeland (he died in Algeria in 1906, a historical fact that puts into sharp relief the pertinence of the story of Behanzin's forced separation from Dahomey/Benin as an allegory of exile), Djéré, his own son, Justin, and the protagonist of the novel, Spero, would continue to claim that nebulous but valued African filiation. That Condé, sometimes mocking in her tone regarding this line of men whom some might see as royal pretenders, also acknowledges in the novel the primacy of Africa in the Caribbean imaginary is suggested by her inclusion, in the tradition of African storytelling, of a "story within the story". Thus, the history of Behanzin's New World sojourn is creatively chronicled in Djéré's "cahiers", notebooks inscribing the child's memories of his African father. These notebooks, interspersed throughout *The Last of the African Kings* without authorial commentary, seem to accord scribal authority to what might sound to some like a fictive tale of origins. And that authority is hardly diminished by the fact that Debbie and Spero fail in their efforts to have the translated text published in the United States; the notebooks rather remain as an alternative history, one that maintains its hold on the ancestor's diasporan progeny.

It would take several generations, however, for an Antillean descendant of the royal émigré to make the return voyage to the quasi-mythical land of origin. Spero would be the first to resume the cycle of sometimes unhappy journeying frequently observed in Condéan fiction: after meeting African American Debbie in his native Guadeloupe, he follows her to Charleston, South Carolina, benefiting, initially, from the aura of legitimacy given him by the story of his ancestry. And yet Spero's fascination with the African ancestor, and therefore with the continent, had been brutally challenged and somewhat diminished when, during his student days in France, he travelled from Lille to Paris to meet with a French colonial civil servant who disdainfully dismissed his claims of royal lineage, offering no validation to the needy West Indian. He was confronted instead with a bureaucratic and existential challenge to which he had no response: "Have you got your grandfather's birth certificate?" (84). Ironically, the refusal by one vested with colonial authority to authenticate the family's claims of lineage seems to confirm the mocking commentary in the communal Guadeloupean voice on the notion that an African could be a monarch, a denial reflecting West Indian alienation, reflecting an ignorance of history beyond that communicated in colonial textbooks. It is in Kreyol that the original French text reflects derisively on the very idea of Behanzin's royalty: " – Un roi africain! *Ka sa yé sa?*"[15] A footnote at the end of the page explains the meaning of the dismissive question in standard French, while in the translation, the explanation is placed in parenthesis: "'An African king! Ka sa yé sa?' (What on earth's that?)" (47).

In addition to the psychic and emotional blow experienced in Paris, Spero's memories of his student days in Lille are generally sombre, associated with "times of solitude, poverty and humiliation of all sorts due to his color" (65). Ignorant of this time of disillusionment, and seduced as much by an enviable myth of origin as by Spero's attractive person, Debbie is happy to present him to her circle in Charleston. Much later, however, a disenchanted Spero "often told himself that Debbie had only married him to have a family tree she could boast about" (97). Unlike Ludovic, moving confidently from place to place (and impregnating women along the way), Spero will come to feel, in his migration journey, like a *follower*, devoid of purpose or agency. Ann Smock is insightful in establishing a connection between Spero's experience and the ancestor's; it is worth emphasizing that the latter's journey away from home is indeed a *banishment*: "Spéro's peregrinations after his marriage – to Jamaica, New York, Charleston, back to New York and back again to Charleston (never at home anywhere, always a stranger) – are not unlike the exiled King's after the burning of his palace in Dahomey."[16]

Not only does this marriage of two radically different but equally needy individuals falter – glorious family trees notwithstanding – but also Spero's expectations of life in America confront the hurdles familiar to many Caribbean migrants. Deemed other by African Americans because he is from "the islands", he does not share, nor does he attempt to understand, the painful sensitivity to racial discrimination born of the history of coexistence with a powerful white majority. Spero is also conspicuous as a *French-speaking* black ("a nigger speaking English with a French accent" [22]), his situation somewhat reminiscent, though in a less hopeful vein, of that of the young Guadeloupean domestic worker Claude in Condé's short story "Three Women in Manhattan",[17] for whom the English language is an obstacle she is determined to overcome: "The evening classes at City College were almost free. She was learning English. Bit by bit, the sounds of New York – which had frightened and deafened her – were becoming intelligible. She was able to decipher the puzzles of neon signs and posters."[18] The difference between Claude and Spero is that the young woman, though apparently on the periphery of American society, *chose* the adventure of the big city, selecting migration to New York rather than the predictability, for a French West Indian, of relocation to Paris under the less than benevolent auspices of the BUMIDOM[19] mass-migration agency. Claude hopes, with the confidence or perhaps the presumption of youth, to make a place for herself not only in New York but in the body of diasporic literature, and her bold journey is suggestive of the particular freedom which urban space may afford the female traveller courageous enough to claim it. That she is unmarried is perhaps significant; one thinks here of an illuminating comment by Carole Boyce Davies in *Black Women, Writing and Identity* on representations of mobility in black women's writing: "Migration as wife, a number of texts such as *Juletane* have shown, does not carry power in cross-cultural contexts."[20] Davies goes on to assert that "the notion of travelling women is not as obscure in African American women's fiction as it may seem on the surface",[21] citing, in particular, novels by Toni Morrison such as *Sula* and *Tar Baby*. Claude, also a travelling woman, might appear powerless in socio-economic terms, but she has a strong sense of self, and she is certainly not without agency (critiquing, for example, the choices of her wealthy employer Elinor and revering instead Vera, the old Haitian writer whose work has never been published). Claude and Anita (daughter of Spero and Debbie), both young women apparently without responsibilities, assert their autonomy by choosing to explore strange lands, in defiance of familial or paternal expectations.

Spero, on the other hand, has not responded to the challenges of separation from the cocoon of his island: at the start of the novel, he has lived for twenty-five years in Charleston, and in the several flashbacks which follow in the non-linear narrative, we learn of the disappointments and failures which have marked his path. His wife's attempts to launch his career as a painter have borne no fruit: "From 1 January to 31 December his paintings, hanging from the rails in his studio, collected dust. Not a single buyer. Not a single collector" (65). And the dream of Africa, inculcated in their beloved daughter by Debbie, seems a remote one for the Guadeloupean overwhelmed by what he perceives as the neediness of African Americans: "He really was suffocating in Charleston! He had had his fill of black churches, black universities and black stories. . . . Sometimes he was taken with the urge to go home. . . . But can you return home empty handed with holes in your pockets? Can you go back with nothing to show but mossy white hair and osteoarthritis?" (27). The reference to the consumerist impulse, to the need to display tangible evidence of having realized some version of the American dream, links this traveller to many Caribbean migrants who also endlessly defer "return"; though privileged in comparison to the itinerant Ludovic and his father, the protagonist of *The Last of the African Kings* is haunted by a sense of failure in the absence of conspicuous material gains. Without that visible success, and without the prestige associated with his royal antecedents, Spero is, at least in his own eyes, a useless wanderer, a ne'er-do-well.

Surprisingly, however, the reverence for the past transmitted to Behanzin's descendants as if in mother's milk seems revived when the beloved only child Anita – a child born and brought up in the United States – announces that she is going to Benin, in her mind a logical outcome to her development studies, but for Spero a doubly transgressive act. Not only is she the first female descendant of King Behanzin to continue what had been a patriarchal tradition of familial reverence for the ancestor, but she chooses to do so in defiance of both her parents, informing them of a life-changing decision during their visit to New York (the location of this discussion is surely significant) to attend her graduation: "It was during this stay in New York that Anita broke his heart by announcing she was leaving for Benin" (81). Anita's attempts to challenge the apparent illogic of the parental resistance unleashed by the news are consistent with the narrative's representation, in the Jules-Juliette family, of a mythmaking impulse: "Hadn't she, Anita, been brought up to worship Africa?" (81).

But Spero answers with a fury as shocking to the reader as it is to Anita. It is here that the narrative voice utters a passionate speech about origins and diasporic identity, which is intriguing in the context of the apparently incurable restlessness that so many of Condé's characters exhibit, inasmuch as it seems to prescribe if not an acceptance of fixity then at least a compromise with the status quo. One might choose to read this as the novelist's own exasperated and at the same time challenging response to what she sees as a futile *passéisme*, as a paralysing preoccupation, in the African diaspora, with retrieving the irretrievable, with reconstructing the past instead of meeting present, *New World* challenges: "Can't we ever live our lives in the present? . . . Wasn't this the misfortune of too many blacks they knew who were so busy building imaginary family trees they had lost out on conquering their own America? What was she hoping for? What did she expect from this voyage to the very beginning of times long ago?" (82) And yet, ironically, Spero, whose life is not without its conspicuous contradictions, has done little himself to try to conquer his "own America", apparently bogged down by the trials and failures of the very past he rails against.

The vague, inclusive term "America" is suggestive here, as it allows both African Americans and Caribbeans to envisage (re)claiming their place in lands to which their ancestors were brought as captives, "conquering" an inalienable identity through cultural or ideological autonomy from mainstream North American society. Here, as elsewhere in Condé's fiction, it is impossible to reduce the text to the writer's "message", and the reader must confront alone the hermeneutical challenges her work offers. Though Condé is eloquent and open in face-to-face communication, her many interviews sometimes offer new perspectives which complicate more than they elucidate. In a conversation with Francoise Pfaff, she reveals an unexpected sympathy for Spero, from which the reader may infer that his inability to "fit in" easily is an extension of the author's own nonconformism: "He is an artist, somewhat a dreamer, perhaps a bit lethargic."[22] And, she goes on to say, recalling his memorable outburst: "He understands that people must live in the present and confront present-day problems."[23]

It is not Spero but Anita, part American and part Antillean, who finally maps out an unorthodox, independent migrant trajectory. Anita's adventure is, I believe, the most compelling of the various journeys comprising *The Last of the African Kings*, in part because of the lacunae evident in its telling: much of our knowledge of her motivation is gleaned from the narration of a father who cannot accept that his daughter, "more courageous or more naïve than any of them" (70), should turn the fantasy of return to Africa – a fantasy that he had been unable to act on – into reality. The reader learns early in the text that Anita has indeed set out on her African pilgrimage of sorts – but her family has little news of her (in a year she has sent them just two postcards), and so this mission is provocatively and, for the abandoned parents, painfully open-ended. Whether the daughter's "migration" or return to Benin has brought resolution to a quest for identity therefore remains uncertain. After writing to the embassy, Spero does learn some reassuring news, but we never hear Anita's voice: "Anita was the pride of the Peace Development Team. . . . Mademoiselle Jules-Juliette did not stop at field work. She had learnt the language of the region and was giving classes in development theory to the men and women" (175). Perhaps *her* version of migration began with an advantage: this new graduate travels without economic challenges, though not without emotional baggage. I have argued elsewhere that "what makes Anita different from the earlier Veronica and Marie-Hélène is that she goes to Africa with a practical purpose, and because she has already challenged the patrilineal heritage of dependence on a regal past, one assumes that she goes with a greater readiness to live in the present. . . . Perhaps indeed Anita will be the near-exemplary voyager of Condé's fiction, the one who travels neither as *conquistadora* or as supplicant."[24] And her capacity to acquire a non-European language, the "language of the region" (in contrast to her father's accented English, persistent marker of his foreignness), is both a practical asset and symbolic of what Spero lacked when he arrived in the United States: a cultural openness, a spirit of adventure, an ability to adapt and even to thrive in the new space.

At the end of the narrative, we are left to ponder the future of Spero, unmoored migrant/traveller, whose marriage, already compromised by his infidelities, is increasingly sterile, and who thinks frequently of how alien America remains for him – but who seems incapable of matching

Anita's audacity in venturing into the unknown, incapable even of pulling up fragile roots and attempting to make peace with "home". The failure of his American adventure is bitterly evoked in a summation of the reasons why – at least from Spero's point of view – his wife has come to despise him: "He was not the worthy heir of his royal ancestor. He himself had no ambition. No ideals! No interest in politics. Nor in the future of the black world. And then he spoke broken English. He came from a godforsaken island that nobody could locate on a map. He didn't like pumpkin pie" (65). Though the reference to the quintessentially American dessert (for Caribbean people, pumpkin is a *vegetable*, accompanying meat dishes) introduces a welcome moment of levity into the narrative, it is also devastating as a symbol of the divisions which make diasporic communities heterogeneous – and sometimes fractured. On the whole, Spero's experiences form a painful allegory of migrant loneliness and dislocation. In one particularly affecting outburst, the migrant seems to abandon the hope of reintegration which is for many a consolation in the years of separation:

> What wouldn't he give to go home? Turn up at Christmas amid the smell of pork casserole and simmering Congo peas!
>
> . . . . Home?
>
> Did these words still have a meaning? After years and years of exile, is any soil still native? And do you still belong? You arrive home and no longer recognize the words or the music. You look but the tree with your placenta is gone. Chopped down by the property developers. (115–16)

The most poignant of these images of belonging is of course the implicit reference, through the word "placenta", to the navel string, the "cordon ombilical" which represents the original, intimate bond with the mother, but which also symbolizes in several countries of the Afro-Caribbean diaspora a visceral connection to the land of birth (the linguist Richard Allsopp defines the term by alluding to "the folk habit of burying an infant's umbilical cord in its parents' homeground"[25]). It is hardly irrelevant, therefore, in terms of narrative strategy, that Spero's mother Marisia dies less than three years after the Guadeloupean's arrival in the United States: he thus loses both biological mother and mother island. His failure to attend Marisia's funeral underscores the obvious but unpalatable reality that separation from geographical home can loosen the bonds of familial intimacy. Though devastated at the news of his mother's death, Spero is unable to go home to support his family in mourning, ostensibly for financial reasons: "At that time you didn't take a plane like you do today. Too expensive! And the boat was too slow. So Spero had had to be content with a magnificent wreath via Interflora" (18).

The sudden death of one's mother is a haunting motif in Condé's work, appearing as a traumatic episode in *A Season in Rihata*,[26] in the later *Tree of Life*,[27] and of course in Condé's own life story.[28] One might contrast this scenario with the equally painful representation in the work of Edwidge Danticat of the loss of her beloved uncle and surrogate father (*Brother, I'm Dying*), of her Aunt Ilyana, guardian of the family home on the mountain, or of her cousin Maxo, killed in the 2010 earthquake. The difference, in the work of the Haitian writer, is that the migrant remains close – as an act of *will* and not simply through chance – to those left behind, travelling home as often as possible and communicating regularly, so that familial bonds remain intact. In Condé's fiction (as in Phillips's *A State of Independence*), one often feels that the gap and the tensions between family members at "home" and abroad, and even between parent and child, cannot be simply attributed to geographical distance.

It is perhaps in *A Season in Rihata* that the lasting impact of the loss of the mother is most powerfully evoked – and it is one of the reasons why Marie-Hélène, Guadeloupean student in Paris, agrees to marry her African suitor Zek and to follow him back to "Mother" Africa:

> Returning to Guadeloupe had meant little more for Marie-Hélène than going back to her mother. . . . But her mother was dead. The grief of having lost her for ever, of not having been near her at the last moment, had made her hate the island and it had become like a sterile womb, never to nurture a foetus again. So Africa, Mother Africa, had appealed to her imagination and raised her expectations.[29]

Commenting specifically on *Segu* and *A Season in Rihata*, Arlette Smith makes the compelling point that while the symbolic association of mother and homeland is common in literature, Condé's treatment of the theme is striking in its focus on absence and lack: "Absence and presence are . . . the structural components which command both the themes of motherhood and exile and other related themes: forced expatriation, nostalgia for the native land . . . The thematic correlation between the mother's disappearance and the inaccessibility of the native land is evident."[30]

The loss of the mother also links the character Spero to Rosélie, the protagonist of *The Story of the Cannibal Woman*, some of whose travelling adventures may be seen as belonging to the category of "migrations of the heart"[31] – journeys inspired by a seductive foreigner – observed in other Condéan fictions. Despite flashbacks to the protagonist's childhood in Guadeloupe, the novel is set mainly in contemporary, post-apartheid and still racist South Africa. Condé, ever inventive, changes the locus of exile from francophone West Africa, apparently freeing her protagonist from the angst of unbelonging, from the challenge of reconnecting with a mythical place of origin, by transplanting her in a country in which no ancestral navel strings reside. At the start of the narrative, Rosélie finds herself suddenly, tragically bereft of her partner, the Englishman Stephen, with whom she has led a nomadic existence for some twenty years – and who has given her the illusion of belonging by sharing with her (or afflicting her with) his imperious need to journey, thus disguising her own alienation from her native Guadeloupe. It is Stephen's violent death which leads his colleague to ask the question cited earlier on regarding the possibility of going "home"; it is his final "abandonment" of her which forces Rosélie to try to make a living – if not a life – in a society in which she has long worn the mask of dispassionate spectator. Here, as in her early novels of displacement such as the controversial *Heremakhonon*, Condé brings to the theme of migration and mobility a gendered perspective, one which makes her female travellers particularly vulnerable and at the same time doubly audacious. At the end of the narrative, finding herself alone again after Stephen's violent death, Rosélie chooses Cape Town (another "hybrid city") rather than Paris or New York, which she knows so well, or what might have seemed the logical destination, her native land.

The circuitous narrative takes us through flashback to a different time, twenty years earlier, when Rosélie left Paris for N'Dossou, the unremarkable capital of a fictitious country in central Africa: a journey undertaken for love, akin to the exile in *I, Tituba* of the Barbadian-born "witch" who follows the enslaved John Indian to Boston, with disastrous consequences. Abandoned, after three years in N'Dossou, by her African lover – who happens to be a reggae musician, and therefore doubly appealing – Rosélie nevertheless avoids blaming her disenchantment on the mother/fatherland: "Africa hadn't always been a prison. She had been eager to make the journey, thinking she was about to launch on the great adventure. Despite her misfortunes she remained loyal to N'Dossou, an unattractive, unpretentious (how could it be anything else?) yet engaging city."[32]

After the defection of the improbably named musician Salama Salama, finding herself alone in a country where she has no familial support, and no means of making a living (at least so she claims), Rosélie resorts to what the narrative terms "the oldest profession in the world" (11), a thinly veiled prostitution. When Stephen meets her, she has been befriended by her neighbours and integrated into a group of women living in precarious circumstances, a sort of community of outcasts which she will finally leave, via his "red, somewhat flashy four-wheel drive" (14), to live in material comfort. This is a provocative and politically incorrect revision of the adventures of the much-defamed protagonist of Condé's first novel, Veronica, accused by her students of being a "whore" because of her involvement with a corrupt minister of government.[33] It is from this unstable life that Stephen *rescues* Rosélie. In some ways, he is an attractive partner, a solid university lecturer, a Briton apparently unburdened by an excessive sense of the merits of Englishness – but then he is half French, a dilution which Condé comments on with a not unmalicious humour: "The French have tainted tastes, for their blood is tainted and over half are mongrels" (8). It is Stephen who takes her to Japan, and to New York, where they spend several unremarkable years while he teaches and she lives the life of the dilettante artist, content enough, but, as in her childhood, something of a misfit. Surprisingly, Rosélie is not seduced by New York's cosmopolitanism: "From the outset, New York had terrified her: its vastness, its shrillness, and its medley of colors. No skin had the same color. No voice the same accent. Which one was the New Yorker? The African? The Indian? The Arab? The Jew? The fair-haired WASP?" (75).

It is Stephen, as well, who initiates their move to another location holding little appeal for Rosélie, reluctant voyager but compliant spouse. She is once again transplanted by a partner whose attraction to Africa is reminiscent of the quest for novelty of early adventurers drawn to the New World: "After seven years in New York, he argued, to see South Africa after apartheid would be like going back in time. Going back to when the United States had just finished muzzling its police dogs and the fight for civil rights was over" (35). So the couple heads "south" – and the choice of South Africa, interesting from several points of view, obviously offers Condé the chance to dismantle north/south binaries, to subvert the colonialist discourse which rashly positions countries in the First and Third World.

The reader is reminded of the inevitable simplifications inherent in the use of the name/notion "Africa": a term frozen in time and enigmatic in relation to place, an appellation obviously charged, for Caribbean people, with mythic power – and yet, for African-born critics, one aggravatingly reductive and dismissive of complex *continental* realities. Condé portrays Cape Town as a city of multiple identities and diverse ethnicities, characterized by flux and yet still bearing the scars of apartheid, a city which is for the interracial couple both comfortable and unsettling. In explaining her choice of this novel as an example of the concern with "la migrance" evident in Condé's work, Marie-Christine Rochmann describes the writer's representation of Cape Town as a "métaphore de la globalité du monde" (metaphor for the globality of the world),[34] and in theory at least, this South African city is remarkable in its openness and its diversity. Strangely, it is here that the light-skinned Rosélie *could* fit in, for her complexion is almost identical to that of her coloured housekeeper and friend Dido, classified as a "Cafre"; and Rosélie herself is dismissively described as such by the hospital authorities who question her after the murder of Stephen. The insulting interrogation to which she is subjected illustrates both the ubiquitous questioning of origins, which other migrant writers (in particular Caryl Phillips) have highlighted, and a specifically South African taxonomy of skin colour: "What relation are you to him? You, his wife? . . . There's nobody else but you? Where are you from in Africa? Guadeloupe? Where's that? Why did you come to Cape Town? What do you do here? You, a painter? A Kaffir, a painter?" (83). Rosélie is certainly not Marie-Hélène, the married protagonist of *A Season in Rihata*, called *"semela"* or "outsider" by in-laws who saw in her light black complexion an undesirable sign of dilution;

she is not as conspicuous in Cape Town as she would have been in a West African community. Despite Rosélie's "Kaffir-like" appearance, however, it would have been implausible for one as sensitive to human unpredictability as Condé to rewrite her earlier quest narratives by portraying such a character as finding solace – if not roots –in this hardly innocuous society. And Rosélie, never really *"bien dans sa peau"* (comfortable in her skin), is particularly uneasy as part of a mixed couple whose heightened visibility she bears with discomfort.

It is after Stephen's death that she realizes the extent to which she had grown accustomed to intrusive and yet distancing stares. After his death, she becomes aware of a new, perhaps welcome, invisibility; but it is an invisibility not equivalent to normalcy: "Rosélie hurried on to avoid being struck down by their looks, then remembered with a start that she was alone. Stephen was no longer walking beside her, arm in arm, or ostentatiously placing an arm around her shoulder. . . . She no longer irritated, she no longer gave offense. She had become invisible" (36–37). Sensitive on her own account, she is also keenly aware – as a "coloured" observer without the lulling status of honorary whiteness, and yet barely integrated into the African community – of the racial hierarchy not easily dismantled by the legal measures which eradicated apartheid. In fact, the narrative opens with a scene which reveals the persistence of old hegemonies in a "new" South Africa:

> The horns of the first ferries split the clouds of mist grazing the sea as they left for Robben Island, once a concentration camp, now transformed into an international tourist attraction. Then the brakes of the overcrowded buses, arriving from the wretchedness of the shantytowns and converging on the splendors of the city center, screeched to a halt at the same stops. The feet of thousands of blacks in cheap shoes tramped toward the subaltern jobs which had always been their lot. (1)

The critique of a South Africa still shackled by its past is even more explicit when the protagonist ventures outside the relatively tolerant cosmopolitan space of Cape Town and is confronted with an old Afrikaner, faithful to the racism of his youth; Rosélie is shocked and unsettled by the utter condescension of a gaze which momentarily returns her to the West Indian past of institutionalized servitude, blurring frontiers of time and space:

> It was then that Jan opened his eyes and she received his gaze full in the face.
> A bluish green gaze, stained in places by fibrils of blood. . . . His gaze pinned
> her rigid against the wall. It seemed he was sending her back to former places,
> to a previous role. . . . Lying, legs spread open, fodder for the master. Back bent,
> lacerated by the overseer's whiplashes. For Jan, time had stopped still. (94–95)

Despite this bruising awareness of objectification in a world where her
"non-whiteness" still defines her, Rosélie shrinks from memories of home,
and even avoids returning for family funerals, less susceptible than Spero
to the temptation to idealize the "rock" often experienced by inhabitants of
Caribbean diasporas. Of note are the narrative's several ellipses regarding
the character's childhood: we only learn, through fragments of biographical detail, almost lost in the plethora of flashbacks, of her deep bitterness
towards a father whom she sees as responsible – because he was a notorious
coureur (womanizer) – for her mother's self-destructive eating, and for the
latter's premature death. Elie is also represented as the controlling father,
surrounded by lawyers as clerk of the court, who wanted his daughter to
study law – her initial motivation for going to Paris, a city of which she, like
Spero, has few fond memories. Yet there are occasional flashes of understanding – on the part of the narrator if not of the protagonist – of another,
more appealing human being: once, searching through old CDs, Rosélie
comes upon the beguine rhythms that her father loved and remembers that
as a young man, he had played the clarinet in a once-popular band, but he
had given up the non-lucrative occupation to earn a "decent" living: "The
band had broken up. Whereas his brothers found jobs wherever they could
– two emigrated to Paris, another to Canada – the valiant Elie sat for the
civil service exam and spent the next forty years in a stuffy office" (109). In
addition to the suggestion that for Elie's generation, migration constituted
an avenue for escape from limitation and tedium, from the confines of
a small society, this section of the narrative offers a rare insight into the
maligned father's point of view, complicating the previous suggestion of
Elie's worthlessness.

It is also hinted that the protagonist will not go home because the pain of
the loss of Camelot – a fleeting time when parents and child lived in perfect
harmony – is too deep, and her awareness of the gap between these early
years and "real life" too keen to allow the necessary adult compromise with

imperfection. Her name, is after all, a combination of the names "Rose" and "Elie", a woman and a man who once loved each other passionately: "She worshiped her husband, and wanted the whole world to know it. How far away those years seemed, almost as if they had never existed. It's true what they say, childhood is a myth, fabricated by senile grown-ups. As for me, I never was a child" (2). There is a provocative ambiguity here, as the narrative voice shifts fluidly between the consciousness of Rosélie and that of an omniscient storyteller, perhaps a communal voice expressing scepticism at the possibility of regaining Eden, whether personally or collectively. Or is it Condé speaking ruefully of her own inability to believe in happy endings? Is it she who refuses nostalgia for the past by claiming that she has "never been a child"? In this, as in other narratives of migration (such as Danticat's *Brother, I'm Dying* – though the tone of that text is radically different from Condé's in its evocation of familial warmth), the irretrievable homeland is closely associated with childhood. The memory of home, whether accurate or embellished by geographical or temporal distance, may become synonymous with an inaccessible state of grace – or, in some of Condé's fictions, with the early death of a beloved if misunderstood mother.

And yet the memories of childhood incorporated in *The Story of the Cannibal Woman* are sparse, and not generally positive: they suggest that Rosélie feels the middle-class milieu in which she (and Condé) grew up in Guadeloupe to be limiting, even stifling, marked by the conspicuous sense of superiority of blacks happy to flaunt their hard-won successes in a neocolonial society. It is a critique of the black bourgeoisie similar to that sketched out in *Heremakhonon*, and also in Condé's semi-autobiographical novel *Tree of Life*, in which the status and prosperity of the Louis family were founded on the time spent working on the Panama Canal and in San Francisco by the patriarch, Albert. When Rosélie finds herself forced to live in a dilapidated apartment building in N'Dossou, for example, befriended by a group of working-class women, she imagines the scandalized reactions of her family: "What would Elie say if he saw her abandoned by her second-rate Bob Marley . . . in this city at the end of the world, in the company of these illiterate women? And Rose? For whom nothing was good enough for her daughter. . . . And her aunts? Especially Aunt Léna, wrapped in her Creole jewelry" (22).

Later on, at a point in Rosélie's life when she has achieved financial security as Stephen's partner, she still envisions home as prison. Particularly surprising is her reaction to the news of her mother's final illness; accompanied by Stephen as far as London, she stalls en route, lingering in Paris for four days, apparently unable to face the final farewell, and arrives in Guadeloupe barely in time to see her mother: "The family had dispatched Aunt Léna to the airport, her face furrowed with reproach" (161). This failure does not prevent Rosélie from falling apart at the funeral, where she is duly supported by an attentive Stephen. But what could have triggered a reconciliation with home leads her to flee once again (without explanation) from the town of La Pointe, where the family resides: it is Stephen's idea to distract Rosélie by taking her to a five-star hotel in the neighbouring tourist island of St Barts. Shortly afterwards, they retreat to the anonymity of New York; and when, after a year of mourning, Aunt Lena phones to communicate the news of Elie's death, Rosélie refuses to travel to pay her respects – a shocking breach, from a Caribbean perspective, of the expectation of familial solidarity, an act that definitively confirms her outsider status.

So if family and home – the Caribbean as home – offer no refuge, how does Rosélie survive and make a living when she is brusquely thrown into the real world of financial necessity, where creativity does not necessarily pay the bills? This time, happily, she avoids bargaining with her body as she had in her early years in N'Dossou, when left to her own financial devices after the desertion of Salama Salama, who, she later acknowledges, "had deafened her with his reggae music" (308). This time around, once more a vulnerable woman alone in an African country which views her as alien, Rosalie embarks on the task of reinventing herself as a sort of New World, late twentieth-century witch, otherwise known as a "medium". It is a nice irony that in so doing, she should draw on the ancestral heritage of the island she no longer claims as hers, practising the visionary, healing gift she has carried since childhood – during which time she had successfully "made a pack of Creole dogs turn tail" (17): "'Rosélie Thibaudin, medium. A cure for the incurable,' proclaimed the rainbow-colored cards printed at a discount on Kloof Street and distributed to the neighborhood shops. . . . Once Stephen was gone, Rosélie was left without any means. All she knew how to do was paint. Painting is not like music. . . . Painting is like literature. No immediate gain or utility" (7). One assumes that here, Condé, the prodigious writer and professor of literature, is writing with tongue in cheek. But whether or not painting could have provided her an adequate income, by accepting this temporary occupation, Rosélie appears to be act- ing out the stereotype of the black witch/Obeah woman, and she surrounds herself with a motley assortment of "objects" designed to persuade her clients of her magical powers (including, for example, a statue of the Hai- tian goddess Erzulie Dantor, bought years previously in New York). One wonders whether Condé is not parodying the ability of some to "play black" to exploit the Other's expectations of exotic performance.

Yet it is possible, too, to read – more positively – in this solution/career Rosélie's alignment, conscious or not, with an African world view, in which divination and traditional healing are free of colonial negativity. And per- haps in this way, she, to some extent like Anita in *The Last of the African Kings*, makes possible for herself a genuine relation, other than that of privi- leged spectator, with the community in which she arrived as a foreigner. Perhaps she is gradually moving away from the fringes of the host coun- try: in this new career as healer, she interacts with a variety of "clients", including some who are non-South Africans, victims of political upheavals in other African countries, such as the native of Rwanda suffering from insomnia, to whom she brings some peace; she also inspires a young girl traumatized by rape, whose mother brings her to Rosélie as a client to take up painting herself.

As suggestive as Rosélie's choice of occupation are several enigmatic ref- erences in the narrative to the story which gives the novel its troubling title. The words "Histoire de la femme cannibale", translated as "The story of the cannibal woman" (though one might be tempted to render the title as "The story of the man-eating woman"), allude to what appears to be only a subplot of the novel – the arrest and trial of Fiela, a South African woman accused of murdering her philandering husband after more than twenty years of an apparently tranquil marriage. Rosélie's near-obsessive interest in the tale of this savage killing invites several possible readings. The emphasis on brutal, inhuman aggression obviously recalls the colonial assumption of African barbarism, and it is telling that the character who has been accused, by both Stephen and Dido, of "see[ing] racism everywhere" (63) also describes herself, after one particularly bitter experience, as "this descendant of cannibals" (96). One may therefore interpret the resounding, slightly intimidating title as a posture of rebellion, and also of sympathy for the underdog; as an "in-your-face" challenge to the colonialist discourse which inscribed black savagery; as an interrogation of racial stereotyping of the same order as the bold affirmation contained in the title, *I, Tituba, Black Witch of Salem.* The francophone reader might also hear an echo of the vehemence of the young Suzanne Césaire, wife of Aimé, who in a 1941 publication commanded Antillean literature to abandon its sweet exoticism with the memorable statement *"La poésie martiniquaise sera cannibale ou ne sera pas"* (Martinican poetry will be man-eating, or it will not exist).[35] (That Condé was struck by Suzanne Césaire's bold words is confirmed by the fact that she herself cites them in an interview published under the challenging title, "Moi, Maryse Condé, libre d'être moi-même" ["I, Maryse Condé, Free to Be Myself"].[36]) Whatever significance one ascribes to Condé's deployment of the trope of cannibalism in the novel, it is impossible to ignore the political implications of the fact that the West Indian, finding herself as observer on the periphery of a society cruelly marked by colonial racism, takes the side of the marginalized, the misunderstood, the demonized.

Quite apart from the issue of race is the matter of whether Rosélie is convinced that this woman, whose husband is said in court to have been physically abusive, is like herself: a silenced victim in an unequal union, one whose long-repressed rage has devastating consequences. Fiela's story and her image in the newspaper certainly haunt Rosélie for much of the narrative, in part because the woman resists all attempts of psychologists and lawyers to have her explain herself; but it is also as a distraction from the more immediate enigma of the circumstances of Stephen's death – and life. Near the end of the text, Fiela's suicide, leaving unexplained the puzzle of her presumed "savagery", seems for a frightening moment to suggest to Rosélie one way out of her own distress, a distress which climaxes with the revelation of Stephen's several infidelities. When the protagonist – and the reader – finally discover the "truth" of her strangely unfulfilling years with Stephen, the news of his homosexuality shatters her; and yet the necessary acknowledgement of the imperfection of what had evidently been for her knight in shining armour a union of convenience is both a painful ending and a new beginning. We are reminded in these last pages that some of Rosélie's journeys had really been forced voyages, and that the "quest", for self and for happiness, might just be starting – in this city of possibility, in this "new" Africa, where cruelty *and* promise abound.

In the introduction to this study, I recalled the realization of the young protagonist of Cristina García's *Dreaming in Cuban* that she is inextricably linked to two "homes": "But sooner or later I'd have to return to New York. I know now it's where I belong – not *instead* of here, but *more* than here."[37] There will be no such epiphanic certainty for Rosélie, no acknowledgement of a tolerable hybridity – for, after all, she is not "bi-cultural" in any real sense. Nor is there the prospect of a "return to the native land", no sweet sigh of homecoming to bring the narrative to happy closure. Condé's protagonist does occasionally contemplate, and fantasize about, a return to Guadeloupe, but she manifestly fears a journey back to a home so long neglected/rejected. More like the character Bertram in Caryl Phillips's *A State of Independence* than like Spero, she has failed to actively cultivate a relationship with loved ones left at home; thus, she holds on to old grievances as an excuse to stay away upon her father's death: "Sealing the quarrel with the family, Rosélie refused to go to Guadeloupe to attend the funeral" (166). The "quarrel with the family" may be seen, in many of Condé's novels, as a quarrel with *home*, with the demands of a small society, sometimes unforgiving of vagrants and rebels.

What remains then for Rosélie is a once-alien city, in which she must emerge from the cocoon of transiency: when Manuel, a new and not unpleasing admirer, offers to take her with him to Cadix, a potential distraction or consolation for Stephen's abandonment (recalling Stephen's own attempt to assuage her grief with mobility after her mother's funeral), she decides to remain in a city in which she positions herself, perhaps presumptuously, as a sort of latter-day *conquistadora*: "She wouldn't leave Cape Town. Suffering is equivalent to entitlement. She had earned this city. She had made it hers by reversing the journey of her ancestors, dispossessed of Africa, who had seen the isles loom up like a mirage to the fore of Columbus's caravels, the isles where the cane and tobacco of their rebirth would germinate" (309). Confident in this new conviction, she rejects the invitation to renewed wandering: "I won't go with you to Cadix. I've never liked traveling. It was Stephen who forced me and I obeyed. Now I want to do as I please" (310).

The notion that she "never liked traveling", at the end of a narrative which has chronicled a life of relocations, not all triggered by Stephen, is difficult to swallow. And Rosélie is manifestly a character whom one cannot always consider a credible witness: the reader may justifiably see her as apathetic follower rather than vulnerable victim. One notes, however, that this newly voiced dislike of travelling may represent a shift in the character's perspective after Stephen's death – so that she assesses her own motivations based on a revisioning of her life history, not a surprising exercise after the devastating *ending* represented by a sudden death. In the introduction to *Signs of Dissent: Maryse Condé and Postcolonial Criticism*, Dawn Fulton underscores the elusiveness of the novelist's characters vis-à-vis efforts to categorize them in the context of contemporary critical discourses: "Figures such as the eponymous protagonist of *Moi, Tituba sorcière . . . noire de Salem* or the widowed Rosélie in *Histoire de la femme cannibale . . .* flirt with categories of oppression by approximating familiar narratives of social ostracism and prejudice, but exhibit in other ways qualities that are inconsistent with visions of oppressed subjects as they are constituted through feminist postcolonial discourse."[38] Thus, it is tempting, but not necessarily justified, to see all Rosélie's "migrations" as trajectories predetermined by the men in her life. Certainly, her first journey to Paris and the subsequent choice of remote N'Dossou were influenced by her father and lover, respectively, but the need to flee Guadeloupe is arguably a powerful motivating factor in Rosélie's travelling routes, and even in her choice of partners.

The narrative includes suggestive silences about her childhood, and particularly about what makes Guadeloupe no more than an accidental birthplace (perhaps akin to the belittled Antigua of Jamaica Kincaid's "small place"[39]): Condé hints at the flaws which have so far allowed Rosélie to *await* "rescuing" rather than to walk confidently along paths of her own choosing. One should not fail to note, however, that Rosélie is a figure with whom the novelist appears to feel some affinity, one implicit in the character's disappointment with a critical misunderstanding of her paintings – a misunderstanding which goes back as far as her father's early reaction to what he saw as "messing about with paint" (32). The author's connection with Rosélie is manifest also in the passion with which the latter finally embraces the challenge of representation and, at the same time, her vocation as artist (the last scene of the narrative shows her boldly beginning a portrait of the *"femme cannibale"*).

This vocation recalls the more ambiguous role played by Spero as artist in exile in South Carolina. While some readers may see this character as no more than an amateur painter using his creativity as an excuse to opt out of the hard struggles which many human beings (and certainly most migrants) face, Lydie Moudileno offers a more sympathetic interpretation in an article bearing the suggestive title "Portrait of the Artist as Dreamer: Maryse Condé's *Traversée de la mangrove* and *Les dernier rois mages*": "The gaze of a Spéro is necessary to the denunciation of the bourgeois-intellectual African American world of Debbie."[40] Certainly, the fact that Spero and Rosélie are both outsiders and artists suggests a nexus between their roles and the sometimes harsh scrutiny Condé directs at the plurality of subjects and societies that her fiction portrays. While Rosélie feels that her work has been undervalued in both New York and Cape Town, the narrator gives reason to conclude that it is original and powerful, and her failure to achieve public recognition may be seen as emblematic of the challenges facing the artist whose focus is not on commercial success. However adroitly one attempts to avoid the trap of conflating author and protagonist, it is hard to ignore the obvious similarities between the concerns of the visual artist and those of the writer, or between the fictional character's final acceptance of insider/outsider status and the redefinition of "home" by a novelist who has for many years "commuted" between geographical regions. It is even harder to dismiss the many critical pronouncements of Maryse Condé, who, for example, commented in an interview conducted a few years after her return to Guadeloupe in the 1980s: "I dare say that a writer should be perpetually on the move, going from one place to another, searching, trying to understand and decipher things different and new all the time."[41]

While not quite constantly on the move, Rosélie is a careful and sometimes critical observer of this country that she seemed to inhabit by chance, but which she seeks to understand, and to which she finally makes a commitment of sorts. In common with other Condéan protagonists, she has previously journeyed at the behest of the man in her life. But finally, bringing this gendered odyssey to a surprising conclusion, Rosélie has declined a new suitor's offer of travel. The text is open-ended, and the reader might have reason to doubt the firmness of the character's resolve. But it is certainly striking that Condé should finally allow her protagonist to express, in however muted a tone, a sense of reconciliation with a "non-native" land.

What we find in Rosélie's account of contemporary South Africa, then, is not the perspective of an "objective" observer/traveller but an Antillean gaze that is relatively – but not completely – unfettered by regional loyalties, focused on things both old and new. The detachment of many migrants living in the United States, which Condé irreverently evoked earlier in the text, is no longer possible for her: "The unexpected thing about America is that you can live there for years without meeting the natives. Nor even speaking their language" (114). Here, in South Africa, Rosélie is gradually drawn closer to the "natives", as concerned observer and not voyeur – though the outward gaze is perhaps an imperfect mask for the need for inward scrutiny. At times, Rosélie's perspective may recall the troubling pseudo-detachment of the colonial travel narrative; but it is also, in fertile contradiction, that of a West Indian who *needs* to see in South Africa a land where the historically dispossessed, the "cannibals", once banished to so-called homelands, can celebrate real reconquest of disputed territory. She is certainly no Ludovic striding from one new space to another, nor the purposeful traveller one finds at one end of the migration spectrum; but neither is she a misfit, nor a stateless refugee truly in exile. Indeed, her situation is located somewhere between the two extremes, and it is a not unrewarding one. Unlike the protagonist of *The Last of the African Kings*, who will presumably continue to dream of a never to be realized return to his birthplace, Rosélie finally appears to accept the habit and condition of impermanence – the impermanence fostered by a life of relative mobility – as creative possibility.

[CHAPTER 5]

CURDELLA FORBES
Of Home Soil in New Lands

THE FIRST STORY IN CURDELLA FORBES'S *A Permanent Freedom* begins on a hill-top, in the sort of dense terrain that Kingston-bound Jamaicans think of affectionately as "country bush", in an environment which, though not quite Edenic, appears to validate some of the old beliefs about the bounty of untouched landscapes and the comfort of communities where genealogy is public property.[1] Bearing the intriguing title "Prologue to an Ending",[2] the narrative maps the first of several journeys structuring the volume: this one might appear on the surface to be that familiar trip "back" to rural Jamaica, which for many Kingstonians remains the heartland, revered place of origin, repository of tradition and values:

> She didn't look up from her work pouring new soil when his shadow loomed over her bent back and the cropped head bent to her cheek. But she rubbed her face with casual affection against the side of his. If her heart leaped a little, she kept it firmly buttoned over, under the old bush jacket that had been a man's.
> "Hi, howdy."
> "Hi howdy. How you do?"
> "So-so. Let me help you with that." He let the crocus bag he carried over his shoulder slide to the ground with a soft thump and took the heavy bucket of soil from her hand.[3]

The present chapter focuses on three stories from *A Permanent Freedom*, "Prologue to an Ending",[4] "For Ishmael" and "Say". The first two of these narratives may be considered separately, but they are intertwined in ways that richly reward an intertextual reading. The male protagonist of

"Prologue" will reappear several stories further on in the collection, if we are to be guided by the discreet clues linking the two texts. Thus, the town-based visitor of the first story becomes the rooted traveller through urban landscape of the penultimate tale, "For Ishmael", a poignant narrative that in several ways seems antithetical to the relatively serene "Prologue" but which deploys tropes indicating and supporting thematic continuities. Journey and, more specifically, migration are central themes in the collection, and it is therefore structurally significant that "Prologue" should begin with travel within the island, from urban centre to one of the many rural districts simply designated, in Jamaican speech, as "country". Forbes's 2002 volume, *Songs of Silence*, ends with movement in the opposite direction, an equally familiar trajectory for a once-colonized people in search of material and educational advancement. As noted in the introduction, departure from home is momentous in most of the narratives considered in this study, whether the traveller is Belicia in *Oscar Wao*, fleeing an oppressive Dominican Republic, or the father in *In the Falling Snow*, leaving his "small island" by boat. Home is frequently remembered, in these fictions of mobility, as a space which, if not nurturing, at least offers the illusion of predictability. In the epilogue to *Songs of Silence*, the young narrator contemplates with what sounds like trepidation an expedition which is also an uprooting: "The morning before I was to leave for Kingston and the teachers college I went down the mango walk to Morris Hole River and looked out to the sea."[5]

The journey envisaged by Jeremy, the male protagonist of "Prologue", is even more of a turning point, since his visit to Maldene, the woman whom he finds "pouring new soil", serves as an oasis of comfort before what will become a long wandering through the desert: his travel to the United States, narrated at the end of "Prologue", prefigures the wanderings/migrations of Jamaican and other travellers, both to and within the United States, in the larger narrative that is *A Permanent Freedom*. This initial text, this "Prologue to an Ending", does end with a separation of sorts, one that the reader, already invested in the tenuous relationship between the protagonists, hopes will be provisional: for after all – in the words of Jeremy, the reluctant migrant poised for flight who must take his leave of a woman he loves – "plane cross water, you know" (14). Departure to New York is not synonymous with definitive separation – although the reader is not sure of that at the end of "Prologue".

Forbes has constructed a volume that can be read as a narrative whole, but *A Permanent Freedom* is also a collection of individual, though hardly discrete, texts, pushing the limits of the short story genre so that the reader's appreciation of character and grasp of situation develop incrementally.[6] Nowhere is this more manifest than in the varied usage in the first two stories considered of the image of soil or earth, sometimes associated with careful, deft hands which garden or plant, and also less explicitly with the hands of a potter, skilfully and creatively moulding clay. It is an image which of course invokes the discourse of racial identity in a colonial/postcolonial context, and specifically the notions of *déracinement*: of diasporic relocation *and* new beginnings. That Forbes's work belongs to a literary discourse which interrogates earlier definitions of Caribbean identity by accepting the possibility of multiple influences and even a certain cosmopolitanism is made clear in the following words from "For Ishmael", in which the traveller yearns for familiar faces and sites while acknowledging that he has not been and cannot be locked into island space: "In his dream these faces gave way to others, the faces of his longing, of people who lived in the place to which he was anchored at the root, though he had traveled paths like rhizomes" (168). Here, the authorial presence is palpable in the allusion to the debates in Caribbean cultural and literary criticism which had opposed "root" to "rhizomes"[7] or Négritude to Antillanité/creolization – and the suggestion that the two are not necessarily mutually exclusive.

That racial belonging cannot be factored out of the problematic of identity is implicit in the second paragraph of "Prologue", as the narrative voice self-consciously links the deep brown earth to the skin of the two protagonists (the "fine earth" is "of their own colour"), and the imagery of colour is reinforced by the reference to the "crocus bag":[8] "He let the crocus bag he carried over his shoulder slide to the ground with a soft thump and took the heavy bucket of soil from her hand. . . . She watched him, the quick, capable brown hands moving in the fine earth of their own colour" (9). The explicit valorization of pigmentation is reminiscent of a section of the Haitian "peasant novel" *Masters of the Dew*, in which the once-exiled hero Manuel gives voice to the author's passionate nationalism by making an emphatic, empowering connection between his racial origin and the earth which has supported their community for generations: "'You know, I'm made out of this, I am.' He touched the earth, caressing its soil. 'That's what I am, this very earth! I've got it in my blood. Look at my color.'"9 But while the characters of Forbes's story are also attached to the dark earth of their native land, neither of them shares Manuel's simple relation to a cherished place of origin: both seem destined to roam, unsettled, whether on a secluded hill away from home and family or travelling to New York.

The tone of quiet concord which might make "Prologue" seem like a gentle romance is soon to be disturbed: retrospectively, the reader will come to see the first two paragraphs (from which the above quotations are taken) as translating a precarious peace, a time emblematic of tranquillity but not fixity. For the lulling simplicity of the setting and the apparent idyll of man and woman alone in untroubled "country bush" are, in fact, deceptive. Manipulating the short story format to provide a minimum of information at a measured pace, Forbes finally reveals that neither Jeremy nor Maldene, the woman he visits, really belongs in this rural community. She has retreated here after her release from prison, following incarceration for a terrible crime – the reasons for which are never elucidated, so that the reader is challenged to show some of the compassion which made her friendship with Jeremy possible in the first place; and he is a priest who met Maldene because he chose to visit the prisons as his "outreach" activity, while also ministering to his uptown parishioners. In the later story, "For Ishmael", Jeremy analyses this divided life, while at the same time exposing some of the very hardships and the schisms in Jamaican society which might make migration an attractive option (though this is not made explicit in the text): "He had lived the same kind of schizophrenia as a priest in Kingston. For three and a half days he gave himself to his work in the prisons and their environs, where the lives of people boiled and seethed. Then from Sunday to Wednesday at midday – his week so neatly cut in half – he performed his service at the uptown altar, neatly cassocked above the polished pews" (166).

What this odd pair – fragile and yet intense in their coupling – seems to embody is Forbes's concern for the marginal, the solitary, the misunderstood. The author frequently avoids explicit statement and in fact seems to revel in the sort of ellipsis inherent in the genre. Forbes's comments on her artistic practice (in response to a question regarding the elusiveness of Maldene's motives) are instructive: "Motive is impossible to read totally, isn't it? The fiction of the omniscient narrator is an untenable one – even the I-narrator doesn't yet fully know why she does what she does. . . . I want to give enough detail for the character to be convincing and easy to empathize with, but not so much that it's all neat and pretty and clear."[10] The narrator of "Prologue" does not in fact explain why Jeremy feels compelled to leave Jamaica, nor who Maldene really is. Though it is suggested that her background is one of relative affluence, her sojourn in Tamarind Farm (Jamaica's minimum-security prison for females) has complicated her social status, so that she is presumably an outcast from conventional Kingston society. Like the deportee character Claude in Danticat's "Night Talkers", Maldene has found a refuge in the hilly retreat; but unlike Claude, she is separated from family and community. She is treated as a benevolent but privileged outsider, one who has "chosen a village, the most gregarious of places, to hide away in" (20), but at the same time, she is sought out for her skills as an herbalist, as if indeed she had remained close to the practices and the skills of those from the heartland. Neither Maldene nor Jeremy, then, is stranger to ambiguity and contradiction, and neither has earned their living by the simple toil of real "country people". In addition to the tension created by the mystery surrounding Maldene's situation – for hers is a form of displacement, despite a superficial integration – there is a quiet tension between the couple, one apparently linked to his imminent departure, to the fact that he chooses to go where she feels unable to follow:

> He said, irrelevantly and yet utterly to the point, "Maldene, I'm leaving. Next Saturday."
>
> . . .
>
> "So it came through? So soon?"
>
> "So soon," he said, his voice gruff, almost angry, and then, with a shrug, "But not really. It's been a long time since I applied. And I have been packed and ready." (12–13)

After this moment's respite, this fertile escape from life's harshness, he must go down to the plain: it is noteworthy here that mountains and hills

are essential to the Caribbean geographical imaginary, particularly for occu-
pants of islands which have a mountainous topography (perhaps for Jamaicans, the hills are as emotionally resonant as "the islands'/bright beaches"[11]
so memorably evoked by Kamau Brathwaite in "South" as emblem of integration with the landscape). In order to reach Maldene, Jeremy had needed
to leave his car (an elderly Fiat[12]) at the bottom of the hill and to make the
last stage of the journey on foot, a detail which underscores the imaging of
the mountain as site and source of a relative liberation – that of the maroon,
of those who were not implicated in/imprisoned by the servitude of the
plantation.[13] Thus, despite his resolutely upbeat affirmation that "you can
always come and visit me. Plane cross water, you know" (14), the character's
descent from the hills appears here as a sort of banishment, though voluntary, from an almost paradisal state, and the final lines of the story seem to
prefigure real dislocation and even rupture.

On the evening of this farewell visit, Maldene pursues, in a newly painful solitude, a project important to her: she works on a bust of Jeremy,
and her potter's hands moulding the clay to form his features evoke, on
the one hand, a lover's caress and, on the other, the earlier scene in which
they both stirred the brown earth with their fingers. But art and the artist
can be overwhelmed by real life: the following morning, Maldene awakes
from a nightmare in which she has walked "for mile after fruitless mile
along a quayside littered with boats and flotsam bobbing on the water" (24)
in search of a now inaccessible Jeremy (Forbes's rewriting of the Orphic
journey?). For his part, Jeremy will undertake his own solitary voyage: "He
arrived in New York in the dead of winter, when there was no stain on the
cold white sky but the pale promise of a rainbow" (24).

When we meet – or think we meet – this character again, in the penultimate tale "For Ishmael", he appears somewhat subdued, journeying without
compass, as a sojourner with little physical baggage. Frequently given the
simple – and yet provocative because ambiguous – label of "the traveller",
Jeremy (or "J.", as he is elliptically called in "For Ishmael") does not quite fit
into the category of displaced persons memorably described by Carole Boyce
Davies as follows: "The figure of the displaced, homeless person is the most
poignant, tragic representation of the transnational, capitalist, postmodern
condition." But Davies goes on to make the pertinent qualification that

"both physical and psychic homelessness exist on a continuum which has as its extreme physical disruptions and outsiderness and a variety of nodal points of displacement through exile, migration, movement".[14] Jeremy is elusively positioned on this continuum, both uncompromising outsider – or, perhaps more accurately, passer-by – in the United States and also, in some ways, almost at ease.

At the beginning of "For Ishmael", the protagonist acknowledges, in a sort of inventory of the heart, that there are a few objects from which he will not be easily parted. About to move from a big city (presumably Washington, DC, based on several elliptical references) to a new, unnamed destination, he must decide which of his possessions will go with him. One of these is a painting, signed "Samuel Reevers and Ishmael", the most precious of several pictures which he values: "There was one picture he would keep. Not the best one; in fact perhaps the least. He stood for a long time looking at it in its cheap plastic frame which he had deliberately not changed after he bought the picture from the artist" (158). Even more important than the painting, though, is a sort of talisman, a pot of earth originally brought from Jamaica, and since then used to cultivate a geranium plant:

> He carefully lifted the plant, now without flower, re-potted it in the city's soil, and placed it on the windowsill. . . . Carefully, he wrapped the original pot of earth in mesh and paper for safe travel in his carry-on luggage. He planned to pour it back in its own place, one day, when he got back to his own country, whenever that would be. (157)

The pot of earth, tended so meticulously, is manifestly a repository of emotion for this solitary figure, somewhat of a loner though travelling through foreign terrain in which his compatriots are found in their numbers. I believe the home soil also serves as a metonym of the much valued "plot" or "family land", the importance of which, in post-emancipation Caribbean societies, is explained elsewhere by Forbes as follows: "The plot was always esteemed not only by family members but also by the whole community, which recognized in each family's plot its own larger hope and identity."[15]

Forbes's protagonist initially seems almost anonymous, though not quite faceless, an elusiveness which allows us to view him as an archetypal traveller figure; at times, the character also has an ascetic quality – a picture complicated, however, by his visceral connection to the woman left behind. We learn that his initial is J., a link with the Jeremy of "Prologue", but details about his identity are strikingly sparse: little is divulged of his family background or – the most provocative of omissions – the reason for his movement from city to city after his arrival in the United States; and so the focus of the story is at least as much on the multiracial, multi-ethnic urban communities in which he finds himself as it is on his Jamaicanness.

Narrative point of view is central to the impression likely to be formed by the reader that J./Jeremy is something of an enigma. Whereas in "Prologue" we see him through the mediating gaze of a loving woman, in "For Ishmael", the only named characters given more than cursory mention are a stranger – the African American Samuel Reevers – and his son; the name Maldene is never used. The woman of "Prologue" was intimately acquainted with the contours of Jeremy's face: her potter's hands were engaged in carving his likeness, and her thoughts, revealed to the reader, provided some insight into his character. In "For Ishmael", on the other hand, J.'s few moments of introspection hardly suffice to tell us what he is doing in the United States and what it will take for him to abandon this journey through a bleak landscape to realize the dream of return. For dream he does, of returning the soil to its source, "one day, when he got back to his own country, whenever that would be" (157).

The yearning for home is thus a sometimes silenced subtext in this narrative of wandering. Perhaps Edward Baugh's assessment of the poet-persona as traveller in his authoritative study of the work of Derek Walcott is applicable to the character J. in Forbes's text: "Just as it is possible to feel exiled at home, so the person in the grip of what Lorna Goodison has called 'quest fever' may be the same one whose home-anchor lies deepest and heaviest."[16] One is reminded too that the term "migrant" is often reductively applied, as if to circumscribe or subsume individuals with complex motivations. Migration may be an economic or political necessity, and it may also be a flight from home, however much that remembered site becomes object of desire and fantasy after departure: the reader is free to surmise that Jeremy's absence from Jamaica is his way of dealing with the limitations of his relationship with Maldene (whose earlier incarceration makes her an unsuitable partner for a minister of religion), that the penance which he appears to inflict on himself might be penance for her sin, not his, or for his "mistake" in loving outside of the dictates of the socially acceptable.

The absence of (a) loved one(s) is not the only void in this unusual migrant's personal relationships. Although "For Ishmael" alludes to the existence of a benevolent institution (comprising a group of volunteers?) with which J. is affiliated, his colleagues remain firmly in their place, on the periphery of the narrative and of his life. We learn in a passing, laconic reference of the existence of a shelter associated with the organization (167) and, more intriguingly, that J. "liked his colleagues, but breaching their liberal certainties had made him tired" (166).

The narrative's other omissions and absences are equally suggestive: with the exception of the conversation with the African American Samuel Reevers, there is little dialogue in "For Ishmael". We hear no nation language establishing complicity and shared nostalgia, no conversations between the protagonist and his fellow Jamaicans. By contrast, if one were to read this story with another remarkable tale of migration in the collection, the longer "Macóné, Macóné, or, Of Age and Innocence", one would note, in the narrative voice of the latter text, a striking example of literary code-switching which is absent from "For Ishmael". Forbes's prodigious gift for moving with an ease which belies effort from standard English to the vernacular language is underscored by Maureen Warner-Lewis in her review of Forbes's earlier volume of stories: "Her *Songs of Silence* (2002) is a collection of eight short stories written with such style that the ear is delightfully startled by the intercalation of poetic and erudite English with the imagery, lexicon, and idioms of Jamaican Creole."[17] It is obvious, however, that diasporic communities are not hermetic entities, and the collection *A Permanent Freedom* does reflect the consequences of a geographical shift: there is conspicuously less Creole used in this new volume than in *Songs of Silence*, of which all the narratives were set in rural Jamaica.

Even in "Macóné, Macóné", an awareness is expressed of the linguistic and other challenges inherent in the condition of the migrant: among the difficulties experienced by the protagonist Maxine, a young Jamaican woman forced by her aunt to migrate to the United States with her brother and grandfather, are nuances of language which spill over in her semi-hostile response to the overtures made to her by an African American schoolmate. Though she is undoubtedly attracted to him, while tentatively negotiating this new relationship, she reacts negatively to the simplistic label of "island girl". For this Jamaican Creole speaker, comfortable in English but nevertheless experiencing a sort of linguistic discontent in the United States, language functions both as real barrier and as trope for unbelonging: "I am caught between languages, registers, tongues. I don't know how to talk across this rubbled canyon of words with me and you on different sides" (65).

Nor are the conflicts threatening to overwhelm Maxine confined to the outer world of foreigners: the reconstituted family has its own share of internal tensions. Ta Lizz, the strong adult figure, masterminded her motherless nephew and niece into migration for the uninspiring reason that "we had to leave [Jamaica] or lose our green cards" (47). But however far away from home fate takes them, the characters of "Macóné, Macóné" are more rooted than those of "For Ishmael", and even those of "Prologue", and the tone of the narrative is less melancholy. (At the other end of the diasporic spectrum, the menace of alienation from homeland hovers in the title story "A Permanent Freedom", in which the husband dying of AIDS is Jamaican, while his wife and lover are originally from Grenada and New Zealand, respectively.) There is a fundamental vibrancy in these characters, perhaps because they travel with an undiluted sense of self, bringing with them to Maryland both past and place – their beloved Brown's Town: "The next day it snowed. We were all at home because there was a weather warning. We joked around between the kitchen and the living room while Ta Lizz baked banana bread, the warm aroma against the winter white somehow affirming something about us as family" (63) They hold fast to their identity – for instance, by savouring the smell of homemade banana bread in the middle of a Maryland snowstorm. But as the younger characters interact with Americans, some degree of compromise and change seems inevitable in the necessary effort to settle into this strange new world.

To return to "For Ishmael", it is striking that Jamaicanness as *essence* (the essence of banana bread!) is in fact largely absent from the narrative, almost as though Forbes has chosen in this story to avoid the simplicity of a narrow nationalism.[18] In fact, were it not for the echoes of "Prologue", the reader might have no idea of the nationality of the protagonist, since there is no reference to Jamaica, Jamaicans or any Jamaican place names. The solitary traveller is not seen to seek out the comfort of home food or familiar accents usually so sustaining to diaspora inhabitants. To some extent, then, the writer deterritorializes J.'s adventure, eschewing the conspicuous markers of difference which one might expect in a migration narrative.

One senses, above all, the author's avoidance of the binarism which would make of all migrations a form of *"sufferation"*:[19] indeed the currency of the term "exile" often obscures the reality that Caribbean people leave their homelands for complex reasons and that many still maintain close ties "back a yard". Though he is sometimes tempted by melancholy, it is hard to cast J. in the simple role of victim of big city blues. If we are far removed from the bleak wintry landscapes of fictions such as Caryl Phillips's *The Final Passage*, perhaps the point here is that this is not to be a "final" passage or crossing: for J. treads lightly on foreign soil, where no navel string[20] has taken root. Perhaps this traveller also has the sense of semi-detachment memorably expressed by Derek Walcott in the Nobel lecture "The Antilles: Fragments of Epic Memory": "The traveller cannot love, since love is stasis and travel is motion."[21] Even more interesting, in the context of the present discussion, is Walcott's description of the point of view of the visitor to the West Indies – and specifically of his own – in relation to the Trinidadian village of Felicity, which he acknowledges viewing as a "compassionate and beguiled outsider". Forbes's traveller is certainly compassionate, despite his yearning for home, and to some extent "beguiled". For the Jamaican priest who travels around with his portion of home soil does savour some aspects of his strange new life in North America: he is fascinated by the diversity of a cosmopolitan city, even by a sort of chaos encountered on the side of town frequented by the "poor and the visibly destroyed":

> On the buses he found another world: encountered the most spontaneous of kindnesses and struck up the most unexpected friendships, some fleeting and whimsical, others surprisingly strong.
>
> He loved the seething chaos: the loud talking, emitting, preaching, easy-greeting, conversation struck with strangers, curses hurled at the unwashed, laughter rolling in waves from passenger to passenger and the drivers' voices freely adding to the noise. (165)

Another aspect of the complexity which challenges easy categorization of J.'s "exile" is that the scene described above is not without parallel to the gritty vibrancy of urban life in Jamaica – with perhaps the provocative difference that while doing his duty in the prisons in Kingston, he would be unlikely to ride a bus to return to his uptown parish. The big city might isolate, but for privileged Jamaicans living with the burden of complicity in a system which continues to marginalize the masses, the anonymity of New York might be a welcome respite, constituting a sort of tabula rasa on which to start afresh without guilt – at least in theory, as if one could ever leave the past behind.

Urban space also offers to J./Jeremy a multiplicity of chance encounters, and with them a magical experience which, though not altogether welcome, reinforces his spirituality[22] and broadens his identity as a human being. Forbes endows her character with a surreal capacity to bear the physical trace on his palms of the many individuals whom he touches, even with a casual handshake (the image of these ultrasensitive palms may recall the stigmata associated with Christ's crucifixion, as if Jeremy is seeking to share some of the suffering of those he encounters):

> Every day now he studied what looked like writing on his palms, which had suddenly changed into a Babylonian stele. The writing changed after certain encounters. . . . Yesterday an old Latino lady had stooped to retrieve a nickel he had dropped, and handed it to him smiling, "God bless you, son" – though his hair was as grizzled as her own. The touch of her fingertips had moved him unbearably. (164)

J. seems drawn to particular individuals who share his sense of isolation, an isolation which may be that of the reluctant migrant barely skimming the surface of the new society which is his temporary home, but which may also evoke other, less easily definable solitudes. Thus, the Jamaican priest establishes a crucial bond with another traveller, an African American who seems no more at home in urban space than he, the father of the child to whom the title alludes.

"For Ishmael", one of the most poignant of these stories of loss and survival, follows the apparently futile peregrination of a non-Caribbean homeless traveller, an individual caught up in the vast movement from rural to urban terrain. The nexus between naming and genealogical certainty is clearly of paramount importance here: the story is dedicated to the child Ishmael, and his name and identity are conspicuously honoured throughout, all the more so because he is lost to Samuel Reevers, the father whom the traveller meets in a public park – a site where transients are provisionally at home. Having observed Reevers painting quietly for several days, J. finally approaches him and expresses interest in his representation of a solitary dancer. The artist explains why the painting bears the names of both father and son, as well as the inscription "For my son". His is a quiet tragedy: he has not seen Ishmael for thirteen years, an estrangement attributable to his involvement with drugs, subsequent imprisonment and failure to try to keep in touch with his mother, his only link with his lost family: "He had done drugs. Whether as seller or taker, he did not say. Been in and out of prison. His wife, tired, had taken his son and left" (162). Having moved from Little Rock (a place name strangely suggestive of the marginality some would ascribe to island space) to the big city where he meets J., having decided to "change [his] life around" (163) and assume responsibility for the care of his ailing sister, Samuel now allows himself the fragile hope that his path will one day cross that of Ishmael and his mother:

> "They lived in Louisiana," he said.
> The sentence lay between them, filled with their unspoken thoughts. People move from place to place all the time; the traveller himself had moved between two cities and was packing now to travel to a third – but by what likelihood would this man's wife and child have travelled here, in answer to his hope? (162)

Looking at the photograph of the baby Ishmael (one might read in Forbes's choice of name for this lost child an allusion to the biblical son of Abraham, sent away with his mother Hagar), sharing the pain of this self-inflicted solitude, J. bestows on the artist the ultimate, consoling gift – the affirmation of fatherhood: "He has a look of you" (159).

This story of an African American separated from family and wandering far away from home recalls the larger peregrinations of blacks in the United States (a topic addressed by Danticat in her essay " Black Bodies in Motion and in Pain"23), and it has something of the poignancy of August

Wilson's *Joe Turner's Come and Gone*, in which a father travels from state to state in search of the wife lost in a form of slavery. Though Forbes's narrative is muted, and scrupulous in its avoidance of a facile sentimentalism, and though it does not identify race as the main factor behind Reevers's dislocation, one may also read this necessarily condensed story as an allegory of enforced nomadism, of the dispersal of rural blacks in search of an elusive place to call home, or even the earlier, decisive uprooting of Africans to be enslaved via the Middle Passage. This episode, foregrounded in the title "For Ishmael", is central to the story, and J. evidently ascribes a value other than the purely aesthetic to the painting which he buys for thirty-five dollars from the itinerant artist. And it is not surprising, then, that Samuel Reevers's palm should leave its mark on the West Indian's own; as they say a quick farewell, the social ritual of the handshake becomes something more: "The traveller caught the other's hand in his just for an instant but he could feel the lines on his own palm changing, as they had done on countless occasions before" (164). One should also note, in this context, the significance of the parallels that can be drawn between Samuel Reevers and Maldene, reminding us that marginalization knows no nationality: both have experienced incarceration; both are artists, (re)fashioning their lives without fanfare, easing their pain through the creativity of gifted hands.

Two days after this encounter with Samuel and with the dream/memory of Ishmael, a catastrophic event intervenes, and the narrative implicitly connects the travels of Caribbean migrants to the displacement of thousands of Americans, newly dispossessed but victims of a long-standing inequality:

> Two days after his meeting with Samuel Reevers and Ishmael, Hurricane Katrina devastated Louisiana. In New Orleans the levees broke; the city drowned. . . . Many people were evacuated to this city. The Red Cross, with which he had volunteered, had taken many in. Helping, he searched faces feverishly for the faces of Ishmael and his mother. He felt that if he saw them, he would know. But he never did. (167)

The public tragedy of Katrina, and its intersection with the familial drama of Samuel and Ishmael, seems to mark a shift in J.'s ability to engage fully with his fellow city dwellers, who have their own stories to tell – and whom he has held at a distance, despite the inherent benevolence of his vocation.

How else might one explain his "sudden decision" to surrender half of the precious soil from home, having become a sort of personal totem which he has carried around with him, and which he had planned to return to its origin intact? The reader realizes towards the end of this carefully crafted story that after the scene related on the first two pages (157–58) in which J. decides to keep the painting by Reevers, the remainder of the narrative is a flashback; the final page (168) brings us back to the present, as J. works on his lovingly tended geranium, now potted in a medium which is a blending not of opposites but of different but similar elements – a process not as dramatic nor as radical as that implicit in the once-popular trope of the "melting pot". Through J.'s gesture of inclusion, the narrative extends the reach of his compassion beyond the prisoners he had cared for in Kingston to embrace those who people "strange" Northern cities:

> Standing now in his empty rooms, remembering, he made a sudden decision. He unwrapped his pot of soil from home and poured half of it back into the pot with the geranium. With his fingers he mixed the soil from home with the city soil in which he had replanted the flower. . . . Tomorrow he would tell his friend to take especial care of that one, because it was planted in the name of a child. (168)

And the story ends with an acknowledgement that, like Samuel, J./Jeremy is sometimes adrift, and this despite his claim to rootedness, despite the shifting lines in his palms which speak of new encounters and a wide compassion. For the traveller who is manifestly adept at listening, but who never tells *his* own story, is doubly bereft – bereft of the deep earth of which the small pot is an inadequate token, and bereft also of the hands of the woman left behind, close to that earth: "When he was lonely for deep companionship, as he often was, he walked beside beautiful gardens at evening and thought of her weeding, sculpting, molding mugs between her small hands. . . . And his longing was a longing for thick black earth and cities grounded, but also part of a larger hunger for rainbow, for sky" (168).

The expression "deep companionship" illuminates what we now feel to be a voluntary isolation; not easily seduced, Jeremy will not compromise, will not surrender to the illusion of emotional connection. Nor can one assume that his "larger hunger" would be easily placated by reintegration with the community of origin: there is considerable ambiguity in the imagery of sky and rainbow – after all, "Prologue" ends with the arrival in New York, against the backdrop of a sky barely marked by a rainbow. (Forbes appears fond of this image – one notes its presence in the epigraph to *A Permanent Freedom*, an extract from the poem "Colour Scheme" by Edward Baugh.) The complex symbolism of the rainbow – sign of God's covenant with the faithful and also, in a secular context, harbinger of new beginnings, token of hope after devastation – suggests that the weight of home soil will always be counterbalanced by the vastness of the sky, by the *possibility* it offers, by the call of a wider world. Forbes's narrative is predictably open-ended: the reader cannot tell whether the character has really arrived at a crossroads – although one would *like* to believe that the returning wanderer of the brief, elliptical "Epilogue" is none other than J./Jeremy.

All we know for sure, at the conclusion of "For Ishmael", is that the cohesion of a fragmented family is restored, in the imagination of a nomadic stranger, by the simple mingling of earth, the creation of what is really "new" soil, an act akin to a sacrament, heralding fusion and rebirth. What remains is Jeremy's implied ambivalence about his "exile", manifest in his inability to embark on the journey back to his own "little rock"; it is an ambivalence perhaps emblematic of the attitude of many West Indians who arrive in North America as neither mendicants nor conquerors, but rather as cautious voyagers looking towards new vistas while always holding within their visual field the dream/memory of home. Despite his ability to feel empathy for fellow travellers and even "natives", like Ishmael's father, Jeremy's relation to the United States therefore remains complex, if not puzzling, at the end of this story.

More easily understandable is the motivation keeping the young protagonist of the narrative "Say" in a country where she has lived for years with her migrant parents. It is important that she is half St Lucian and half Jamaican, that she holds on, as to a lifeline, to a very specific sense of place, even at her most fragile, so that she is able to affirm, "I grew up in St. Lucia, in a place called Anse la Raye. I lived there until I was twelve years old" (140). This tale of a disturbed student, isolated in a creative writing class where she is the only black person, widens the spectrum of displaced Caribbean people who are the subjects of *A Permanent Freedom*. Gysette is not alone, nor really "in exile", in the United States: she first travelled there with her parents at the age of twelve, and she dreams of returning to Jamaica when she has completed her studies. Yet, while the parents, who do not live in Iowa where she attends college, are confident that all is well with her, the distant Jamaican grandmother senses the young woman's distress.

At the start of the text, Gysette is manifestly troubled, precariously so; she is apparently the victim of the abuse of a distinguished writer in residence from the United Kingdom, the professor in her creative writing course. In the story "Say", and in the companion text which follows, "Nocturne in Blue", the reader is challenged to put the pieces together, to try to understand Gysette's fragility. It would be easy, but in this case perhaps not justifiable, to impute her malaise to the widely held Jamaican belief in the concept of "foreign sending you mad"; at one point, the protagonist wryly alludes to that notion, saying to herself, "I am really hallucinating now. This is the kind of thing that used to happen to people who went to England in the old days – you know England is a place that used to make black people mad. But I am not in England, I am in America" (128).

Though the trauma she experiences is clearly aggravated by the longing for her beloved "country bush" and, above all, for the grandmother with whom she has maintained a strong bond, the sort of simplification which would conveniently represent the young woman as victim of being a black foreigner is noticeably absent here. The professor who has triggered in her what appears to be an emotional and psychological breakdown is the very embodiment of alienation – a colourless West Indian transformed into a "Briton". He is himself of West Indian origin, though it is an origin that he has long denied, draping himself instead in the acquired identity of black Briton, proud of being the recipient of an MBE, "of being recognized at last as a British writer" (131). Forbes tiptoes around some aspects of this particular character's pain, leaving the reader to re-create the full story masked by the text's several ellipses, a story which emerges as a gendered migration narrative, as it becomes clear that Gysette's conversations/discussions with the professor of creative writing have gone far beyond the normal in a purely academic context. (It is only in the following "Nocturne in Blue" that the suspected transgression is confirmed: the visitor, who tells his story in the first person, has in fact forced his attentions on Gysette.) In this season of distress, a wounded Gysette dreams of a return home, either to St Lucia or to Jamaica; but she is also realistic about the impossibility of going back to a past no longer accessible to her: "Grandma I would like to come to you, or go to walk on the beach at Anse, but I have nobody left in Anse. Everybody is here" (120).

Then, magically to some but believably to many Afro-Caribbean readers, Gysette's devoted grandmother back in Jamaica "dreams" her and imagines offering her the classic gestures of comfort and healing: "'See I wash you in the river. . . . Drink the peas soup'" (123). The pull of homeland is stronger in this story than in any other in the collection, as an extraordinary communication between fragile granddaughter "in foreign" and nurturing grandmother on the rock becomes a struggle for the sanity and even for the survival of the young woman. Gysette is closely linked, in spirit and through the intimacy of the Creole language, to her Jamaican grandmother. The author collapses the boundaries between real and imagined so that the young woman feels Grandma's presence, communicating through a magical medium which includes dreams and visions: "Two nights now I dream her. . . . I don't hear from her but I keep on writing, for I says sometimes when you down and out and you hear a voice, a voice of somebody who love you, even if it is from far, it hold you up like a rope that somebody string cross a precipice" (117).

At the start of the story, Gan Gan visualizes her return in vivid terms; the narrative offers examples of how adroitly Forbes gives free expression to Jamaican Creole in an apparently effortless demonstration of code-switching and code-mixing: "From the moment she get off the taxi I know something wrong" (112). The grandmother remembers their intimate bond, from the time of Gysette's babyhood: "I practically grow that little girl, for every Augas holiday the mother uses to send her to me . . . from she small till she big and they go away to America" (112). And in constructing this dream scenario of the return of the much-missed grandchild, Forbes lovingly piles on the details in a listing which makes palpable the cherished gastronomy of the Jamaican heartland, even including the fortifying mannish water:[24] "I make toto and bammy and drops and grater cake[25] with the red colouring just how she like it, I even call Jew Boy to make mannish water as only he can make it, but though she try hard she can't eat much" (113).

It is interesting how the voice and, specifically, the orality conveyed through letter writing figure here as a support and a remedy for the lonely (in contrast to the persistent isolation of the Haitian nurse Nadine in Danticat's "Water Child"); in "Say", there is initially a gap in communication, as the grandmother writes in agitation to a granddaughter too depressed to write back.[26] But in this time of Gysette's affliction, both she and her Gan Gan "dream each other", and it is striking that the young woman, though recently mute in her creative writing class, is not stripped of the gift of speech. Isabel Hoving, commenting on the importance of voice in the work of migrant Caribbean women writers, makes the compelling point that "one's identification of oneself as a speaking subject is highly dependent on one's sense of place".[27] Retaining that sense of place, Gysette is able to eloquently articulate her dream of a journey home, in which the neighbours greet her enthusiastically, focused on what she might have brought them from "foreign", but also carrying out the ritual salutation marking the return to the fold of one who has crossed the water:

> Grandma, I see myself on a minibus driving to come to you. . . . People in the piazza, sitting on the stone wall, will call to me and say, "Miss Mimma granddaughter, pretty girl, you come to look for the old people? But you look nice, how nice you look, foreign gree with you!"
>
> I will be glad to hear their voices, even though I know it is not true. Foreign don't gree with me. (126)

It is only at the end of the story that we realize that the detailed account of Gysette's return home is entirely imaginary. But the supernatural connection is vital, even lifesaving, as Gysette is "hanging on to the navel string that connecting her 'cross the rainbow to Gan Gan, Mammy, Miss Mimma Barclay letter dem", then going on to pledge that "she will write to her grandmother in the morning" (128). At the close of the narrative, the reader senses that without a physical journey, Gysette has achieved a form of healing by reconnecting with home and that, no subaltern, she will survive and continue her sojourn in "foreign". And Gan Gan/Mimma Barclay is able to confirm to the young man who is taxi driver and so much more in the tightly knit community that "my granddaughter awright, praise God" (129).

As for the itinerant priest with whom the collection began, who travelled light, but always clinging to a portion of home soil, he appears to be the only character in *A Permanent Freedom* who returns permanently to his place of origin. We assume that his is the road-weary figure of the brief "Epilogue". In that text, a woman (his Penelope/Maldene?) positioned at the top of a hill is to be reunited with a long-lost traveller, one described as "walking now with a limp because of the experience of feet in the cold . . . a man of great hope, and little expectation" (195). The textual clues to his identity, though minimal, are memorable, including the fact that he walks up a hill and towards a woman who one would like to think is the potter of the prologue, a woman who, "startled, will shade her eyes from the sun" (195). Much of the epilogue is narrated in the future tense, which does not necessarily make the implied outcome less certain: rather, the choice of tense might give the text the weight of prophecy, or at least of a dream/vision, especially since the earlier story "Say" made evident that, from Forbes's perspective, dreams can have value and efficacy. Another reassuring detail is that the traveller "will pour soil like libation from a jar" (194) into the soil at the roots of a large guango tree. So we are tempted to believe that this is indeed Jeremy: "tomorrow a man will walk up this hill, shading his face from the sun. He will love the remembered warmth beating down on his shoulders, his skin, but he has lived for a long time in a different life; the brightness hurts his eyes" (194).

That the two characters known to the reader from the collection's beginning are not named in "Epilogue" might undermine a wished-for certainty that Jeremy is able to pick up where he left off, after fulfilling what appears as the penance of years of wandering. One notes also that while the landscape is clearly tropical, no identifying markers situate this final scene in Jamaica. Forbes's deliberate vagueness adds power to her conclusion, giving the uphill trajectory of a single limping man the force of allegory, and offering the hope that even if changed by the years of displacement, other real-life travellers might find their way home. In a very different text, Junot Díaz's *The Brief Wondrous Life of Oscar Wao*, the character Belicia, who had been obliged to flee the Dominican Republic as a very young woman, seemed to brush off an old man's attempt at reassurance: "Santo Domingo will always be there."[28] But the need to believe in the *possibility* of return is a common theme in most of the narratives considered in this study: it is a need linking characters as disparate as Díaz's Yunior to the granddaughter in "Say" and, finally, to Curdella Forbes's travelling priest, who has always held on in memory, and perhaps in hopeful anticipation, to "the place to which he was anchored at the root, though he had travelled paths like rhizomes" (168).

CHAPTER 6

AFTER THE JOURNEY

Reinventing the Self?

What are we bringing from home? What is going to help hold us together here?
—Junot Díaz, "Junot Díaz Reads Edwidge Danticat", *New Yorker* Fiction
Podcast, 1 February 2017

IN "REQUIEM", ONE OF THE STORIES in Forbes's *A Permanent Freedom*, a Jamaican
returning to her village of origin after a family funeral is troubled by the
fear that her dispersed siblings will one day abandon the ritual journey of
reconnection, and that the death of the elders means the loss of a dream
of home, of *"the home to which year after year we all pretend that we'll return
for a bang-up pick-up lick-dung grand reunion but nobody except me has come,
and me not since Da died, for what is the point, if Ma and Da aren't there any
more"*.[1] It is a fear of dilution[2] of Antillean identity which I think haunts
much of the literature studied in the preceding chapters, though it is least
evident in the work of Maryse Condé and in that of Caryl Phillips – the
latter appearing to finally embrace his Englishness, to claim a linkage with
the slave castles of Ghana *and* to honour a familial connection to the small
island which he left as an infant. The black Briton, who has imagined his
ashes being scattered half way across the Atlantic,[3] is certainly far removed
in his concept of identity from Curdella Forbes, in whose stories the *soil* of
her native Jamaica seems a persistent presence, insistent on its materiality.
Each writer's trajectory is singular; each relates differently to the notion
of diaspora. Indeed, an observation by the Ghanaian-born/Jamaican poet

Kwame Dawes reminds us that there are, for some diasporic writers, even more complex definitions of home than those founded on a choice between binaries, between two familiar countries. For Dawes, whose childhood was divided between Ghana and Jamaica, and who has lived and worked for two decades in South Carolina[4] while travelling frequently back and forth to Jamaica,[5] acknowledges that all these three locations have meaning for him: "I have always lived as if I am from somewhere else or as if there is somewhere else to which I belong". On the other hand, it is perhaps a personal history of nomadism which has led the Guadeloupean Maryse Condé to an acceptance of a sort of homelessness (though in most of Condé's fiction, including *The Last of the African Kings*, examined in chapter 4, the native island remains compelling in the individual's imagination, even when the pathway home remains "the road not taken").

Inherent in the quotation above from *A Permanent Freedom* is the postcolonial subject's fear of loss of the land – which was after all, in the West Indies, the precious, tangible evidence of "full freedom" for the once enslaved. It is a concern which appears in less melancholy form in Danticat's essay "Walk Straight", in which the writer acknowledges the role of her beloved elderly aunt as faithful keeper of ancestral space, guardian of a familial sanctuary which is hardly a lost Eden, but nevertheless a site essential to the traveller's sense of self. Almost in the same breath, as she prepares to leave Haiti, and to say goodbye to Tante Ilyana (for what would turn out to be the final time), the narrator struggles to shrug off a perhaps self-indulgent sentimentalism regarding her situation as migrant: "There are already so many separations in our family, constant departures and returns. We cannot afford to curse or avoid these exits and migrations, however, because they have earned us whatever type of advancement we have made."[6]

Danticat's *appearance* of pragmatism exemplifies the ambivalence which most of these writers reflect, as they oscillate in their fiction and in their life writing between longing for a "home" and recognizing the changes wrought by exposure to and even, to some extent, integration into a new land. In the unsettling words quoted at the start of chapter 1, Danticat seems to ask herself – and, implicitly, her fellow migrants of whatever nationality – how much of the connection to home is the fruit of the imagination rather than of memory; yet this emotional formulation, echoing a section of Toni Morrison's Nobel speech, makes it clear that, for Danticat at least, the bond, however tenuous or elastic it might appear, is very real: "Will we ever have a home in this place, or will we always be set adrift from the home we knew? Or the home we have never known."[7] To this haunting, unanswerable question, perhaps the most appropriate response is Díaz's enigmatic affirmation that "home is vast".[8]

I would elaborate on this elliptical statement by suggesting that "versions" of home remain in the consciousness of both first- and second-generation migrants – versions likely to be rewritten in what may be surprising ways with the passing of the years. In Edwidge Danticat's case, one feels with certainty that "the great black country"[9] will never be sidelined, even though the writer does not elide the political turmoil which triggered her elderly uncle's travel to the United States, nor her own privilege, as resident of a country where she has achieved fame and made memories (*Brother, I'm Dying*). Yet, to the generation of "migrants" whose knowledge of home is only gleaned second hand, such as those in Phillips's *In the Falling Snow*, or in Condé's *Desirada*, the Caribbean island is a remote, if not obscure, location, brought alive through the oral testimony of those who first crossed the waters or, less commonly, by a journey "back" to an unfamiliar landscape.

The writers considered in this study began publishing their work in the late twentieth/early twenty-first century, well after the era of accession to statehood and optimism about the prospects of newly independent nations, and also after the time of prolonged migrant separation from the region because of the high cost of travel – factors that might have influenced their relation to the Caribbean. In her discussion of "The Poetics of Wandering", Odile Ferly argues that West Indian expatriate writers of an earlier generation tended to idealize their island of origin:[10] "A strong tendency to idealize the homeland is found among early diaspora writers across the region."[11] Although one should be prudent in venturing to make a generalization on the basis of a limited corpus of texts, it would seem that contemporary diasporic writers, and particularly those located in the United States, are more likely to be frequent travellers to the Caribbean. This evolution is underlined by Paul Jay, in *Global Matters: The Transnational Turn in Literary*

Studies, as he points out that the novels discussed in his study, including Díaz's *Oscar Wao*, "underscore how the structure and rhythm of migration is changing as globalization accelerates".[12] One would assume that such habitual travellers are likely to be more aware of changing realities, less invested in the dream/mirage of the past and, therefore, less disappointed at the sort of transformation that Lorna Goodison fears/regrets in the poignant poem, "Change if You Must Just Change Slow":

> please don't change or change if you must
> just change slow. Old countryman riding
> jackass, big woman watering the dry peas
> ....
> Little bit of country village place or woodland
> name of Content, Wire Fence, Stetin, Allsides,
> far from domain of gunman and town strife.
> Country we leave from to go and make life.[13]

I have always found compelling the title of Condé's *Desirada*, in which the young protagonist, transplanted to Paris as a child, makes a solitary journey back to Désirade, the island off the coast of Guadeloupe where her grandmother still lives. After this return to "roots", Marie-Noelle is able to make peace with her "non-native" status in the Antilles, returning to Boston and to her university job. In a Caribbean where, among other changes, the "domain of gunman and town strife" seems to be expanding relentlessly, it is far from certain that, especially for younger second-generation migrants, the island to which their family traces their origin is in fact a *desired* land.

Yet I was struck, in analysing the selection of narratives on which this study focuses, by the sense that no departure from a Caribbean homeland can ever be seen as truly definitive. I was struck by each writer's representation of the irreducible singularity of the land of origin, and by the tenacity of a sense of cultural and linguistic specificity. More than half a century ago, the French president Général de Gaulle infamously described the islands of the French Antilles as *des poussières sur l'océan* (specks on the ocean). This rashly dismissive declaration, which would be much interrogated in French Caribbean writing, reminds us even today of the discursive impact of the colonialist vision of *relatively* small islands as peripheral. The contemporary literature of migration studied in the preceding chapters implicitly refutes that marginalization, that trivialization of island space, however potent the lure of the "metropolis" remains in the Caribbean imaginary. Even as the authors discussed in this study sometimes blur the lines between native and other lands, they could hardly be described as either insular *or* deterritorialized; rather, they exploit and illustrate, through their fiction and non-fiction, the creative possibilities of an ambiguous situation. They are frequently guarded in their expression of nostalgia, as in this description by Junot Díaz of a young fictional migrant's longing for home: "It is probably her son she misses, or the father. Or our whole country, which you never think of until it's gone, which you never love until you're no longer there".[14] But the resistance of the mythmaking impulse is certainly not synonymous with an absence of attachment, or with the abandonment of *memory*.

A few years ago, as I was embarking on the research which led to this study, I found myself strangely drawn to a song by the Jamaican dance hall artist Laden (with Stephen "Di Genius" McGregor), "We Remember". It began with the words

> No, wi neva figet weh wi come from
> No, we neva regret weh wi come from
> Wi remember everyday
> Just remember every ting.[15]

These catchy lyrics spoke of a journey away from a small place of origin, but their focus was, I think, not necessarily on migration[16] but rather on the move between rural Jamaica and an urban centre, presumably the site of opportunity and social mobility, but also a gritty place, barely masking novel dangers. Although the relation to origins is clearly more complex, especially for those diasporic writers who first journeyed as children, than the pledge to "never forget", these defiant words have continued to resonate for me:

> Even when mi go away you know mi affi go back, yeah
> 'Cause wi nah run away, no! Wi coulda neva do dat
> No way![17]

The allusion in this part of the song to the fear of being cast as "runaways" echoes the complex sentiments expressed by migratory characters in all the texts studied about the ways in which they are perceived at home, and the taunts such as that of "gringo", in the Spanish-speaking world, or dyaspora, in the Haitian context, which other the returning resident anxious to fit in.

For those who left their islands, and also, importantly, for those who remain, this diasporic literature offers a potent reminder of the need, in this era of indefinable, evolving or transnational identities, to honour rather than to efface difference; to excavate and document even while appearing to move on; to reaffirm and to reconstruct. One may argue that this is not a novel challenge for those inhabiting the "new" diasporas of North America and Europe, given the original collective experience of *déracinement*. The task of traversing and adapting to a "new world" while looking in two directions[18] is, I believe, less radical than the process of creolization described by Edouard Glissant in terms reminiscent of Stuart Hall's emphasis on identity as process:[19] "In the West Indies, the region where I was born, it can be said that a people is engaged in the positive process of constructing itself."[20] Embracing new crossings, these writers – from the Afro-Hispanic Díaz to the black British Phillips, from the recent migrant Forbes, to Danticat, with "feet planted in both worlds", to the perennial traveller/nomad Condé – remind us that some journeys are liberating, or simply *necessary*, even when they lead to shifting or hyphenated identities. At the same time, their fictions highlight the not insignificant challenge of reinventing *and* holding on to the self, as they narrativize a remembered/imagined/refashioned connection to their rocks of origin.

NOTES

INTRODUCTION

1. Maryse Condé, *The Story of the Cannibal Woman*, trans. Richard Philcox (New York: Simon and Schuster, 2007), 30.
2. Dennis Scott, "Homecoming", in *Uncle Time* (Pittsburgh: University of Pittsburgh Press, 1973), 7.
3. Cristina García, *Dreaming in Cuban* (New York: Ballantine, 1993), 236.
4. Caryl Phillips, *The Atlantic Sound* (New York: Faber, 2000), 15.
5. This law, which transformed Martinique, Guadeloupe, Reunion and French Guyana into departments of France, was presented to the French Assemblée nationale by Aimé Césaire.
6. In the anti-colonial discourse of the time, this phrase was ironically inverted to read *"des Francais entièrement a part"* (Frenchmen kept completely apart).
7. Bureau pour le développement des migrations dans les départements d'outre-mer.
8. United States Office of Immigration Statistics, *2013 Yearbook of Immigration Statistics* (Washington, DC: US Department of Homeland Security, August 2014), 8. The same document gives the following immigration statistics for the final decade of the twentieth century: Cuba – 159,037; Haiti – 177,446; and Jamaica – 177,143.
9. Gilbert Müller, *New Strangers in Paradise: The Immigrant Experience and Contemporary American Fiction* (Lexington: University Press of Kentucky, 2008), 2–3.
10. Elleke Boehmer, *Colonial and Postcolonial Literature: Migrant Metaphors* (New York: Oxford University Press, 2005), 226.
11. Curdella Forbes, *A Permanent Freedom* (Leeds: Peepal Tree Press, 2008), 22.
12. The term "imagined communities", which clearly alludes to Benedict Anderson's influential text on nationalism, is used here to refer specifically to the reconstitution of communities through virtual, electronic media.
13. Robert T. Tally Jr, preface to *Literature's Sensuous Geographies: Postcolonial*

Matters of Place, by Sten Pultz Moslund (New York: Palgrave Macmillan, 2015), x.

14. Kezia Page, *Transnational Negotiations in Caribbean Diasporic Literature: Remitting the Text* (London: Routledge, 2010), 3. See also Page's discussion of Danticat's work, especially her focus on voice, in the chapter "Migrant Bodies, Scars and Tattoos".

15. Pluto Shervington, "I Man Born Ya", *Again,* KR, 1982, LP.

16. Lorna Goodison, *Goldengrove: New and Selected Poems* (Manchester, UK: Carcanet, 2006), 111.

17. It is recognized that this study does not take into consideration the substantial body of texts represented by Indo-Caribbean literature: the decision to focus on Afro-Caribbean writers was made because of a concern with coherence in an analysis already including several language areas.

18. James Clifford, *Routes: Travel and Translation in the Late Twentieth Century* (Cambridge, MA: Harvard University Press, 1997), 251.

19. Avtah Brah, "Thinking through the Concept of Diaspora", in *The Post-Colonial Studies Reader,* ed. Bill Ashcroft, Gareth Griffiths and Helen Tiffin (London: Routledge, 2007; first published 1995), 444.

20. Ibid.

21. Forbes, *Permanent Freedom,* 50.

22. Ibid., 157.

23. J. Michael Dash, "Fictions of Displacement: Locating Modern Haitian Narratives", *Small Axe* 12, no. 3 (October 2008): 41.

24. The exception is Maryse Condé's *The Last of the African Kings* (trans. Richard Philcox [Lincoln: University of Nebraska Press, 1997]), chosen because it provides interesting points of comparison with the later work.

25. Phillips, *Atlantic Sound,* 98.

26. Edwidge Danticat, "Haiti: A Bi-cultural Experience", *Encuentros* 12 (December 1995): 1–9.

27. Ibid., 7.

28. Maryse Condé, *The Journey of a Caribbean Writer,* trans. Richard Philcox (London: Seagull Books, 2014), 61.

29. H. Adlai Murdoch, *Creolising the Metropole: Migrant Caribbean Identities in Literature and Film* (Bloomington: Indiana University Press, 2012), 3.

30. For details, see, for example, "Author Junot Diaz Stripped of Honor after Speaking out against the Dominican Republic", *Los Angeles Times,* 23 October 2015.

31. Odile Ferly, *A Poetics of Relation: Caribbean Women Writing at the Millennium* (New York: Palgrave Macmillan, 2012), 131.

32. Edward Said, "The Mind of Winter", in *The Post-Colonial Studies Reader,* ed. Bill

Ashcroft, Gareth Griffiths and Helen Tiffin (London: Routledge, 2007), 439.

33. This term, of biblical origin, is also associated with the song "By the Rivers of Babylon", popular with Rastafarians.

34. These words inevitably bring to mind the iconic text *The Pleasures of Exile* (London: Michael Joseph, 1960) by George Lamming.

35. Said, "Mind of Winter", 442.

36. Kamau Brathwaite, *The Arrivants: A New World Trilogy* (Oxford: Oxford University Press, 1973), 57.

37. Junot Díaz, *This Is How You Lose Her* (New York: Riverhead, 2012), 9–10.

38. Brathwaite, *Arrivants*, 60.

39. Ibid., 60–61.

40. See, for example, Jamaica Kincaid, *A Small Place* (New York: Farrar, Straus and Giroux, 2000); Jamaica Kincaid, *My Brother* (New York: Farrar, Straus and Giroux, 1997).

41. Julia Alvarez, *Something to Declare* (Chapel Hill, NC: Algonquin Books, 1998), 172–73.

42. Having first left Guadeloupe at age sixteen, Condé has spent most of her adult life abroad. At present, she lives in New York and Paris.

43. This text, seen as the literary manifesto of the Créolité movement, was jointly authored by Jean Bernabé, Patrick Chamoiseau and Raphael Confiant.

44. Maryse Condé and Madeleine Cottenet-Hage, eds., *Penser la Créolité* (Paris: Eds Karthala, 1995), 310.

45. Homi Bhabha, *The Location of Culture* (London: Routledge, 1994), 35–36.

46. For the 1989 novel *The Mambo Kings Play Songs of Love*. Oscar Hijuelos died in October 2013.

47. Oscar Hijuelos, "Lost in Time and Words, a Child Begins Anew", *New York Times*, 15 June 2011.

48. Ibid.

49. Marshall cites the Polish emigrant writer in her essay "From the Poets in the Kitchen", *New York Times*, 9 January 1983.

50. Patrick Chamoiseau, "Reflections on Maryse Condé's *Traversée de la mangrove*", trans. Kathleen M. Balutansky, *Callaloo* 14, no. 2 (Spring 1991): 393–94.

51. Ibid., 394.

52. Junot Díaz, "Fiction Is the Poor Man's Cinema: An Interview with Junot Díaz", *Callaloo* 23, no. 3 (2000): 904.

53. Edwidge Danticat, "The Art of Not Belonging", interview with Dwyer Murphy, *Guernica*, 3 September 2013, https://www.guernicamag.com/the-art-of-not-belonging.

54. In Rebecca Mead, "Stepmother Tongue", *New Yorker*, 20 November 1995.

55. Stuart Hall, "Negotiating Caribbean Identities", *New Left Review* (January–February 1995): 14.

56. Ibid., 1.

57. "Ask the Author Live: Edwidge Danticat", *New Yorker*, 22 January 2010, https://www.newyorker.com/books/ask-the-author/ask-the-author-live-edwidge-danticat.

58. Ibid.

59. Christopher González, *Reading Junot Díaz* (Pittsburgh: University of Pittsburgh Press, 2015), 78.

60. Maryse Condé, "Je me suis réconciliée avec mon île", interview with Vèvè Clark, *Callaloo* 12, no. 1 (1989): 86–132.

61. Maryse Condé, "O Brave New World", in *Multiculturalism and Hybridity in African Literatures*, ed. Hal Wylie and Bernth Lindfors (Trenton, NJ: Africa World Press, 2000), 31.

62. Brent Hayes Edwards, *The Practice of Diaspora: Literature, Translation and the Rise of Black Internationalism* (Cambridge, MA: Harvard University Press, 2003).

63. Ibid., 118.

64. Stewart Brown and Mark McWatt, eds., *The Oxford Book of Caribbean Verse* (Oxford: Oxford University Press, 2009), 252–53.

65. Ferly, *Poetics of Relation*, 135.

66. Elizabeth Thomas-Hope, ed., *Freedom and Constraint in Caribbean Migration and Diaspora* (Kingston: Ian Randle, 2009), xxxv.

67. This famous and courageous activist, having had to flee Haiti twice for political reasons, was murdered in front of his radio station, Radio Haiti, on 3 April 2000.

68. Edwidge Danticat, *The Butterfly's Way: Voices from the Haitian Dyaspora in the United States* (New York: Soho Press, 2001), xv.

CHAPTER 1

1. Edwidge Danticat, "Black Bodies in Motion and in Pain", *New Yorker*, 22 June 2015.

2. Claude McKay, "The Tropics in New York", in *Selected Poems* (Mineola, NY: Dover, 1999), 30–31.

3. Alison Donnell, *Twentieth-Century Caribbean Literature* (London: Routledge, 2006), 127.

4. *New York Times*, 29 October 2013.

5. Edwidge Danticat, "A Harrowing Turning Point for Haitian Immigrants", *New Yorker*, 12 May 2017.

6. Danticat explains her use of the term in an interview with Renée Shea in *Callaloo* 19, no. 2 (1996): 387.

7. Danticat, "Haiti", 7.

8. Ibid., 4.

9. Ibid., 6.

10. *La Constitution de la République d'Haïti, 1987*, https://www.oas.org/juridico /mla/fr/hti/fr_hti-int-txt-const.html.

11. Marie-Hélène Laforest, *Diasporic Encounters: Remapping the Caribbean* (Naples: Liguori, 2000), 158.

12. Edwidge Danticat, *Breath, Eyes, Memory* (New York: Soho Press, 1994), 162.

13. Interview conducted via email in August 2010. I am grateful to the author for her generosity in this regard.

14. Quoted in Garry Pierre-Pierre, "Facing Prejudice: Edwidge Danticat: Chronicling the Haitian-American Experience", in *Libète: A Haiti Anthology*, ed. Charles Arthur and J. Michael Dash (Princeton, NJ: Markus Wiener, 1999), 202.

15. Danticat, "Art".

16. Mary Gallagher, "Concealment, Displacement and Disconnection: Danticat's *The Dew Breaker*", in *Edwidge Danticat: A Reader's Guide*, ed. Martin Munro (Charlottesville: University of Virginia Press, 2010), 155.

17. Edwidge Danticat, *The Dew Breaker* (New York: Vintage, 2005), 38–39. Subsequent citations to *The Dew Breaker* appear parenthetically in the text.

18. Edwidge Danticat, *Create Dangerously: The Immigrant Artist at Work* (Princeton, NJ: Princeton University Press, 2010), 36.

19. Ibid., 39.

20. Edwidge Danticat, "Enfant d'eau", *Passerelles* 21 (2000): 231–39.

21. Edwidge Danticat, *Krik? Krak!* (New York: Vintage, 1996; first published 1991), 9, 14.

22. The formula is found in all the former French colonies, but also used on some anglophone islands such as Trinidad.

23. Aitor Ibarrola-Armendariz, "The Language of Wounds and Scars in Edwidge Danticat's *The Dew Breaker*: A Case Study in Trauma Symptoms and the Recovery Process", *Journal of English Studies* 8 (2010): 40.

24. For an interesting study of the importance of the letter format in Danticat's work, see Brenna Munro's article "Letters Lost at Sea: Edwidge Danticat and Orality", in *Echoes of the Haitian Revolution, 1804–2004*, ed. Martin Munro and Elizabeth Walcott-Hackshaw (Kingston: University of the West Indies Press, 2008).

25. For a literary representation of this habit, see Simone Schwarz-Bart's *Ton beau capitaine* (Paris: Seuil, 1987), which also deals with the issue of infidelity affecting a Haitian couple separated by migration.

26. Edwidge Danticat, *Brother, I'm Dying* (New York: Vintage, 2008), 34. Subsequent citations to *Brother, I'm Dying* appear parenthetically in the text.

27. At least to the readers of her creative work; the ordeal of Joseph Dantica had already been the subject of newspaper articles.

28. Danticat, "Haiti", 8.

29. Sandra Pouchet Paquet, *Caribbean Autobiography: Cultural Identity and Self-Representation* (Madison: University of Wisconsin Press, 2002), 257.

30. Danticat speaks of her successful efforts, involving legal process, to gain access to government files relating to her uncle's death. Edwidge Danticat, "A Family Story", interview with Renee H. Shea, in *Edwidge Danticat: A Reader's Guide*, ed. Martin Munro (Charlottesville: University of Virginia Press, 2010), 187–93.

31. Evelyne Trouillot, "The Right Side of History", in *Edwidge Danticat: A Reader's Guide*, ed. Martin Munro (Charlottesville: University of Virginia Press, 2010), 169.

32. Ibid., 171.

33. Wyclef Jean lifted the mood at the end of the telethon "Hope for Haiti" held on 22 January 2010, first by singing a version of "By the Rivers of Babylon", and then with an upbeat performance in Creole.

34. Danticat, email interview, conducted in 2010.

35. Danticat, *Create Dangerously*, 5. Subsequent citations to *Create Dangerously* in this chapter appear parenthetically in the text.

36. Edwidge Danticat, "We Are All Going to Die", interview with Nathalie Handal, *Guernica*, 15 January 2011, https://www.guernicamag.com/danticat_1_15_11/.

37. One thinks, for example, of the symbolic function of the mountains in Roger Mais's *The Hills Were Joyful Together* (London: Heinemann, 1981; first published 1953); or in Edouard Glissant's *La Lézarde* (*The Ripening*) (Paris: Seuil, 1958). In commenting on the latter text, in which the protagonist, Thael, will follow the course of the river down towards the sea in order to carry out his heroic mission, Beverley Ormerod describes the mountain as "a lofty place of origin which suggests a symbolic superiority over the fallen flatlands of cane". *Introduction to the French Caribbean Novel* (London: Heinemann, 1985), 41.

38. Elizabeth Walcott-Hackshaw, "Home Is Where the Heart Is: Danticat's Landscapes of Return", *Small Axe* 12, no. 3 (October 2008): 81.

39. "Ask the Author Live: Edwidge Danticat." *New Yorker*, 22 January 2010, https://www.newyorker.com/books/ask-the-author/ask-the-author-live-edwidge-danticat.

40. The original French title is "Les Nègres".
41. Toni Morrison, *Song of Solomon* (New York: Vintage, 2004; first published 1977).
42. Laferrière is the author of, for example, *How to Make Love to a Black Man without Getting Tired* (*Comment faire l'amour avec un nègre sans se fatiguer*).
43. Dany Laferrière, "Foreword: A Heart of Serenity in the Storm", in *Edwidge Danticat: A Reader's Guide*, ed. Martin Munro (Charlottesville: University of Virginia Press, 2010), viii.
44. Aimé Césaire, *Cahier d'un retour au pays natal* (Paris: Présence Africaine, 2000; first published 1939), 24.
45. Valerie Kaussen, "Migration, Exclusion and 'Home' in Edwidge Danticat's Narratives of Return", in *Identity, Diaspora and Return in American Literature*, ed. Maria Antonia Oliver-Rotger (London: Routledge, 2014), 37.
46. Edwidge Danticat, *Claire of the Sea Light* (New York: Knopf, 2013), 8.
47. Ibid., 221.
48. Ibid., 228.
49. Alscess Lewis-Brown, "'Bearing Witness': An Interview with Edwidge Danticat", *Caribbean Writer* 28 (2014): 12.
50. That Danticat also continues to "create dangerously", to advocate for Haitian and other immigrants, is evident in her essay in the *New Yorker*, "Poetry in a Time of Protest", 31 January 2017, referring to protests at the Miami International Airport against the newly imposed "travel ban".

CHAPTER 2

1. See, as a recent example of this collaboration, the *Los Angeles Times* op-ed "In the Dominican Republic, Suddenly Stateless", 10 November 2013. The two writers had previously co-authored an essay entitled "The Dominican Republic's War on Haitian Workers" published in the *New York Times* on 20 November 1999. Of the latter piece, Christopher González comments, "Of the same generation, Diaz and Danticat are as committed to political activism as they are to their writing." *Reading Junot Díaz*, 146.
2. Díaz, "Fiction", 900.
3. For example, they both read, on the same evening, at the 2014 staging of the international literary festival Calabash in Treasure Beach, Jamaica. Interestingly, on that occasion, a member of the audience called out a reminder that children were in the gathering after Díaz began a reading which included his usual "colourful" language.

4. Díaz became the first Dominican and the second Latino to receive the Pulitzer Prize (2008); both he and Danticat have been beneficiaries of the MacArthur Fellows Program (the so-called genius award).

5. Edwards, *Practice of Diaspora*.

6. Anne Margaret Castro, "Caribbean Collusion: Junot Díaz, Edwidge Danticat and the *New Yorker* Fiction Podcast", *Afro-Hispanic Review* 32, no. 2 (Fall 2013): 23.

7. "Junot Díaz Reads Edwidge Danticat", with Deborah Treisman, *New Yorker* Fiction Podcast, 1 February 2017, MP3 audio, 55:51, https://www.newyorker .com/podcast/fiction/junot-diaz-reads-edwidge-danticat-2.

8. Ibid.

9. Junot Díaz, *The Brief Wondrous Life of Oscar Wao* (New York: Riverhead, 2007); this title is henceforth referred to as *Oscar Wao*.

10. Díaz, "Fiction", 896. Díaz develops this point by explaining that this was an era during which Latinos were affirming their identity: "In this country that's what you're called if you are not called other things first. But I also think I came of age at a time when people were affirming themselves" (896).

11. Díaz, *Oscar Wao*, 59–60. Subsequent citations to *Oscar Wao* appear parenthetically in the text.

12. González, *Reading Junot Díaz*, 59.

13. The language of colour and shade differentiation varies from territory to territory: in Jamaica, one who is termed "brown" is seen as closer to the white than to the black stratum, and may be accorded privileges and respect in a society where light skin is still given value.

14. Tommy L. Lott, "When Diasporas Meet: Black Solidarity and Inter-ethnic Intersections in the United States of America", in *Dimensions of African and Other Diasporas*, ed. Franklin W. Knight and Ruth Iyob (Kingston: University of the West Indies Press, 2014), 224. Lott explains that the expression was first used by Orlando Patterson.

15. However, in an interview with Edwidge Danticat in *Bomb Magazine*, Díaz has expressed his strong opposition to an article claiming that Dominican migrants frequently deny their African origin.

16. Lott, "When Diasporas Meet", 220.

17. I am of course alluding to the lyrics "Oh island in the sun" from the nostalgic song "Jamaica Farewell", made popular by Harry Belafonte.

18. The word "*gringa*" is used, often pejoratively, in Spanish-speaking countries of the Caribbean and Latin America to refer to non-Hispanic (white) foreigners.

19. Césaire, *Cahier*.

20. Junot Díaz, interview with Edwidge Danticat, *Bomb Magazine*, 1 October 2007.

21. Díaz, *This Is How*, 8. Subsequent citations to *This Is How You Lose Her* in this chapter appear parenthetically in the text.
22. This is also common on flights between North America or England and Jamaica; on a transatlantic journey last year, I was struck by the fact that while returning nationals clapped enthusiastically when landing in Kingston, no similar applause was offered by a planeload of Jamaicans arriving in London.
23. Junot Díaz, *Drown* (New York: Riverhead, 1997).
24. Ibid., 163.
25. Ibid., 167.
26. Ibid., 177.
27. Ibid., 190.
28. Díaz, "Fiction".
29. Díaz, *Drown*, 208.
30. Junot Díaz, interview with Hilton Als, *Literary Hub*, 18 March 2016.
31. Paule Marshall, *Brown Girl, Brownstones* (New York: Feminist Press, 2006; first published 1956).
32. In the discussion of "Seven" with Deborah Treisman, "Junot Díaz Reads Edwidge Danticat".
33. Santiago Vaquera-Vásquez, "'The Inextinguishable Longings for Elsewheres': The Impossibility of Return in Junot Díaz", in *Identity, Diaspora and Return in American Literature*, ed. Maria Antonia Oliver-Rotger (London: Routledge, 2014), 170.
34. Ibid.
35. Paul Jay, *Global Matters: The Transnational Turn in Literary Studies* (Ithaca, NY: Cornell University Press, 2010), 193.
36. González, *Reading Junot Díaz*, 10.
37. Alvarez joined Díaz and Danticat in critiquing the legal marginalization of Dominicans of Haitian descent.
38. Alvarez, *Something to Declare*, 173.
39. Ibid., 175.
40. Junot Díaz, *Islandborn* (New York: Dial, 2018).

CHAPTER 3

1. Scott, *Uncle Time*, 5.
2. Danticat, "Haiti", 7.
3. Condé, "O Brave New World", 34.
4. Bénédicte Ledent, *Caryl Phillips* (Manchester: Manchester University Press, 2002), 5.

5. Miller's remarks are quoted in the *Guardian* in an article entitled "Nobel Laureate, Poet and Playwright Derek Walcott Dead, Aged 87" (17 March 2017); he also says of Walcott: "Walcott always insisted that he was a Caribbean writer . . . and that this wasn't a limit, that it didn't make his work parochial."

6. Renée T. Schattemann, *Conversations with Caryl Phillips* (Jackson: University Press of Mississippi, 2009), 122–23.

7. Caryl Phillips, *A New World Order* (New York: Vintage, 2002).

8. Caryl Phillips, *A State of Independence* (New York: Vintage International, 1986).

9. Caryl Phillips, *The Final Passage* (London: Faber, 1985).

10. The novel *Cambridge* (New York: Vintage, 1993) foregrounds the impressions of an Englishwoman who travels to her father's plantation in the West Indies.

11. Phillips, *State of Independence*, 150.

12. Ibid., 152.

13. The term "returning resident" is commonly used in Jamaica to refer to emigrants choosing to resettle in the country after years of absence.

14. J. Dillon Brown, "A State of Interdependence: Caryl Phillips and the Postwar World Order", *Ariel* 44, no. 2–3 (April–July 2013): 100.

15. Scott, *Uncle Time*, 5.

16. Caryl Phillips, *In the Falling Snow* (New York: Vintage, 2010). Subsequent citations to *In the Falling Snow* appear parenthetically in the text.

17. Christopher Tayler, review of *In the Falling Snow*, *Guardian*, 30 May 2009.

18. Gordon Collier, "The Dynamic of Revelation and Concealment: *In the Falling Snow* and the Narrational Architecture of Blighted Existences", in *Caryl Phillips: Writing in the Key of Life*, ed. Bénédicte Ledent and Daria Tunca (Amsterdam: Rodopi, 2012), 398.

19. Caryl Phillips, "*The Final Passage*: An Interview with Writer Caryl Phillips", by Maya Jaggi, in *Black British Culture and Society: A Text Reader*, ed. Kwesi Owusu (London: Routledge, 2000), 166.

20. Maria Antonia Oliver-Rotger, introduction to *Identity, Diaspora and Return in American Literature* (London: Routledge, 2014), 2.

21. Richard Patteson, *Caribbean Passages: A Critical Perspective on New Fiction from the West Indies* (Boulder: Lynne Rienner, 1998), 127.

22. Olive Senior, *Discerner of Hearts* (Toronto: McClelland and Stewart, 1995). The theme of madness in West Indian literature has been the object of considerable critical attention; see for example Evelyn O'Callaghan's "Interior Schisms Dramatised: The Treatment of the 'Mad' Woman in the Work of Some Female Caribbean Novelists" (in *Out of the Kumbla*, ed. Carole Boyce Davies and Elaine Savory Fido [Trenton, NJ: Africa Word Press, 1990], 89–110) and Kelly Baker Josephs, *Disturbers of the Peace: Representations of Madness in Anglophone Carib-*

bean Literature (Charlottesville and London: University of Virginia Press, 2013).

23. Kasia Boddy, review of *In the Falling Snow, Telegraph*, 7 July 2009.

24. Brah, "Thinking", 444.

25. Stuart Hall, "Frontlines and Backyards: The Terms of Change", in *Black British Culture and Society: A Text Reader*, ed. Kwesi Owusu (London: Routledge, 2000), 127.

26. Ibid., 128.

27. I am grateful to Rhonda Cobham-Sander and other participants in a panel discussion at the 2016 Association for Commonwealth Literature and Language Studies (ACLALS) conference, at which I presented a preliminary version of a part of this chapter, for their insights on this point.

28. Sam Selvon's *The Lonely Londoners* (Harlow: Longman, 1985; first published 1956) is an outstanding example, but of course there are many others.

29. Caryl Phillips, *Color Me English: Migration and Belonging before and after 9/11* (New York: New Press, 2011), 16.

30. Interview with Leonard Lopate, in Renée T. Schatteman, *Conversations with Caryl Phillips*, 67.

31. "Caryl Phillips: Reflections on the Past Twenty-Five Years", interview with Renee T. Schatteman, in Renée T. Schatteman, *Conversations with Caryl Phillips*, 165.

32. One might contrast this for example with the opening pages of Jean Rhys's *Voyage in the Dark* (first published London: Constable, 1934; reprint, London: Norton, 1982) in which the protagonist is overwhelmed by the grey blandness of England.

33. Phillips, *Atlantic Sound*, 16.

34. Ibid., 98.

35. Hall, *Familiar Stranger*, 199.

36. Phillips, *New World Order*, 305.

37. Phillips, *Atlantic Sound*, 212–13.

38. Wendy Knepper, "Caryl Phillips's Seascapes of the Imaginary", in *Caryl Phillips: Writing in the Key of Life*, ed. Bénédicte Ledent and Daria Tunca (Amsterdam: Rodopi, 2012), 230–31.

39. Toni Morrison was present at this moving ceremony in honour of the writer and in memory of the Africans who arrived, as strangers on the island, to be "prepared" for slavery. I felt fortunate to witness the ceremony, in the context of the Fifth Biennial Conference of the Toni Morrison Society (2008). See the article in the *New York Times*, "Bench of Memory at Slavery's Gateway", 28 July 2008.

40. In an interview published in *The World* (January–February 1989).

41. Phillips, *Atlantic Sound*, 207.
42. This documentary highlights the concern of the French-Ivorian filmmaker with racism affecting those brought up, like her, in metropolitan France but feeling the sting of a discourse which makes them other.
43. Phillips, *Color Me English*, 24. Subsequent citations to *Color Me English* appear parenthetically in the text.
44. Brown, "State of Interdependence", 102.
45. One chapter, for instance, is a tribute to the late musician Luther Vandross.
46. I am of course alluding to Phillips's non-fiction volume *Extravagant Strangers: A Literature of Belonging* (London: Faber, 1997).
47. Phillips has written elsewhere about Elmina Castle (see the last chapter of *New World Order*, 305) – a building and an ancestral past which clearly haunt him.
48. The door of no return is a powerful element of this memorial to slavery at Elmina, since it was through this door that the Africans passed before boarding the ships which would take them away from their homeland.
49. Fred D'Aguiar, "Home Is Always Elsewhere", in *Black British Culture and Society: A Text Reader*, ed. Kwesi Owusu (London: Routledge, 2000), 197.
50. Alscess Lewis-Brown, "A Conversation with Derek Walcott", *Caribbean Writer* 28 (2014): 206.

CHAPTER 4

1. Condé, "Je me suis réconciliée".
2. Subsequently republished under the title *En attendant le bonheur*.
3. Maryse Condé, *Desirada*, trans. Richard Philcox (New York: Soho Press, 2000; first published in Paris: Laffont, 1997), 28.
4. See, for example, the place of Haiti in *Tree of Life*, trans. Victoria Reiter (New York: Ballantine, 1992). Condé has also declared in an article entitled "Haiti Chérie", in *Haiti Rising: Haitian History, Culture and the Earthquake of 2010*, ed. Martin Munro (Kingston: University of the West Indies Press, 2010), 153, "I would say that Haiti played a key role, as key as that of Africa, in my personal development".
5. The meaning of the word "*Heremakhonon*" is "waiting for happiness".
6. Condé, *Journey*, 161–62.
7. "I had decided never to write about Africa again because the book was so terribly received by Africans and Africanists." Interview in *I, Tituba, Black Witch of Salem*, trans. Richard Philcox (New York: Ballantine Books, 1994), 204.

8. Césaire's 1939 epic poem *Cahier d'un retour au pays natal* traced a journey from the poet's native Martinique to France, and then imagined an emotional "return" to the island – but more importantly to the African roots.

9. Condé, *Story of the Cannibal Woman*, 30.

10. See Phillips, *Atlantic Sound*, 98.

11. Condé, *Journey*, 7.

12. Maryse Condé, *Les derniers rois mages* (Paris: Mercure de France, 1992), 106.

13. Condé, *Last of the African Kings*, 70. Subsequent references to *The Last of the African Kings* appear parenthetically in the text.

14. In reality, Condé's narrator tells us that the king did petition the French government for permission to take his youngest son with him to Algeria, but his requests were denied. This crucial piece of information was unknown to the Martinican family and to his descendants, including Spero.

15. Condé, *Les derniers rois mages*, 75.

16. Ann Smock, "Maryse Condé's *Les derniers rois mages*", *Callaloo* 18, no. 3 (Summer 1995): 676.

17. Maryse Condé, "Three Women in Manhattan", in *Green Cane and Juicy Flotsam: Short Stories by Caribbean Women*, ed. Carmen Esteves and Lizabeth Paravisini-Gebert (New Brunswick, NJ: Rutgers University Press, 1991), 56–67.

18. Ibid., 64.

19. The Bureau pour le développement des migrations dans les départements d'outre-mer.

20. Carole Boyce Davies, *Black Women, Writing and Identity: Migrations of the Subject* (New York: Routledge, 1994), 148.

21. Ibid.

22. Francoise Pfaff, *Conversations with Maryse Condé* (Lincoln: University of Nebraska Press, 1996), 93.

23. Ibid., 95.

24. Anthea Morrison, "Archives of the Heart or 'Imaginary Family Trees?' Maryse Condé's Ambiguous Quest for Origins", paper presented at the Atlantic Crossings Workshop, Dartmouth College, Hanover, NH, May 2001.

25. Richard Allsopp, *Dictionary of Caribbean English Usage* (Oxford: Oxford University Press, 1996), 401.

26. Maryse Condé, *A Season in Rihata*, trans. Richard Philcox (London: Heinemann, 1987; first published as *Une saison à Rihata* in 1981). Married to an African, the protagonist bitterly regrets that she did not know of her mother's death when it occurred.

27. Maryse Condé, *La vie scélérate* (Paris: Seghers, 1987; translation published in 1992).

28. Condé was travelling in Europe at the time of her mother's death (she was only twenty years old at the time) and did not learn of her loss until it was too late to attend the funeral.

29. Condé, *Season*, 63.

30. Arlette Smith, "The Semiotics of Exile in Maryse Condé's Fictional Works", *Callaloo* 14, no. 2 (Spring 1991): 383.

31. This term borrows from the title of African American Marita Golden's autobiography: *Migrations of the Heart* (New York: Ballantine, 1987); it also provides a literal translation of the title of Condé's 1995 novel *La migration des coeurs* (of which the English translation is entitled *Windward Heights*).

32. Condé, *Story of the Cannibal Woman*, 15. Subsequent citations to *The Story of the Cannibal Woman* appear parenthetically in the text.

33. Maryse Condé, *Heremakhonon* (Boulder: Lynne Rienner, 2000; first published 1976).

34. Marie-Christine Rochmann, "Migrance et identité: Au miroir de l'analepse dans *Histoire de la femme cannibale*", in *Maryse Condé en tous ses ailleurs*, ed. Françoise Simastochi-Bronès (Paris: Editions L'Improviste, 2014), 50.

35. Suzanne Césaire, cited by Lilyan Kesteloot, *Les écrivains noirs de langue française: naissance d'une littérature* (Brussels: Editions de l'Institut de Sociologie, 1963), 42.

36. Maryse Condé, "Moi, Maryse Condé, libre d'être moi-même", interview with Lydie Moudileno, *Women in French Studies* 10 (2002): 121–26.

37. García, *Dreaming in Cuban*, 236.

38. Dawn Fulton, *Signs of Dissent: Maryse Condé and Postcolonial Criticism* (Charlottesville: University of Virginia Press, 2008), 10.

39. Kincaid, *Small Place*.

40. Lydie Moudileno, "Portrait of the Artist as Dreamer: Maryse Condé's *Traversée de la mangrove* and *Les derniers rois mages*", *Callaloo* 18, no. 3 (Summer 1995): 629.

41. Condé, *I, Tituba*, 208.

CHAPTER 5

This chapter is a revised and extended version of an essay first published under the title "Of Home Soil and Rainbows: Rooted Travelers in Curdella Forbes' *A Permanent Freedom*", *Journal of Caribbean Literatures* 6, no. 3 (Spring 2010): 23–36.

1. Forbes, *Permanent Freedom*.

2. This title is an interesting inversion of that of the brief final story of Forbes's

previous collection, *Songs of Silence* (London: Heinemann, 2002), 152, entitled "Epilogue: A Beginning".

3. Forbes, *Permanent Freedom*, 9. Subsequent citations to *A Permanent Freedom* appear parenthetically in the text.

4. Referred to from this point on as "Prologue".

5. Forbes, *Songs of Silence*, 152.

6. One may compare the collection, in this regard, with Danticat's *Dew Breaker*.

7. See, for example, Richard Clarke's article, "Root versus Rhizome: An 'Epistemological Break' in (Francophone) Caribbean Thought", *Journal of West Indian Literature* 9, no. 1 (2000): 12–41.

8. A crocus bag is a brown sack made of jute, originally used in Jamaica for the transportation of agricultural products; for further details, consult Olive Senior's *Encyclopedia of Jamaican Heritage* (St Andrew, Jamaica: Twin Guinep, October 2003).

9. Jacques Roumain, *Masters of the Dew*, trans. Langston Hughes and Mercer Cook (Oxford: Heinemann, 1978), 74. The image of the dark soil is repeated in Roumain's novel to form a structuring motif, culminating in the burial of the body of Manuel, the rolling stone who had spent many years as an agricultural labourer in Cuba, in that earth. Forbes's symbolism is less obvious, and the time and setting different, yet the two examples are not dissimilar in ideological implication.

10. Email correspondence with Curdella Forbes, 18 May 2010.

11. "But today I recapture the islands' / bright beaches: blue mist from the ocean / rolling into the fishermen's houses / By these shores I was born." Brathwaite, *Arrivants*, 57.

12. The Jamaican reader will note that this detail situates the narrative in the late twentieth century, since this make of vehicle is no longer to be found on Jamaican roads, even in its most aged form.

13. One thinks here of the dramatic contrast established between mountain and plain in Glissant's *La Lézarde* (*The Ripening*), in which the hills are associated with the independence of the maroon, while the flattened plains beneath evoke a compromise with the reality of colonial/postcolonial society.

14. Davies, *Black Women*, 113–14.

15. See the discussion "Politics of Space and Property in the Historical and Contemporary Caribbean", in Curdella Forbes's "Between Plot and Plantation, Trespass and Trangression: Caribbean Migratory Disobedience in Fiction and Internet Traffic", *Small Axe* 16, no. 2 (July 2012): 25.

16. Edward Baugh, *Derek Walcott* (Cambridge: Cambridge University Press, 2006), 173.

17. Maureen Warner-Lewis, review of *Songs of Silence*. *Jamaica Journal* 30, no. 1–2 (2006): 77.
18. In the critical text *From Nation to Diaspora: Samuel Selvon, George Lamming and the Cultural Performance of Gender* (Kingston: University of the West Indies Press, 2005), Forbes offers valuable insights on migrant literature and specifically on the movement away from the nationalist era.
19. "*Sufferation*" is a Jamaican Creole term meaning "suffering".
20. This is an allusion to the Caribbean tradition – an African retention – of burying the umbilical cord (navel string) after birth in a location that is to become a symbol of the child's belonging.
21. Derek Walcott, *What the Twilight Says* (London: Faber, 1998), 77. For a thoughtful treatment of the figure of the traveller in Walcott's work, see Jeffrey Gray's article "Walcott's Traveler and the Problem of Witness", *Callaloo* 28, no. 1 (2005): 117–28, in which he quotes the line "The traveller cannot love, since love is stasis and travel is motion."
22. The spiritual underpinnings of *A Permanent Freedom* are complex and syncretic: a divinity called Aliun (invented by the author) watches over the wanderers who people the narrative. The author explains in the acknowledgements at the start of the collection that she discovered, long after completing the manuscript, that "not only did the name Aluin, meaning 'supernatural being' or 'elf', exist, it had almost twenty variants".
23. Danticat, "Black Bodies".
24. Mannish water is a much-prized soup made from goat meat.
25. Bammy is a very popular Jamaican food, a sort of bread made from cassava; the other items are sweet delicacies of which coconut is an essential ingredient.
26. The theme of letter writing and its importance to the relationship between families separated by migration is central to Paulette Ramsay's epistolary novel *Aunt Jen* (Oxford: Heinemann, 2002), in which it is a young girl left behind in rural Jamaica who reaches out – in vain – to the mother gone to England.
27. Isabel Hoving, *In Praise of New Travelers* (Stanford, CA: Stanford University Press, 2001), 29.
28. Díaz, *Oscar Wao*, 210.

CHAPTER 6

1. Forbes, *Permanent Freedom*, 188.
2. I am thinking here of Aimé Césaire's comment, in leaving the French Communist Party in 1956, that he feared the "dilution dans 'l'universel'" ("dilution

in the 'universal'") of Martinican identity. *Lettre à Maurice Thorez* (Paris: Seuil, 1956), 15.

3. See Phillips, *New World Order*, 304.
4. Dawes lectured at the University of South Carolina from 1992 to 2012; he is currently a Chancellor's Professor of English at the University of Nebraska.
5. Kwame Dawes, "Writing Home Away from Home", in *Writing Life*, ed. Mervyn Morris and Carolyn Allen (Kingston: Ian Randle, 2007), 52–53. Kwame Dawes was one of the founders (in 2001) of the now famous Calabash International Literary Festival, held biennially in Treasure Beach, Jamaica, and remains one of its principal organizers.
6. Danticat, *Create Dangerously*, 35.
7. Danticat, "Black Bodies".
8. "Junot Díaz Reads Edwidge Danticat".
9. See chapter 1, page 53.
10. Ferly makes an exception of Selvon's *Lonely Londoners* in discussing this tendency.
11. Ferly, *Poetics of Relation*, 136.
12. Jay, *Global Matters*, 177.
13. Lorna Goodison, *Collected Poems* (Manchester, UK: Carcanet, 2017), 405–6.
14. Díaz, "Otravida, Otravez", *This Is How*, 60.
15. Laden, "We Remember" (ft. Stephen "Di Genius" McGregor), Jah Lyrics, 2019, https://www.jah-lyrics.com/song/laden-we-remember. The creolization of the transcription of the lyrics is mine.
16. In the song, Laden foregrounds the journey from a childhood home in a "ghetto" in Kingston to Junction, St Elizabeth.
17. Laden, "We Remember".
18. I am echoing here the metaphor used by Edwidge Danticat in defining a "bi-cultural" identity.
19. See the introduction to this book, page 19.
20. "Or aux Antilles, d'où je viens, on peut dire qu'un peuple positivement se construit." Edouard Glissant, *Soleil de la conscience* (Paris: Seuil, 1960), 15.

BIBLIOGRAPHY

Allsopp, Richard. *Dictionary of Caribbean English Usage*. Oxford: Oxford University Press, 1996.

Alvarez, Julia. *Something to Declare*. Chapel Hill, NC: Algonquin Books, 1998.

Arthur, Charles, and J. Michael Dash, eds. *Libète: A Haitian Anthology*. Princeton, NJ: Markus Wiener, 1999.

"Ask the Author Live: Edwidge Danticat." *New Yorker*, 22 January 2010.

Baugh, Edward. *Derek Walcott*. Cambridge: Cambridge University Press, 2006.

Bernabé, Jacques, Patrick Chamoiseau and Raphael Confiant. *Eloge de la créolité*. Paris: Gallimard, 1993.

Bhabha, Homi K. *The Location of Culture*. London: Routledge, 1994.

Boddy, Kasia. "Review of *In the Falling Snow*". *Telegraph*, 7 July 2009.

Boehmer, Elleke. *Colonial and Postcolonial Literature: Migrant Metaphors*. New York: Oxford University Press, 2005.

Brah, Avtah. "Thinking through the Concept of Diaspora". In *The Post-Colonial Studies Reader*, edited by Bill Ashcroft, Gareth Griffiths and Helen Tiffin, 443–46. London: Routledge, 2007. First published 1995.

Brathwaite, Kamau. *The Arrivants: A New World Trilogy*. Oxford: Oxford University Press, 1973.

Brown, J. Dillon. "A State of Interdependence: Caryl Phillips and the Postwar World Order". *Ariel* 44, no. 2–3 (April–July 2013): 85–111.

Brown, Stewart, and Mark McWatt, eds. *The Oxford Book of Caribbean Verse*. Oxford: Oxford University Press, 2009. First published 2005.

Castro, Anne Margaret. "Caribbean Collusion: Junot Díaz, Edwidge Danticat and the *New Yorker* Fiction Podcast". *Afro-Hispanic Review* 32, no. 2 (Fall 2013): 11–26.

Césaire, Aimé. *Cahier d'un retour au pays natal*. Paris: Présence Africaine, 2000. First published 1939.

———. *Lettre à Maurice Thorez*. Paris: Seuil, 1956.

Chamoiseau, Patrick. "Reflections on Maryse Condé's *Traversée de la mangrove*". Translated by Kathleen M. Balutansky. *Callaloo* 14, no. 2 (Spring 1991): 389–95.

————. *Texaco*. Paris: Gallimard, 1992.

Clarke, Richard. "Root versus Rhizome: An 'Epistemological Break' in (Francophone) Caribbean Thought". *Journal of West Indian Literature* 9, no. 1 (2000): 12–41.

Clifford, James. *Routes: Travel and Translation in the Late Twentieth Century*. Cambridge, MA: Harvard University Press, 1997.

Collier, Gordon. "The Dynamic of Revelation and Concealment: *In the Falling Snow* and the Narrational Architecture of Blighted Existences". In *Caryl Phillips: Writing in the Key of Life*, edited by Bénédicte Ledent and Daria Tunca, 375–406. Amsterdam: Rodopi, 2012.

Condé, Maryse. *Crossing the Mangrove*. Translated by Richard Philcox. New York: Random House, 1995.

————. *Desirada*. Paris: Laffont, 1997.

————. *Desirada*. Translated by Richard Philcox. New York: Soho Press, 2000.

————. "Haiti Chérie". In *Haiti Rising: Haitian History, Culture and the Earthquake of 2010*, edited by Martin Munro, 147–54. Kingston: University of the West Indies Press, 2010.

————. *Heremakhonon*. Boulder: Lynne Rienner, 2000. First published 1976.

————. *Histoire de la femme cannibale*. Paris: Mercure de France, 2003.

————. *I, Tituba, Black Witch of Salem*. Translated by Richard Philcox. New York: Ballantine, 1994.

————. "Je me suis réconciliée avec mon île". Interview with Vèvè Clark. *Callaloo* 12, no. 1 (1989): 86–132.

————. "Moi, Maryse Condé, libre d'être moi-même". Interview with Lydie Moudileno. *Women in French Studies* 10 (2002): 121–26.

————. *The Journey of a Caribbean Writer*. Translated by Richard Philcox. London: Seagull Books, 2014.

————. *The Last of the African Kings*. Translated by Richard Philcox. Lincoln: University of Nebraska Press, 1997.

————. *La vie scélérate*. Paris: Seghers, 1987.

————. *Les derniers rois mages*. Paris: Mercure de France, 1992.

————. "O Brave New World". In *Multiculturalism and Hybridity in African Literatures*, edited by Hal Wylie and Bernth Lindfors, 29–36. Trenton, NJ: Africa World Press, 2000.

————. *A Season in Rihata*. Translated by Richard Philcox. London: Heinemann, 1987.

————. *The Story of the Cannibal Woman*. Translated by Richard Philcox. New York: Simon and Schuster, 2007.

————. "Three Women in Manhattan". In *Green Cane and Juicy Flotsam*, edited by Carmen C. Esteves and Lizabeth Paravisini-Gebert, 56–67. New Brunswick, NJ: Rutgers University Press, 1991.

———. *Traversée de la mangrove*. Paris: Mercure de France, 1989.

———. *Tree of Life*. Translated by Victoria Reiter. New York: Ballantine, 1992.

Condé, Maryse, and Madeleine Cottenet-Hage, eds. *Penser la Créolité*. Paris: Eds Karthala, 1995.

La Constitution de la République d'Haïti, 1987. https://www.oas.org/juridico/mla/fr/hti/fr_hti-int-txt-const.html.

D'Aguiar, Fred. "Home Is Always Elsewhere: Individual and Communal Regenerative Capacities of Loss". In *Black British Culture and Society: A Text Reader*, edited by Kwesi Owusu, 195–206. London: Routledge, 2000.

Danticat, Edwidge. "The Art of Not Belonging". Interview with Dwyer Murphy. *Guernica*, 3 September 2013. https://www.guernicamag.com/the-art-of-not-belonging/.

———. "Black Bodies in Motion and in Pain". *New Yorker*, 22 June 2015.

———. *Breath, Eyes, Memory*. New York: Soho Press, 1994.

———. *Brother, I'm Dying*. New York: Vintage, 2008. First published 2007.

———. *The Butterfly's Way: Voices from the Haitian Dyaspora in the United States*. New York: Soho Press, 2001.

———. *Claire of the Sea Light*. New York: Knopf, 2013.

———. *Create Dangerously: The Immigrant Artist at Work*. Princeton, NJ: Princeton University Press. 2010.

———. "The Dangerous Job of Edwidge Danticat". Interview with Renee Shea. *Callaloo* 19, no. 2 (1996): 382–89.

———. *The Dew Breaker*. New York: Vintage, 2005. First published 2004.

———. "Enfant d'eau". *Passerelles* 21 (2000): 231–39.

———. "A Family Story: Danticat Talks about Her Newest – and Most Personal – Work". Interview with Renee H. Shea. In *Edwidge Danticat: A Reader's Guide*, edited by Martin Munro, 187–93. Charlottesville: University of Virginia Press, 2010.

———. "Haiti: A Bi-cultural Experience". *Encuentros* 12 (December 1995): 1–9.

———. "A Harrowing Turning Point for Haitian Immigrants". *New Yorker*, 12 May 2017.

———. *Krik? Krak!* New York: Vintage, 1996. First published 1991.

———. "Poetry in a Time of Protest". *New Yorker*, 31 January 2017.

———. "We Are All Going To Die". Interview with Nathalie Handal. *Guernica*, 15 January 2011. https://www.guernicamag.com/danticat_1_15_11/.

Dash, J. Michael. "Fictions of Displacement: Locating Modern Haitian Narratives". *Small Axe* 12, no. 3 (October 2008): 32–41.

Davies, Carole Boyce. *Black Women, Writing and Identity: Migrations of the Subject*. New York: Routledge, 1994.

Dawes, Kwame. "Writing Home Away From Home". In *Writing Life: Reflections by West Indian Writers*, edited by Mervyn Morris and Carolyn Allen, 51–58. Kingston: Ian Randle, 2007.

Díaz, Junot. *The Brief Wondrous Life of Oscar Wao*. New York: Riverhead, 2007.

———. *Drown*. New York: Riverhead, 1997. First published 1996.

———. "Fiction Is the Poor Man's Cinema. An Interview with Junot Díaz". *Callaloo* 23, no. 3 (2000): 892–907.

———. "Junot Díaz Reads Edwidge Danticat", with Deborah Treisman. *New Yorker* Fiction Podcast, 1 February 2017. MP3 audio, 55:51, https://www.newyorker.com/podcast/fiction/junot-diaz-reads-edwidge-danticat-2.

———. Interview with Edwidge Danticat. *Bomb Magazine*, 1 October 2007.

———. Interview with Hilton Als. *Literary Hub*, 18 March 2016.

———. *Islandborn*. New York: Dial, 2018.

———. *This Is How You Lose Her*. New York: Riverhead, 2012.

Donnell, Alison. *Twentieth-Century Caribbean Literature*. London: Routledge, 2006.

Edwards, Brent Hayes. *The Practice of Diaspora: Literature, Translation and the Rise of Black Internationalism*. Cambridge, MA: Harvard University Press, 2003.

Ferly, Odile. *A Poetics of Relation: Caribbean Women Writing at the Millennium*. New York: Palgrave Macmillan, 2012.

Forbes, Curdella. "Between Plot and Plantation, Trespass and Trangression: Caribbean Migratory Disobedience in Fiction and Internet Traffic". *Small Axe* 16, no. 2 (July 2012): 23–42.

———. *From Nation to Diaspora: Samuel Selvon, George Lamming and the Cultural Performance of Gender*. Kingston: University of the West Indies Press, 2005.

———. *A Permanent Freedom*. Leeds: Peepal Tree Press, 2008.

———. *Songs of Silence*. London: Heinemann, 2002.

Fulton, Dawn. *Signs of Dissent: Maryse Condé and Postcolonial Criticism*. Charlottesville: University of Virginia Press, 2008.

Gallagher, Mary. "Concealment, Displacement and Disconnection: Danticat's *The Dew Breaker*". In *Edwidge Danticat: A Reader's Guide*, edited by Martin Munro, 147–60. Charlottesville: University of Virginia Press, 2010.

García, Cristina. *Dreaming in Cuban*. New York: Ballantine, 1993.

Glissant, Edouard. *La Lézarde*. Paris: Seuil, 1958.

———. *Le Soleil de la conscience*. Paris: Seuil, 1960.

Golden, Marita. *Migrations of the Heart*. New York: Ballantine, 1987.

González, Christopher. *Reading Junot Díaz*. Pittsburgh: University of Pittsburgh Press, 2015.

Goodison, Lorna. *Collected Poems*. Manchester, UK: Carcanet, 2017.

———. *Goldengrove: New and Selected Poems*. Manchester, UK: Carcanet, 2006.

Grey, Jeffrey. "Walcott's Traveler and the Problem of Witness". *Callaloo* 28, no. 1 (2005): 117–28.

Hall, Stuart. *Familiar Stranger: A Life between Two Islands*. Durham, NC: Duke University Press, 2017.

———. "Frontlines and Backyards: The Terms of Change". In *Black British Culture and Society: A Text Reader*, edited by Kwesi Owusu, 127–30. London: Routledge, 2000.

———. "Negotiating Caribbean Identities". *New Left Review* (January–February 1995): 1–14.

Hijuelos, Oscar. "Lost in Time and Words, a Child Begins Anew." *New York Times*, 15 June 2011.

Hoving, Isabel. *In Praise of New Travelers*. Stanford, CA: Stanford University Press, 2001.

Ibarrola-Armendariz, Aitor. "The Language of Wounds and Scars in Edwidge Danticat's *The Dew Breaker*: A Case Study in Trauma Symptoms and the Recovery Process". *Journal of English Studies* 8 (2010): 23–56.

Jay, Paul. *Global Matters: The Transnational Turn in Literary Studies*. Ithaca, NY: Cornell University Press, 2010.

Josephs, Kelly Baker. *Disturbers of the Peace: Representations of Madness in Anglophone Caribbean Literature*. Charlottesville: University of Virginia Press, 2013.

Kaussen, Valerie. "Migration, Exclusion and 'Home' in Edwidge Danticat's Narratives of Return". In *Identity, Diaspora and Return in American Literature*, edited by Maria Antonia Oliver-Rotger, 25–43. London: Routledge, 2014.

Kesteloot, Lilyan. *Les écrivains noirs de langue francaise: Naissance d'une littérature.* Brussels: Editions de l'Institut de Sociologie, 1963.

Kincaid, Jamaica. *A Small Place*. New York: Farrar, Straus and Giroux, 1988.

———. *My Brother*. New York: Farrar, Straus and Giroux, 1997.

Knepper, Wendy. "Caryl Phillips's Seascapes of the Imaginary". In *Caryl Phillips: Writing in the Key of Life*, edited by Bénédicte Ledent and Daria Tunca, 213–33. Amsterdam: Rodopi, 2012.

Laden. "We Remember (ft. Stephen 'Di Genius' McGregor)". Jah Lyrics, 2019. https://www.jah-lyrics.com/song/laden-we-remember.

Laferrière, Dany. *Comment faire l'amour avec un nègre sans se fatiguer.* Paris: Serpent à plumes, 1999.

———. "Foreword: A Heart of Serenity in the Storm". In *Edwidge Danticat: A Reader's Guide*, edited by Martin Munro, vii–viii. Charlottesville: University of Virginia Press, 2010.

Laforest, Marie-Hélène. *Diasporic Encounters: Remapping the Caribbean*. Naples: Liguori, 2000.

Lamming, George. *The Pleasures of Exile*. London: Michael Joseph, 1960.

Lea, Richard. Tribute to Derek Walcott. *Guardian*, 17 March 2017.

Ledent, Bénédicte. *Caryl Phillips*. Manchester: Manchester University Press, 2002.

Lewis-Brown, Alscess. "A Conversation with Derek Walcott". *Caribbean Writer* 28 (2014): 203–7.

———. "'Bearing Witness': An Interview with Edwidge Danticat". *Caribbean Writer* 28 (2014): 208–12.

Lott, Tommy L. "When Diasporas Meet: Black Solidarity and Inter-ethnic Intersections in the United States of America". *Dimensions of African and Other Diasporas*, edited by Franklin W. Knight and Ruth Iyob, 216–35. Kingston: University of the West Indies Press, 2014.

Mais, Roger. *The Hills Were Joyful Together*. London: Heinemann, 1981. First published 1953.

Marshall, Paule. *Brown Girl, Brownstones*. New York: Feminist Press, 2006. First published 1956.

———. "From the Poets in the Kitchen". *New York Times*, 9 January 1983.

McKay, Claude. *Selected Poems*. Mineola, NY: Dover, 1999. First published 1953.

Mead, Rebecca. "Stepmother Tongue". *New Yorker*, 20 November 1995: 50–51.

Morrison, Anthea. "Archives of the Heart or 'Imaginary Family Trees?' Maryse Condé's Ambiguous Quest for Origins". Paper presented at the Atlantic Crossings Workshop, Dartmouth College, Hanover, NH, May 2001.

———. "Of Home Soil and Rainbows: Rooted Travelers in Curdella Forbes' *A Permanent Freedom*". *Journal of Caribbean Literatures* 6, no. 3 (Spring 2010): 23–36.

Morrison, Toni. *Song of Solomon*. New York: Vintage, 2004. First published 1977.

Moslund, Sten Pultz. *Literature's Sensuous Geographies: Postcolonial Matters of Place*. New York: Palgrave Macmillan, 2015.

Moudileno, Lydie. "Portrait of the Artist as Dreamer: Maryse Condé's *Traversée de la mangrove* and *Les derniers rois mages*". *Callaloo* 18, no. 3 (Summer 1995): 626–40.

Müller, Gilbert. *New Strangers in Paradise: The Immigrant Experience and Contemporary American Fiction*. Lexington: University Press of Kentucky, 2008.

Munro, Brenna. "Letters Lost at Sea: Edwidge Danticat and Orality". In *Echoes of the Haitian Revolution, 1804–2004*, edited by Martin Munro and Elizabeth Walcott-Hackshaw, 122–33. Kingston: University of the West Indies Press, 2008.

Munro, Martin, ed. *Edwidge Danticat: A Reader's Guide*. Charlottesville: University of Virginia Press, 2010.

———, ed. *Haiti Rising: Haitian History, Culture and the Earthquake of 2010*. Kingston: University of the West Indies Press, 2010.

Murdoch, H. Adlai. *Creolising the Metropole: Migrant Caribbean Identities in Literature and Film*. Bloomington: Indiana University Press, 2012.

O'Callaghan, Evelyn. "Interior Schisms Dramatised: The Treatment of the 'Mad' Woman in the Work of Some Female Caribbean Novelists". In *Out of the Kumbla: Caribbean Women and Literature*, edited by Carole Boyce Davies and Elaine Savory Fido, 89–110. Trenton, NJ: Africa Word Press, 1990.

Oliver-Rotger, Maria Antonia, ed. *Identity, Diaspora and Return in American Literature.* London: Routledge, 2014.

Ormerod, Beverley. *Introduction to the French Caribbean Novel.* London: Heinemann, 1985.

Owusu, Kwesi, ed. *Black British Culture and Society: A Text Reader.* London: Routledge, 2000.

Page, Kezia. *Transnational Negotiations in Caribbean Diasporic Literature: Remitting the Text.* London: Routledge, 2010.

Patteson, Richard. *Caribbean Passages: A Critical Perspective on New Fiction from the West Indies.* Boulder: Lynne Rienner, 1998.

Pfaff, Francoise. *Conversations with Maryse Condé.* Lincoln: University of Nebraska Press, 1996.

Phillips, Caryl. *The Atlantic Sound.* New York: Faber, 2000.

———. *Cambridge.* New York: Vintage, 1993. First published 1991.

———. *Color Me English. Migration and Belonging before and after 9/11.* New York: New Press, 2011.

———. *Extravagant Strangers: A Literature of Belonging.* London: Faber, 1997.

———. *The Final Passage.* London: Faber, 1985.

———. *"The Final Passage*: An Interview with Writer Caryl Phillips". By Maya Jaggi, in *Black British Culture and Society: A Text Reader*, edited by Kwesi Owusu, 157–68. London: Routledge, 2000.

———. *In the Falling Snow.* New York: Vintage International, 2010. First published 2009.

———. *A New World Order.* New York: Vintage, 2002.

———. *A State of Independence.* New York: Vintage International, 1986.

Pierre-Pierre, Garry. "Facing Prejudice: Edwidge Danticat: Chronicling the Haitian-American Experience", in *Libète: A Haiti Anthology*, ed. Charles Arthur and J. Michael Dash, 201–2. Princeton, NJ: Markus Wiener, 1999.

Pouchet Paquet, Sandra. *Caribbean Autobiography: Cultural Identity and Self-Representation.* Madison: University of Wisconsin Press, 2002.

Ramsay, Paulette. *Aunt Jen.* Oxford: Heinemann, 2002.

Rhys, Jean. *Voyage in the Dark.* London: Norton, 1982. First published 1934.

Rochmann, Marie-Christine. "Migrance et identité: au miroir de l'analepse dans *Histoire de la femme cannibale*". In *Maryse Condé en tous ses ailleurs*, edited by Françoise Simastochi-Bronès, 49–61. Paris: Editions L'Improviste, 2014.

Roumain, Jacques. *Masters of the Dew*. Translated by Langston Hughes and Mercer Cook. Oxford: Heinemann, 1978.

Said, Edward. "The Mind of Winter". In *The Post-Colonial Studies Reader*, edited by Bill Ashcroft, Gareth Griffiths and Helen Tiffin, 439–42. London: Routledge, 2007. First published 1995.

Schattemann, Renée T. *Conversations with Caryl Phillips*. Jackson: University Press of Mississippi, 2009.

Schwarz-Bart, Simone. *Ton beau capitaine*. Paris: Seuil, 1987.

Scott, Dennis. *Uncle Time*. Pittsburgh: University of Pittsburgh Press, 1973.

Selvon, Sam. *The Lonely Londoners*. Harlow: Longman, 1985. First published 1956.

Senior, Olive. *Discerner of Hearts*. Toronto: McClelland and Stewart, 1995.

————. *Encylopedia of Jamaican Heritage*. St Andrew, Jamaica: Twin Guinep, 2003.

Shervington, Pluto. "I Man Born Ya". *Again*, KR, 1982. LP.

Smith, Arlette. "The Semiotics of Exile in Maryse Condé's Fictional Works". *Callaloo* 14, no. 2 (Spring 1991): 381–88.

Smock, Ann. "Maryse Condé's *Les derniers rois mages*". *Callaloo* 18, no. 3 (Summer 1995): 668–80.

Tally, Robert T., Jr. Preface to *Literature's Sensuous Geographies: Postcolonial Matters of Place*, by Sten Pultz Moslund, ix–x. New York: Palgrave Macmillan, 2015.

Tayler, Christopher. Review of *In the Falling Snow*. *Guardian*, 30 May 2009.

Thomas-Hope, Elizabeth, ed. *Freedom and Constraint in Caribbean Migration and Diaspora*. Kingston: Ian Randle, 2009.

Trop noire pour être française? Directed by Isabelle Boni-Claverie, 2015.

Trouillot, Evelyne. "The Right Side of History". In *Edwidge Danticat: A Reader's Guide*, edited by Martin Munro, 168–174. Charlottesville: University of Virginia Press, 2010.

United States Office of Immigration Statistics. *2013 Yearbook of Immigration Statistics*. Washington, DC: US Department of Homeland Security, August 2014. https://www.dhs.gov/sites/default/files/publications/Yearbook_Immigration _Statistics_2013_0.pdf.

Vaquera-Vásquez, Santiago. "'The Inextinguishable Longings for Elsewheres': The Impossibility of Return in Junot Díaz". In *Identity, Diaspora and Return in American Literature*, edited by Maria Antonia Oliver-Rotger, 170–88. London: Routledge, 2014.

Walcott, Derek. *What the Twilight Says*. London: Faber, 1998.

Walcott-Hackshaw, Elizabeth. "Home Is Where the Heart Is: Danticat's Landscapes of Return". *Small Axe* 12, no. 3 (October 2008): 71–82.

Warner-Lewis, Maureen. *Review of Songs of Silence*. *Jamaica Journal* 30, no. 1–2 (2006): 77–78.

INDEX

www.ingramcontent.com/pod-product-compliance
Lightning Source LLC
Chambersburg PA
CBHW030308060726
47498CB00002BB/550